JESUS
THE MESSIAH
— and —
THE PERSON

OMAR AHMAD

Copyright © 2023 Omar Ahmad.

First Edition-2015
Second Edition- 2023

All rights reserved. No part of this book may be reproduced, stored, or transmitted by any means—whether auditory, graphic, mechanical, or electronic—without written permission of both publisher and author, except in the case of brief excerpts used in critical articles and reviews. Unauthorized reproduction of any part of this work is illegal and is punishable by law.

ISBN: 979-8-88640-962-8 (sc)
ISBN: 979-8-88640-963-5 (hc)
ISBN: 979-8-88640-964-2 (e)

Because of the dynamic nature of the Internet, any web addresses or links contained in this book may have changed since publication and may no longer be valid. The views expressed in this work are solely those of the author and do not necessarily reflect the views of the publisher, and the publisher hereby disclaims any responsibility for them.

One Galleria Blvd., Suite 1900, Metairie, LA 70001
1-888-421-2397

CONTENTS

Commemorations v

Preface ix

Introduction: Jesus, The Messiah And The Person xiii

Chapter 1   *The Use of the Metaphor as Used by the Prophets and Saints* 1

Chapter 2   *The Death of Jesus as Indicated that it Occurred From the Gospels and the Quran* 37

Chapter 3   *The Birth of Jesus as Taught by the Quran and the Teachings of the Gospels* 76

Chapter 4   *Evolution of Man and the Creation of Adam as an Evolved Homo Sapien* 96

Chapter 5   *Some Facebook Articles By Me Here* 119

Chapter 6   *The Teachings Of Christ As Understood By Us In Islam* 183

Chapter 7   *Biblical And Islamic Eschatatology As It Refers To Ahmadiyyat And The Second Coming Of Christ* 215

Chapter 8   *Conclusions To My Book And Comments From Myself To You* 227

COMMEMORATIONS

I would like to dedicate this book to the unborn child who through no fault of his or herself was killed in utero by methods barbaric here and they know legislation is passed in Oklahoma and other states where they know my literature is sacred and now the child is safe there from their callous disregard of the law there with the ideology of aborting an infant in arms they have, as they are in her arms at birth so why not before, but it is true it is a cradle for her and him in her uterus which they abandon with compunction not in this state of evil ideology they promote still in some lands of the country but it is clear they are outcast now as the Supreme Court has ousted their ideology of kill me, as all are killed who do this abortion thing they say, and it is clear with Roe being overturned a new era of sanity will emerge where sexual promiscuity will be outcast as one thing leads to another and sex can't be separated from issues of abortion and this land not but worldwide abortion and sex outside marriage vows is looked down upon as against norms of decency now emerging in this land of earth forum here. Further, it is clear sex is outmode because it leads to other sins as well and the soul depreciates it in its woes on one and candor and forthright behavior result not in one because of it.

Also, this book is for her who tries unceasingly to bring it about reform to the Muslim world sitting in her chamber there but I know she has sinned but has the heart to repent and not do it again so that fornication can end in the world and the world can become a better place because of her and her child, as she carries through now, and hopes for him to be a world leader, like myself, teaching statutes are inherent in us and we must allow freedom of speech to people averse to our faith and so forth so it occurs We are one Entity now in perversity not but still with issues as girls know we have but we work for the greater cause for Allah and the Prophet to subserve us in their needs and so forth I am Dabbat Al-Ard because of the girl's insist he brought him and herself a structure of piety he has and there is peace in that thought as you are with the one you love according to his teach on her and others in Islam they have. It is so, much work has to be done here and life is busy with teach of others and responsibility to child is inherent now in her and so they come through in unison in one body, all girl kind the world over, as they network My views to them in China and India and other countries and how is it so I won't forgive her says Allah there and so forth you know I am forgiving actual if you are pious in it.

Please see many world leaders support Omar's mu but the most important man for Omar's destiny there has been Donald Trump who got him out of prison when they incarcerated him and poisoning began, so he told them to inhibit him but don't poison our faith the future holds for us and he made phone calls there to the judiciary to enable release on insanity issues he has, he says, but we know he is kind and knows Omar is astute but it so occurs Omar really had insanity issues according to family structure he has and so it occurred he acted a part for Him, the Creator, to do so, as they were killing him otherwise and death had been written by the former government agency so he relented to being put away but lost faith in it as medication cause that in him but now he is free, but is he, we will see what the future holds and there is little an ex-president can do if they come after his car as they have done repeatedly in the past but tankeen is safe and we don't give anyone authority over him as according to people's thoughts he is Bond actually and takes orders direct from Allah and His Prophet and so forth now only.

It is also clear that the Chinese Premier Xi Jinping has come through because of the girl's shaur that he is king actually they're just saying he is bipolar to please people as he is unpopular because of the law of abortion coming forth and adultery is outmode now and fornication is over for the most part, in girls at least, and so it occurs they have an idea to make it gradual but absolute that it is over sex in their country and sex is no longer permitted for them in schools and women are not allowed abortion as it is clear American shaur has occurred Omar is law-giver from them, sahaba of Him Who is Allah there, as they understand the metaphor he is teaching them and so they are one with him as they protect her who is girl who wants poverty in things and knows money corrupts her so they shed wealth and live simply like Omar did even though he had riches there.

Please know the world is a better place they know since Omar appeared but it is clear there are many adversaries yet and now is the time for gradual assimilation of his ideas to be propagated to the masses so they can educate themselves in principles of equality and love between them as the time is immediate or never, according to girl's shaur there, but let it be gradual, Allah is patient with man and his companion as they bring fidelity in their relationships as they know God punishes those sins, as the Quran says.

Further, world leaders know they have done it, brought Omar back to life as they were unanimous he should live so they relented in the government here and released him but stipulated he must be medicated to inhibit sainthood in him, so they agreed then, but now is the time for peace and tranquility between him and man so they relent to him and let him medicate with less though not as the statutes allow.

Please know it's the American government agenda to inhibit him but there is good there with the American people who know he is free by them since he doesn't teach by force and allows gradual assimilation as he did when they put him to bed but it is clear it is unjust to do so to a man of peace to us who gave us the identity of worship again, we were a dead earth and he came to revive us and bring fidelity again, so it occurred they released him there when the US government wanted to arrest him.

Please see the girl and others there with her are abound and protect him in tasdeeq law they have of verifying issues that occur with him and transmit them accurately to court there so that he is protected by him in courtroom procedure that they try nonetheless to inhibit with poison to him and take his car repeatedly and then relent on a daily basis even though they guarantee the American people daily on issues and then backtrack but it is so they are getting better but a lot needs to be accomplished yet and the government must fall to his clan of Mehdi men and womenkind who fight for his cause in courtrooms and government offices they have and try to bring a semblance of justice to him in his room and home where he is allowed to read in peace you say, nay, but it is better than before where he was extrude from life practical ways with them in the government dick on him.

Please see it is the girl and the boy in the future who submit to him, no, it is all of us in world forum since he is kind there and insists that love will supersede all things and girls know to take his wealth and use it for a good cause of spreading Islam there, something they can all do with the shahada prayer in them, as they know in Omar's shaur some prayer is better than none and gradually qitar will occur with them when they are stronger in repose but it is so for now early worship of Islam is permitted and sanity prevails when we keep Allah with them in their thoughts to him and her so that He can take care of their affairs when He guides them in thoughts to them and so it is prayer is abrogated not but implemented this way and Islam will prosper with it worldwide inshallah or God willing.

Please also see we are one entity now with Allah in our midst so obey Him in issues otherwise you will see adversary from some in mankind as they take over land and you saw what a failed experiment it is to use a law structure of your own rather than His laws as you killed many child with this faith that you know better than Him, yes you were gods and not His sons in issues of law on you. Omar.

PREFACE

The placing of my posts on Facebook began in mid-2013 when I started to teach my viewpoints to those that followed me. I was fairly active and gradually my Facebook page became known to others. I developed a repertoire of articles that I placed there on diverse topics but mainly about religious viewpoints facing us in this country.

Please know I have been ardent in my views and have propagated them here with the intent to bring my readership to you.

In this book are certain things that I have posted on my Facebook page in 2014 and onwards and it is these items that I have placed in there along with their introduction. It is for the reader to appreciate my intellect as I have been derided as a person with mental disease who is a not a coherent individual and I have been committed on many occasions during the time this book was compiled. It was for this reason the publication of the book was delayed, the first edition was published in 2015 and so forth results this is the second edition now.

Please understand my ardor in bringing you this book is for myself as I will be asked what did I accomplish for Him during my tenure here on earth.

Please understand this is my attempt to bring you the food for your life in the Hereafter and it is now for you to partake in it and understand there was some fallacy that came about in the teachings of Christ and that these things are clarified here. I know Paul was a man of integrity not as he changed the teachings of your savior Jesus there as he recognized truth in him but he had a pernicious nature and wanted to change religion around to monotheism not as he liked adultery in things and knew he could make them subservient to him, the devil he had in him, by teaching Islam was different and they should worship idols like the Romans did in their gods and so forth he is extruded as a man of credit by you now as your comprehension has occurred that monotheism was before and he made a hybrid form that makes sense to no one. Later scholars followed suit on the same principle so that the principle teachings of Christ regarding the Oneness of His Entity were altered bringing about a discrepancy from the church that James, the Just, headed after Jesus left Palestine. The original church of James considered Jesus to be a prophet and messiah to her and him who fought Paul in issues but it was so they lost and the church gained ground in monotheism not and eventually abrogated Paul in issues of godhead in man since I arrived to teach in this country and did not allow Paul's teachings of Godhead in him to be present in their dogma, at least unofficially. It is for the reader to understand that changes in the teachings of the prophets do occur and our Prophet Muhammad was no exception, allowing a deviant viewpoint in the teachings regarding the law of apostasy to enter in mainstream Islam, amongst several other deviances as well. It is no shame to correct yourself and understand that the metaphor was applied as real in the teachings of Christ.

Please know if we commit a mistake we are asked to apologize and correct ourselves. It is that way here and for us to realize that an error was made and rectify our claims of godhead in mankind. In all religions these sorts of errors have taken place where man has been elevated to the rank of God and it is time to use circumspection and try to understand that these are errors. Please know Krishna has been taken as God and Buddha is revered as one.

Please see the caption there in their homes.

Please know I am sad I am wrong.

Please try to understand I am wrong if you call me to be so. I am not in error in these matters that I bring to you in this book. I would like an unbiased critique of my book to take place and with due circumspection you will see I am accurate in factual data and my assumptions are based on logic and a deep understanding of our religious beliefs.

Please know my readership includes those who don't understand English well but they seemed to have an interest in my page due to diverse nature of the literature which was original in format, and something that probably no scholar has done in the past. It appears my page gained the attention of scholars and I was able to convey to them my viewpoints in Ahmadiyya Islam in way they found they could understand. It appears our viewpoints regarding Jesus gained ground and recent literature that has been published have shown him to be a man-like entity rather than as a God-like person. I will however allow the leeway of time to judge whether I have made an impact on the community here in this country or elsewhere where my posts are followed.

Ure son in repose is a term I use when I show affinity to your group here though there may be people who are averse to my view in the sentence. Your son in repose is used when I am humble to your community thoughts and there is a sentiment of affinity there as well. Please know these are codes that I use in my literature to enhance it readership interest. In this way I use the term in repose to Him indicating my affinity is towards my Creator when I write the sentence. I know repose is a complex word; suffice it to say that when I use it it signifies I am working towards my peace when I perform the deed or writing. It means that we rest in repose or my thoughts are from Him on a matter and it also means our intent or purpose when I use that word. In this way it is my peace that occurs when I write these words and is in repose to Him that I complete this book in His appreciation and for my satisfaction by doing this work as well. So, when I benefit myself and your community it is in repose to you while when I perform a deed for Him and my peace occurs then it is in repose to my Creator and Benefactor Who rewards those who work for Him. Repose simply means our thoughts from Him, our Creator to us, and we have repose when we think about issues in our minds. It is like saying we rest on these thoughts and these are messages from Him when we think things through, it is hid for some but for me these messages are real and I follow through with them.

Please know my vernacular is specific and the words are carefully chosen. Some of the meanings may be archaic while others are in common usage. I have used my literature in a style that would please you and my aim is to get the meaning across using the least amount of words. In this way the language is powerful and brief. I have tried to follow the format of the Quran with some repetition of words and the brief but powerful way of communicating. The language does require concentration and an adept intellect. Please perform ablution before *you read my work here but I know some do but many won't but I know you understand me more then.*

Please know there has been usage of literature already published. I am grateful to those who I have copied verbatim.

Please know that I appreciate those who have helped me compile this book.

Please know the translation of the Quran that I have used is from my great-grandfather, Muhammad Ali's translation and notes. I have used translation and literature from the internet and I am in regard for using these resources. I will make a brief introduction and start with the book that has in it my articles and Facebook comments for the most part.

Omar Ahmad.

INTRODUCTION

JESUS, THE MESSIAH AND THE PERSON

The term Messiah is meant to represent the savior for a group of people.

Please know in the Hebrew literature it is one who anointed. In this way several kings or leaders were named before Jesus.

Please know for the Jews he was known to be the one who would end the occupation of their lands. In this they were surprised that no one liberated them, in fact Jerusalem was sacked by the Romans around 70 AD. In this they were dismayed. However, God had a different plan. In the passing away of Jesus from Palestine there came a gradual hold of his teachings through the Roman Empire and eventually Constantine, the Roman Emperor, became a Christian after which Rome and its people converted to Christianity. In this way the teachings of Jesus gained ground and he was the person they looked towards for their knowledge of religion. In this way the Messiah conquered a nation like the Romans and Jesus' role as the Messiah became established. In the later centuries his teachings of compassion and mercy took hold and Christian nations aspired to follow his example in their dealings with others.

Please know that pragmatism took hold of the Christian nations and the Messianic period took hold when they became world conquerors in the eighteenth and nineteenth century. They conquered in the name of Jesus and though they had some elements of brutality in their dealings with others they were by and large merciful and compassionate. In this way the teachings of Jesus came to the forefront in the world and a new era of civilization followed which is seen nowadays where governments work together to promote world peace. In the world today, there are elements that do not keep compassion in the mainstream of their focus and this is a sign of Anti-Christ elements in the working of governments.

We know the teachings of Christ are ignored by some but by and large the people of the communities here in the West follow the principle of care and compassion for others which are the hallmarks of the Messiah's message. In the same way the teachings of Prophet Muhammad have gained ground and he is recognized as a world Prophet with the Last Testament for mankind.

In Islam there is strict monotheism and gradually this concept will gain ground, hopefully with the teachings of the Ahmadiyya Jamaat and Illihoon Islam emerging in the West where association of God is done by raising Christ to Godhead as it was done in the past. It is my attempt to clarify how this misconception took place and it began when I wrote the article regarding the Godhead of Christ being in the sense of a metaphor. In this way we see peace as it is my attempt to bring the community of Christians into the monotheistic frame of mind so they better understand their savior Jesus Christ, the Messiah, who is foretold in the Old Testament and verified as the Messiah in the Quran and is the identity of worship not anymore in the land we live in and they export views we have worldwide to Christians living abroad that he has come, listen to him, and they have, bending over backwards in the sense of acquiescal as they know it is over now and trinity and atonement are no longer valued as sane, as the Quran says otherwise, further these teachings gained ground because the Quran was there and they accepted him who was Muhammad there because of the qualities he has of quiet fortitude, which I inculcate in others here.

Please see there are several Messiahs actually in the Muslim world and I include Jesus as one as well here as he was a Muslim to us in Islam and I am the one who brought Christianity of trinity teachings to an end when my book gained ground in the recent years and it is through the help of Prophet Muhammad who teaches things to us from his seat in heaven these have come about. He is the Messiah actual the Muslim world has and Mirza's claim to be the Messiah as well is not unfounded to him and he was the stepping stone to myself as he taught me what Islam really meant and so forth results I am a Muslim because of him and his baith-nama was sane to follow and I have my own baith of accepting my teachings and protecting me in regards to law proceedings on me which are cumbersome and tiring as Mirza some knew as his tribe was subjected to humiliation because of it since he differed in view about the death of Christ and so forth he was ousted from Islam there by talkeen or deceptive mode they adopted that he was a Non-Muslim and so forth he was banished from view as a decent human being because of talkeen they had, and as the book of Revelations says his head was chopped off in the metaphorical sense of the word.

There are 3 of us in the Messiah identity in Ahmadiyya who have the spirit of Christ to explain his teachings so the world would become a better place because of it and One God will appear in your shaur as sane but it is so they think they are all Messiahs who taught us the Word from Him, the Creat, and our Jamaat is the Messiah group the world was expecting to reform the teachings of Christ about trinity concepts they have and so in that sense our group came to reform us in Islam as well and so are Messiahs there too. It is because of this I say the credit goes to Muhammad Ali in particular as he reformed Ahmadism when it went astray by calling him who was mentor there a prophet actual and it came about their descent from grace they had and now you know it a debacle afflicted them and when I clarified it to the world order of men they became interested in our group and started to read him who was Mirza and found him to be cogent and astute and his branch of Qadianism to be not sane in calling him prophet of God.

It is clear there are some in the Ahmadiyya Jamaat who are upset I have usurped his place who is Mirza, don't be, I am a saint like him and we are the virgin class of people you admire, so it occurs you will admonish those who insist he is a kafir by sanctions on you as he is a world leader in the future as people come to his people to learn what the metaphor was that Allah used for him when He said he was one body with Him and His arms and legs, yes, he was a metaphor Him but not like me or Isa Ibn Maryam who were complete in it and so henceforth you admonish those who talkeen it that he is kafir while they know better and take away their privileges in things.

In 2014, when my book first gained grounds some of my teachings had not come to light but now I am established as the saint of Paradise foretold in your book as well as in ours as saint or auliya Dabbat Al-Ard *who is mentioned there as Omar who will appear at the end of times to bring Illihoon ideology to you where our teachings will instruct boys and girls fundamental truths are sane for us in our following of Him, our Creator, on Whom be peace that it has come about monotheism here and our Prophet is recognized as the leader of mankind because of purity he had as he never touched a woman's body outside marriage rites and so forth he is the leader of us from there in Heaven abode he has. Also, he was the faithful spirit who never spoke a lie and never broke a trust as was well known in his time. These things are known from my Facebook comments in recent years but I know acclaim is mine because I brought them to the forefront and now he rests in peace there knowing the world has come to an end and Islam reigns worldwide as the kalima shahada is recited in prayers we have and Islam is recognized as our religion.*

Please know it has occurred and we are one nation now worldwide and we can pray in unison there in Mecca as too many people have occurred there and it is not safe in rites as yet as too arduous occurs and we break our fiber in it, Hajj is hard anyway, now it is not possible to have peace in it so forego it they think but it is so you will still go there but tankeen or delay it awhile until things settle down there.

These comments of mine are well known and judicial courts recognize our Prophet's law in the Quran as sane and well founded in logic and so forth results he is the law-giver of man in the embodiment of the Quran and in my works in the quran I use on Facebook to guide those who read me.

Omar.
November 2022.

CHAPTER ONE

THE USE OF THE METAPHOR AS USED BY THE PROPHETS AND SAINTS

Introduction here.

I initiated my Facebook page in May 2013. Initially I was writing comments mainly on Pamela Geller's website. Subsequently I posted my comments on the entity Jesus Christ as he is envisaged in Islam. My comments made headway and I received international acclaim as a writer of tehreer or changes in thought about issues about Islamic issues and about the life and death of our savior Jesus Christ. I started my campaign with my article Godhead as a metaphor as indicated in the teachings of Jesus. After the publication of my data I received acclaim in a negative sense as well as in a positive sense from the community I reside in. Unfortunately, they took away my medical license and committed me repeatedly to the mental asylum on charges of mental aberration of thought for pursuing this thought that I can change the minds of people regarding the savior Jesus who indicated the metaphor in his teachings to the Pharisees before the crucifixion occurred. He indicated this, as indicated in the article below, that was published on or around October 2013. Omar.

The dogma of Christ as God is wrong, as indicated from the Quran and the Bible.

While this a premise we have that Jesus lived and died as a Muslim it is clear from historical data that can't be refuted that most of the ideas promulgated by Christians nowadays are either from Paul or later scholars like Ignatus who mentioned the three entities that now entail God: Jesus the son, the Holy Spirit and God himself, who is relegated to the third of the entities of worship of the Christian faith.

While Theophilus indicated trinity it was not until the Council of Nicaea in 325 AD and later that the concept was formulated as dogma of the Christian church of Catholicism.

In Islam, we consider the words to be an error as indicated in the chapter four or Women where He asks us not to raise Christ to Godhead, as indicated in the words: 'desist from saying three,' which is the concept of trinity the Christians have nowadays. As Christ himself is not guilty in this regard we should desist from calling him a heretic to our beliefs of Islam where strict monotheism is the rule of our life. In Islam we serve our Creator Who wishes us to be lenient on them until they realize the fault in our people is due to an error in the interpretations of the teaching of Christ as he himself used the metaphor in his relationship with Him, Whom we serve.

I have devised a simple method of communicating my views regarding the sonship of Christ is only a metaphor as indicated in his words to the People of the Book when they were planning to stone him; he indicated in his words to them that he should not be held accountable for the error they were making as the metaphor was clearly implied when he used the words of him being the son of our Creator, as in John; 10:34, where he indicated in the Psalms God referred to the rabbis and doctors of law as gods, as indicated by the words "ye are gods", in Psalms 82:6, indicating they were acting in their own godhead by ignoring His commandments, vouchsafing forever the concept of the metaphor when leaders of mankind refuse to bow down to His will and follow their own laws ignoring His edicts.

This concept is also clear where he also mentioned that he can circumvent the godhead of one or two individuals when they decide to disobey His verdict in a certain matter however when there are three gods then he was unable to circumvent their opinion, as indicated in his words in the Gospel of Thomas and elsewhere. While it is clear the metaphor is meant here Christian apologists have made an error in these interpretations as is indicated in their writings, documented in their literature. Omar.

Though it was not published in our local paper where I usually publish my articles it received international acclaim for the precepts that I taught in it. The article indicates that our savior Jesus indicated the metaphor in his teachings regarding him being the son of God. He also indicated it in the literal sense as being the chief Rabbi or in the sense of a metaphor to be the king of the Jews or Bani-Israel. We understand this to be a title given to the chief rabbi or scholar of the People of the Book of his time. I understand this to be in the concept of metaphor as we are all children of our Creator when He teaches us things to do and we live according to the practices that He teaches us. The term son of God is the title that He gave to the chief rabbi and it is a generic term for a childlike state that we have when we have repose in Him that he will teach us the precepts of Islam as He wishes them to be taught to His children as in the sense of the metaphor. The ideology of Islam permits this precept that we are the children of Him in the concept of an entity that is nurtured by Him onto perfection just like a father would nurture a child or son in his repose or intention. We're akin to the child, like our savior Jesus or Mohammed, or for that matter any Prophet or saint-like entity who wishes to please his Creator and fulfill His goals in his endeavors here.

We wish to please our Creator when we strive in His way. It is with this intention that we teach Islam to your people so that they may enter Paradise with us and those who please Him. It is indicated in the saying of our Prophet that the People of the Book will enter paradise just like other Muslims. This indicates we have the prerogative to inform others that their savior Jesus Christ can permit them entry into Paradise after he teaches them the truth about their beliefs. This may occur on the Day of Judgment for some while for others they may see the truth with our endeavors here where we teach you the precepts of Islam as indicated by Him in his teachings in the gospels and elsewhere. Omar.

Please see the Facebook article on this note we are one entity if we understand the teachings of Christ in the concept of One God, Who we associate with metaphorically.

The teachings of the Oneness of God have come through to all the prophets. The Quran states that all the prophets taught monotheism. In Islam, this concept is codified as law. It is not possible to be a Muslim without believing in the strict monotheism of Him. The teachings in Christianity of trinity were not taught by their leader James the Just, the brother of Jesus. It was Paul in the Diaspora that stated the teaching the Godhead in Christ, which James was against. It will be seen thus from historical data that James was a strict monotheist and would not have been so if Jesus taught of godhead in himself in a manner other than the metaphor.

The following is a post placed on my Facebook page where I elaborate on these terms and some of the historical data on the teachings of trinity from your books and the Quran.

Please understand there was no leeway given in regard to the Oneness of our Creator given in the Quran.

Please see the following caption there in Palestine in the times of Jesus.

Please know there was clarity that he was a prophet and not God.

Please know the words of a prophet may be taken in an out of context manner after he leaves however in the case of Jesus there was an attempt to portray him as divine in order to suit the needs of the people to have a God-like entity in their midst in order that they may know it is the truth from Him.

Please know trinity was not formulated by the scholars until years after Jesus and it was not introduced until the Council of Nicaea in 325 AD when it was formed initially though dogma occurred later in a subsequent council meeting.

Please understand even Paul had not mentioned trinity in his works and Jesus does not talk about it either and the reference to it in the Bible appears to be fictional according to modern scholarship there.

Please understand that we are His repose or purpose if we serve Him and it is in that context we are Him.

Please know these are spiritual terms and not to be taken in the actual sense as they were by the trinity writers over the ensuing times as these concepts make sense when the metaphor is understood as we are Him if we walk and talk for Him. Omar.

Nisa.

4:170 O mankind, the Messenger has indeed come to you with truth from your Lord, so believe, it is better for you. And if you disbelieve, then surely to Allah belongs whatever is in the heavens and the earth. And Allah is ever Knowing, Wise.

4:171 O People of the Book, exceed not the limits in your religion nor speak anything about Allah, but the truth. The Messiah, Jesus, son of Mary, is only a messenger of Allah and His word which He communicated to Mary and a mercy from Him. So believe in Allah and His messengers. And say not, Three. Desist, it is better for you. Allah is only One God. Far be it from His glory to have a son. To Him belongs whatever is in the heavens and whatever is in the earth. And sufficient is Allah as having charge of affairs.

Preamble to the second article here.

Some concept with us that we are His Entity when we serve Him in our world pursuits. There is a saying of our Prophet Mohammed that paradise is vouchsafed for those who believe inherently in the One Entity to be worshiped by mankind. There is no leeway in this regard and the One Entity to be worshiped is sacrosanct in all religions in their original format. We believe, in the Hereafter some modification of thought process will occur before the Day of Judgment and on the Day that we are Reckoned we will be tested and tried severely for our wrong doings.

This is indicated in all major religious beliefs from time immemorial and indicates that we are to be responsible for our deeds that were performed in our lower life here on earth. There is no carte blanche forgiveness of sins or atonement as its taught in the current day Christian lore. We understand just as a child is responsible for its actions we too are accountable for our deeds here no matter what the masses think to be otherwise. We have accountability in our deeds here on earth so how is it possible that we do not have accountability for them in the Hereafter? I consider this in an anomaly that has crept in the Christian lore after the passing away of Jesus Christ from the area that he preached in before he migrated to the present-day Indian subcontinent.

It is clear from our lore in Islam that there is a discrepancy in the understanding of life and death of Jesus Christ even among Muslims. It *is clear that Christian sentiments crept into the Muslim mindset early on in its history. The verses of the Quran are similarly misinterpreted by early Muslim scholars regarding this entity of Jesus, the son of Mary. Jesus was clearly a mortal whose life and birth was the life of a Muslim man, just like Muslim men before his time. He was not a distinct entity like is thought currently by mainstream Muslim men and in the Christian lore as well.*

There are many discrepancies that crept into the mind of people after Jesus Christ passed on as has been indicated in recent literature on the topic. Some men were willing to understand that a difference of opinion is a benefit to the community of Muslims worldwide. This is indicated in a saying of Prophet Mohammed where it was indicated to him as such when he prayed for unity in belief. The verses of the Quran are incorrectly interpreted by Muslim scholars for eons. It was only with the passage of time that Muslim scholars realized that there may be a difference of opinion regarding the birth and demise of Jesus Christ that may be valid there in the centers of excellence in the Middle East, particularly Mecca and Medina, where research is ongoing in this matter as we speak.

Islam subserves mankind who strive for excellence in their works or deeds. It is for this purpose that we teach man and woman the precepts of religious belief that we understand to be correct. It is for the discerning mind to see if we are correct in our beliefs as to what we say makes sense to them. It is with this fundamental principle of communication that I bring forth to you our beliefs as hopefully they will have the presumed effect of coherence in your mindsets.

If any error has crept in the Christian or Muslim mind over eons, as we speak, then it is time for a rectification of this error to occur. We hope to clarify any discrepancy that may be in the mind of an individual regarding the entity Jesus Christ and know we have repose that he will come through as man for you before the end of time, as indicated in our works on him. We are only His slave when we teach you the truth about his entity, as he himself would like us to do. It is no credit to him that he should be considered Godhead in the actual sense of the word as to be a god is a distinct indistinction for him, in his repose in paradise, where he waits his comprehension coming forth that in the Bible his reference to godhead was in the sense of a metaphor or being one with Him, the Creator of us, and not in the literal sense of his word of like it was being stated before I started teaching here..

Islam only indicates the truth when it says that he is a human that has no corporeal connection with the Creator and that his sonship is in the metaphorical sense only. It is clear from the Quran that there is no discrepancy in this matter and that his entity is distinct from his Creator's as indicated in several areas of the Quran. There are numerous sayings of the Prophet Mohammed that talk about the unity of our Creator and His relationship to man and mankind. In this way Islam is a pure monotheistic faith that does not allow any association in the literal sense of the word with our Creator, Allah, or God, or whatever you may know him by.

The sonship of Christ is in the sense of the metaphor as indicated before. The use of the metaphor is extensive in the teachings of prophets and saints from time immemorial as indicated here. The following is an article that was written after the first article regarding the Godhead as a metaphor indicated here for your perusal and review.

The second article about the metaphor in 2014.

This is the second of a series of articles on the use of the metaphor by Jesus in our literature as we know it today as he is known as a God as indicated by his lineage of his Creator by some individuals. As it is clear he was a teacher of His Creator's gospels he used the metaphor extensively in his sayings, as indicated before in my previous article on the use of the metaphor by him. Here we will dissect out the implications of the word godhead in our religion of Islam where the words are used as a metaphor or in their spiritual sense. There is a saying or hadith of our Prophet Muhammad, on him be peace in which he teaches us the analogy of godhead in us mortals, "When a servant like him who achieves excellence in his religion walks, he walks with the legs of Allah and when he talks, he talks with the words of Allah." This indicates that their purpose is the same as His, as was indicated in the words of Isa Ibn Maryam mentioned below.

While Islamic lore allows this concept it is clear the metaphor is meant in the statement of Isa, as in the previous article, where he referred to the words 'son of God' as one who is taught by His Creator, just as a son is taught by a father, who wishes him best in his worldly endeavors. This is here as was indicated in the saying of Christ when he referred himself to his Father Who takes care of him in his worldly endeavors which was to teach the message of God to his follower John and other disciples, as indicated extensively in the Gospel of John and other sources of his teaching.

While it is clear the metaphor is used Jesus is taken out of context to imply that he represents himself as God, he is only saying he is His emissary as indicated in his words in John; 14:6, "I am the way and the truth and the life. No man shall come to the Father except through me." The concept is clear in our religion as no one can ignore the prophet of the time, he delivers His Word, if it is not followed then he will not enter the Heavenly abode of the Hereafter. It also indicates his repose or purpose is the same as His Father Who created him out of nothing as we are all nothing until we are born in the physical sense, though our soul has traveled before as indicated here where he says "he was there before the creation of Abraham in the world" when he said "I am" to the disciples not of his ilk. This indicates that the souls are numbered even before they appear in our bodies. This is indicated in Islamic lore as well when the Prophet Muhammad indicated he was a traveler who spent some time in the cool shade of the world where his desire was to fill His repose that Islam would prosper and man would learn our repose is to fulfill His Word.

It is obvious that it is because of the metaphor in our language many people have been led astray by some men and heresy in the belief of the One Creator has entered in the belief system of many religions, which indicates that the belief before that was inculcated in us by our Creator is universal of Himself as Ahd or One. This is circumvented by teachings of men who circumvent the truth by telling the people to associate their prophet with Him so they can circumvent the teachings of His- in order to glorify the one they wish to be raised higher than Him- who the prophets themselves were obedient to in their endeavors.

Our Prophet was careful in this regard as he used the metaphor rarely regarding godhead in mankind, which has been documented in past literature of the notables we speak about here in this discourse. As this concept is universal in religions we see it has led to polytheism prevalent nowadays in nearly all religions, other than present day Islam and Judaism. This has been corrupted somewhat where the people idolize our Prophet and where the words of the scholars are taken literally as the word of God, without a basis in the scripture of the books or the teachings of the prophets. In Islam, the Quran indicates the matter in no uncertain terms and only allows the concept of 'Us', as His associates, when He uses the term 'We' to address Himself in His dialogue to us indicating the term only that as His servants we serve His purpose in the worldly life, as indicated in chapter 7, surah Araf, verse 33. Here He allows this association in the spiritual concept only and not as incarnates of His Being, when we serve Him in our deeds and worldly pursuits which is what His repose is for us here on earth. This is also seen in the words of Jesus where in his conversation with his disciple in the Gospel of John; 14 and elsewhere that he wishes to serve Him by being His representative, indicating that when you come to him you actually serve Him, as to serve him is to serve his Creator, as his repose is the same as his Creator's, above him in His heavenly abode.

It appears the teachings of Jesus are taken out of context quite extensively by his followers in the Christian faith as he only applied the terms indicating godhead in man in the metaphorical concept, as indicated in John; 10:34 and 35, where he described the terms as metaphors to the Pharisees when he chose for them the passage of Psalms to indicate his displeasure to them as they were taking his words out of context and indicating he was guilty of the crime of heresy of association of himself with his Creator. Here he told them clearly that he was not to be held accountable for his works as they were taking his words out of context, as is the practice of his followers nowadays in the Christian world. This statement of his is verified in the words of the Quran where his Creator asks him if he was guilty of calling himself a deity and he replied in the negative in surah Maida verse 116.

This is also stated in his conversation with his favorite disciple, the apostle Phillip, in John; 14:10, where his words are misconstrued as when he says "he is in his Father and his Father is in Him." This only indicates he is His servant doing His works, as all the prophets of God do, the latter part of the statement states only his soul is from Him. There is an error there in the first part as can be seen that words are not carefully transposed at a later time or that Jesus made an error of thought in it and the Quran here states this here that our soul is transposed later as well where our Creator breathes His spirit into us giving us life thereby in surah 15, The Rock, verse 29.

Our Prophet made it clear that godhead in us, as indicated in the teachings of Christ, is only as a metaphor and is not to be construed as actual. This is indicated in the hadith of our Prophet Muhammad when he inquired from a woman if she knew who he was, she acquiesced he was the Prophet of our Creator. He then inquired if she knew who was her Creator and she replied in the affirmative, she did and pointed to the heavens above. He then released her from the bondage of slavery she was compelled to perform indicating the reality of His Being is above us in Heaven and we live and die on earth as servants of His.

In Christianity, we are able to understand how this variation occurred in His Oneness when we realize that the term of God and son of God were coined in actuality by Paul and were not a part of the early Christian church of James who was appointed by Jesus to be the leader after him, and other apostles, some of whom deviated apparently and implied the literal concept to further the teachings of Jesus as the savior of the world. It was however understood by him that to take the metaphor as literal would turn people away from the teachings of Jesus, in their spirituality as he knew that to corrupt the teachings of his mentor would lead to the despair that is prevalent nowadays where worldly pursuits are the mainstay of worship and not the other way around, where the world is kept in abeyance. This is indicated in his teachings and in the teachings of all the prophets of our Creator, all of whom serve the purpose of their Creator and it is His repose they rest in the Hereafter.

In our quest for excellence if we use the words of the hadith quoted above regarding the servant who walks with His legs and talks His words or His repose it is the same sense we see in the teachings of Jesus himself when he indicates he is His repose, as in John: 8, and other places in the Bible where we will realize their metaphorical origin as no human is in actuality the Creator, only His servant, who reaches His repose in their endeavors as a righteous slave can if they persevere in His purpose.

There are other instances in the Old Testament where these terms of son of God or even godhead are rife as other prophets have been called sons of God though it is the metaphorical concept only or in the sense of being His representative, as a leader or king would be nowadays if he followed His edicts in his endeavors as we are all His sons if we show obedience to His edicts.

In chapter 82; the Psalms of the chapter Asaph, verse 6, the terms gods referred to unjust among the rabbis and doctors of law who were disobedient to the edicts of their Creator, as were the people of the Book of his time, as a corollary, who were stoning him, while the words that follow "while you are His sons" indicates the metaphor where a pious servant is like an obedient son who listens and obeys his Father's edicts, indicative of our natures as submissive to Him which is where the term of Islam arrives at as Islam means to submit. This is how the concept appeared in us that when we submit to Him we achieve solace in His words and peace in our deeds here which are indicative we will achieve a Heavenly abode if we submit to His teachings, as indicated in words of Jesus and Prophet Muhammad, on them be peace. Omar.

Please see this comment that created the end of trinity in March 2015.

Please see this occurs the judiciary is upset that the exact date is known that trinity concepts dissipated some but it is clear it is talkeen if I do post it but it is so it was on that date of March that year that they finally understood by what it meant when you say you are one with your Creator and so forth results I am jailed not now or in future as you are pleased it occurred and you came into Islam formally then, which is what I thought but it did occur jail in me because of this issue.

Please see it was my mother who gave me this concept that changed world history and it became obvious trinity was misapplied there when they interpreted this verse 'I and the Father are one' as 1 god in Islam they had for 3 entities and so forth you left trinity concepts forever then and became Islam on that day as it was my Sunday sermon to you then early morning after being toxed that night in bed.

Comment in March 2015 that created history, the rest was follow through and jail time for doing this to Islam they had.

Please know I am asked if your Creator is One.

Please know He is.

Please understand Him,

Please know He creates us from Him,

Please know we are Him if we are to be in His repose or His thoughts on us.

Please know fuse with Him,

Please know it is to be one with Him,

Please know when we forsake us we are in essence Him if we do His work and are Him in repose or intent.

Please know the statement of our Prophet that when we walk we walk with His legs and when we communicate we communicate from Him,

Please know the intent is meant here.

Please know repose,

Please know it is His intent that we do everything or we are one with Him.

Please know our savior Christ was one with Him in repose or intent.

Please know He was in essence Him,

Please know the metaphor,

Please know our Creator is the Creator of us.

Please know more,

Please know He expects us to be this metaphor that we are His intent or one with Him,

Please see this,

Please see that we are His repose.

Please know Jesus and his spirit were one with his Beloved. I know you hope to be like him one day. Omar.

Preamble to son of God section.

As you can see from this article the use of the metaphor is extensive and is used by Prophet Mohammed as well as later saints, like my mentor Mirza Ghulam Ahmad and myself in our works. Jesus was adept in use of the metaphor though it appears to have caused trouble to him and he decided to forgo it before the crucifixion process as indicated in the Gospel of John and other places.

There is also an article in Wikipedia which details the use of the term son of God in the Hebrew literature as well as in the pagan custom of calling a leader a god in the literal sense. I am enclosing references from this article. Omar.

Referral to the term of godhead and son of God in the Old Testament.

There is a comprehension here that the terms 'sons of God' are generic and refer to His sonship as an obedient slave, while the term 'god' in men refers to His disobedient one who alters His word or teachings from Him. Jesus was no different as he taught the metaphor in his works adding some vernacular, like David, by indicating that being His slave his Father was his savior who taught him how to teach others, like He taught him, thereby referring to the metaphor of a Father Who is a mentor to him. Your son in repose to Him knows the metaphors have been used from time immemorial and were misconstrued as real by the lay followers of these personages who used these terms as honorific titles in the context of acting in His repose or purpose in their works.

Please see some of the passages from the Old Testament here that refers to the metaphor when using the terms son of God or Godhead in man. Please know this list is not complete and only gives a reference that these terms were widely used for the prophets and kings of our Creator.

This section in Genesis talks about the sons of God marrying the daughters of men. It probably refers to the obedient men were given women in marriage.

Genesis chapter 6.

"When human beings began to increase in number on the earth and daughters were born to them, the sons of God saw that the daughters of humans were beautiful, and they married any of them they chose."

Please know Israel is the prophet. It refers to the nation of Israel in this passage from Exodus.

Please know the firstborn child refers to the position of eminence they have with Him. In this way it is placed in similar places in the Old Testament and refers to prophets and saints who have eminence with Him.

Exodus chapter 4.

22 Then say to Pharaoh, "This is what the Lord says: 'Israel is my firstborn son.'"

David in psalms 89 calls our Creator his Father just like Jesus did in his vernacular. In return, God calls David his firstborn son to whom He will give preeminence. In this way we see the vernacular of Jesus was not unique to him and in no way should connote that Jesus was referring to a corporeal father in Heaven, just like David was not. In similar ways we see the extent of the usage in the Old Testament was similar to the gospels and it is obvious that these words were taken out of context for Jesus and godhead was applied.

26 He will call out to me, "You are my Father, my God, the Rock my Savior.

27 And I will appoint him to be my firstborn, the most exalted of the kings of the earth."

In psalms 2 our Creator anoints the king as His son and states that He will be his Father. It is clear the son of God here is an honorific title that is given to the king in charge of the nation, similar to the title given to David. In this way we see that our Creator uses the title 'son of His' as a title of honored servants, as indicated in the Quran later in the chapter.

6 "I have installed my king on Zion, my holy mountain."

7 I will proclaim the Lord's decree: He said to me, "You are my son; today I have become your father."

In this way we see Samuel has also been called the firstborn of his Creator. Adam in the Bible has been called son of His and Abraham too.

In the Old Testament we see thus the usage of the terms son of God to be replete and indicative of the prophet or king in charge of the Israeli nation. In this way we know Jesus used the terms himself like he clarified in his communication with the People of the Book when they were about to stone him.

Please know when Jesus used the term 'son of God' for himself he did not state he was the only son of His Eminence, indicating continuity in the usage of the term.

Please understand these references were derived from a source on Wikipedia by the heading 'son of God.' These references were then checked by the biblical text. In addition to these references there are some others that an interested reader can see on their webpage.

Please see the following caption there.

Please know these terms are rife in our book so why change facts for your purpose.

Please know that we encourage the reader to do their research and verify for themselves that what I state here is factual and not in any way contrived. Omar.

Another post here.

The oath of Ecclesiasticus is safe for us in Islam in that it gives the heartbroken man grief not but joy that he will find God with him in Heaven when he serves others in faith they have of helping out them who are needy.

Please see this passage from Ecclesiasticus where it is mentioned that a righteous servant is a son of His Eminence,

Please know this is the complete post from my Facebook page,

Please know there is an impression that son of God was specific to Jesus while that is not the case,

Please know the term 'begotten' is an interposition and not in the original teachings of Christ,

Please know Christ never used the term 'begotten' for himself and he never said worship me and so forth it is a heresy you do.

Please know son of God was used by Christ and reiterated as being in sync with Him as a righteous slave is,

Please know the interposition is real and evil to do.

Please see the note below,

Please know it is about a righteous man,

Please know our savior fulfilled the oath for Him and was called son of God,

Please know you can all fulfill the mold,

Please know our Prophet was similar.

Please see this verse from Ecclesiasticus,

Please know our Creator beckons us to be righteous,

Please know He calls us His son,

Please see the footnote here,

Please know it is to mean He loves us more than her who begets,

Please give in,

Please know it is a common word in Hebrew texts,

Please know He will call us to account for using it in an out of context manner,

Please know Jesus was no son of His in the actual sense but a righteous man who fulfilled the Ecclesiasticus oath for Him. Omar.

Bible source.

1 "My son, defraud not the poor of his living and make not the needy eyes to wait long.

2 Make not an hungry soul sorrowful; neither provoke a man in his distress.

3 Add not more trouble to an heart that is vexed; and defer not to give to him that is in need.

4 Reject not the supplication of the afflicted; neither turn away thy face from a poor man.

5 Turn not away thine eye from the needy and give him none occasion to curse thee:

6 For if he curse thee in the bitterness of his soul his prayer shall be heard of him that made him.

7 Get thyself the love of the congregation and bow thy head to a great man.

8 Let it not grieve thee to bow down thine ear to the poor and give him a friendly answer with meekness.

9 Deliver him that suffereth wrong from the hand of the oppressor and be not fainthearted when thou sittest in judgment.

10 Be as a father unto the fatherless, and instead of an husband unto their mother: so shalt thou be as the son of the most High and he shall love thee more than thy mother doth."

Metaphors in the Quran and the Bible, current concepts we have.

Please see this article sums up our concepts in Islam on metaphors used in the Bible, Quran and other texts where trinity occurs in the minds of people as correct though it makes little sense to most people I have conversed with.

There is some repetition here with topics I have covered elsewhere but it is clear this article made headway when I was a practicing doctor in September of 2021 and they sought to take away my license once again, which they did when I was committed by them for bringing Illihoon ideology in vogue.

1 Godhead as a positive metaphor.

Hadith of prophet Muhammad,

When a servant walks he walks with the feet of the Creator and when he talks he says His words.

In other words you have fused with Him and are one with Him. In this way as a metaphor you are Him but it is not true that you actually become Him. He is on His throne in Paradise and we are here on earth and we can never become His Absolute Self.

Please see it an honorific title we are Allah's metaphor.

Please also see Anfal where we fuse with Him in action.

8:17 So you slew them not but Allah slew them, and thou smotest not when thou didst smite (the enemy), but Allah smote (him), and that He might confer upon the believers a benefit from Himself. Surely Allah is Hearing, Knowing.

In other words they are one with Him or His agents.

Jesus had a similar state. He was one with Him in repose or His agent working in concert with His desires as seen in John (10:30) where he says those words to the Jews that "I and the Father are one." We can see in this section he was performing God's deeds so he was one with Him in action or deeds. It is misconstrued by theologians to indicate he was one substance but that is not the context of his words.

Please see the passage below when he says those words and the context they are in:

John 10.

24 Then came the Jews round about him and said unto him, "How long dost thou make us to doubt? If thou be the Christ, tell us plainly."

25 Jesus answered them, "I told you and ye believed not: the works that I do in my Father's name, they bear witness of me.

26 But ye believe not because ye are not of my sheep, as I said unto you.

27 My sheep hear my voice and I know them, and they follow me:

28 And I give unto them eternal life and they shall never perish, neither shall any man pluck them out of my hand.

29 My Father, which gave them me, is greater than all and no man is able to pluck them out of my Father's hand.

30 I and my Father are one."

31 Then the Jews took up stones again to stone him.

32 Jesus answered them, "Many good works have I shewed you from my Father, for which of those works do ye stone me?"

33 The Jews answered him saying, "For a good work we stone thee not; but for blasphemy; and because that thou, being a man, act like a god."

34 Jesus answered them, "Is it not written in your law, I said, Ye are gods?"

35 If he called them gods, unto whom the word of God came and the scripture cannot be broken;

36 "Say ye of him whom the Father hath sanctified and sent into the world 'Thou blasphemest' because I said, I am the Son of God?

37 If I do not the works of my Father, believe me not."

Please see here that God's hand is fused with that of Jesus thus verifying that when the Creator loves you you become Him in repose or action. The Jews did not understand this was a metaphor and when Jesus explained to them these are metaphorical terms they understood as when he quote the scripture in Psalms 82 indicating they were gods as they knew the metaphor was meant.

I know they were upset but Jesus further goes on to say he was sanctified and would not commit blasphemy by saying actually those terms like son of God, which was a metaphor to them, still they misimplied it and stoned not as he escaped that that day but eventually hung him.

2 Godhead as a negative metaphor.
Psalm of Asaph

1 God presides in the great assembly. He judges among the gods.

2 "How long will you judge unjustly, and show partiality to the wicked?

3 Defend the weak, the poor, and the fatherless. Maintain the rights of the poor and oppressed.

4 Rescue the weak and needy. Deliver them out of the hand of the wicked."

5 They don't know, neither do they understand. They walk back and forth in darkness. All the foundations of the earth are shaken.

6 I said, "You are gods, while all of you are sons of the Most High."

In other words sons are His agents while gods are wicked disobedient ones.

In these verses of Asaph there is conviction that son of God is His agent, as Jesus was in his life works. A god or disobedient one is one who agrees to disagree with the Creator and finds him repulsed in his works. In other words he is agent in a negative sense or disobedient to Him in his works of life. A scholar is similar if he disregards the works of Him and if he transposes a meaning other than what is meant by Him in His entirety on him or the scholar reads into it another meaning than what is meant.

The verse that follows corroborates with that view.

The Quran from The Immunity

9:31 They take their doctors of law and their monks for lords besides Allah, and (also) the Messiah, son of Mary. And they were enjoined that they should serve One God only — there is no god but He. Be He glorified from what they set up (with Him)!

Excerpt from the Quran translation by Muhammad Ali.

Note on 9:31. Most of the commentators agree that it does not mean that they took them actually for gods; the meaning is that they followed them blindly in what they enjoined and what they forbade, and therefore they are described as having taken them for lords, on account of attaching to them a Divine dignity. It is related in a hadith that, when this verse was revealed, 'Adi ibn Hatim, a convert from Christianity, asked the Holy Prophet as to the significance of this verse, for, he said, we did not worship our doctors of law and monks. The Holy Prophet's reply was: Was it not that the people considered lawful what their priests declared to be lawful, though it was forbidden by God. Hatim replied in the affirmative. That, the Prophet said, was what the verse meant (Tr. 44:9; IJ). Muslims who accord a similar dignity to their scholars have a similar view of them as gods in the negative sense of the word.

Thus, we see in the Bible the word god refers to the disobedient one. This is distinct from the scholar works who is disobedient to God's works as a disobedient slave works in his own accord against the wishes of his God or Creator. In other words, he is acting as his own god, disobedient to Him who created him. Also, we know God words are inherently sane for us and we enter heresy when we go against His words on us. I teach this by saying if we disobey Him by going against His will on us then we are disobedient ones or gods in our make.

3 Son of God in the Bible as corroborated by the Quran.

The son is a positive metaphor in the case of Asaph as it appears they have the repose to serve Him in their works. In other words their life is dedicated to the service of humanity.

Please see the context below that we are servants of God in that we serve Him in our works. This is the meaning of son in the Bible.

Please see the Bible contains many references to son of God. Adam and Abraham have been called His son, as is a righteous servant of His Eminence. Jesus himself used to refer to God as his Father and also portrayed to some of his companions to pray to Him Who is Father there. In this sense he called them children of God.

It is clear this metaphor was taken out of context by Christian theologians and they implied Godhead in him because of it as a son is

JESUS THE MESSIAH AND THE PERSON

of the makeup of the father. Furthermore, it is obvious Jesus meant it as metaphor as he calls himself repeatedly in it, the Bible I mean, that he was son of man, meaning he had an earthly father.

Corroboration from the Quran
Al-Anbiya
21:26 And they say: The Beneficent has taken to Himself a son. Glory be to Him! Nay, they are honored servants—
21:27 They speak not before He speaks, and according to His command they act.

Please see here the metaphor is indicated. Messengers are called sons but they are actually honored servants of His.

4 Father in the Bible is equated with Rabb in Islam.

Children of God in the Christian lore and relation to Abba and Rabb:

In the Quran the word used for God is Rabb or Creator to us while in the biblical lore it is Abba or Father, both providing the context that He is the father or nourisher unto perfection, just as a father perfects his son or daughter to be good to others, so does the nourisher or Rabb.

5 Oneness of God as taught by Jesus in the Bible lore they have.

Jesus himself believed in the Oneness of his Creator as mentioned in the Bible on several locations. Here are some excerpts of his works from the Bible, a book which is valid to you and Jesus' followers of the Christian faith.

Matthew 4
9 He said to him, "I will give you all of these things if you will fall down and worship me."
10 Then Jesus said to him, "Get behind me, Satan! For it is written, 'You shall worship the Lord your God, and you shall serve him only."

John 17
1 Jesus said these things and lifting up his eyes to heaven, he said, "Father, the time has come. Glorify your Son that your Son may also glorify you;

2 even as you gave him authority over all flesh he will give eternal life to all whom you have given him.

3 This is eternal life that they should know you, the only true God, and him whom you sent, Jesus Christ.

4 I glorified you on the earth. I have accomplished the work which you have given me to do."

The Quran corroborates this view that he was innocent in regard to his teachings about One God in their life's works. He says in Maida the following.

5:116 And when Allah will say: O Jesus, son of Mary, didst thou say to men, Take me and my mother for two gods besides Allah? He will say: Glory be to Thee! it was not for me to say what I had no right to (say). If I had said it, Thou wouldst indeed have known it. Thou knowest what is in my mind, and I know not what is in Thy mind. Surely Thou art the great Knower of the unseen.

5:117 I said to them naught save as Thou didst command me: Serve Allah, my Lord and your Lord; and I was a witness of them so long as I was among them, but when Thou didst cause me to die Thou wast the Watcher over them. And Thou art Witness of all things.

6 The unity of the message of the Torah, Jesus' teachings and the Quran.

The Old Testament is replete with the teachings of One God in them but it is clear that Jesus did not deviate in the message of the Old Testament that he taught the One God teachings in his works, as I have shown here. It was Ignatus and others who raised him to godhead in the literal sense of the word in trinity concepts and other works.

Please see the concept of One God is not new in Christianity. Early followers of Christ believed in One God concepts like the Ebionites and other sects they had and were different from the Jews only in that they took him for Christ who was Jesus. Furthermore, this concept prevailed in early Christianity until James was killed and for some time thereafter and it was in the Nicene creed that he was son literally and that god also appeared there in literature they had from Paul and later trinity *was formulated but early Islam there was monotheistic for the most part and Paul was considered heretical, as James had indicated to them.*

Please see that early Christians believed as we do in Islam, they took Jesus to be a prophet and would not pray to him, admitted in the Holy of Holies in the temple of the Jews they were and they taught Paul and others were wrong in their teachings of him being God or son of His Eminence in the literal sense of the word.

Islam confirms the message of Jesus somewhat as it gives precedence to the literal word of One God literally and uses metaphors sparingly in this context. This is why Muslims and Jews use the metaphor sparingly and Christians deviate in it by calling him who is Jesus God actually. It is so in other religions as well as they metaphor him literally who is their prophet-God sense. As he teaches God's word to them they sense Him in their prophet's teachings. This is how the metaphor is applied here.

Please see the caption on their hearts repose of things.

There is no God but Allah but he must be god as well.

The image of God transposes them to think he must be God literally while he is His servant repose of things in him. This is clear that God is One Entity and we are all His satellite clinics of things we teach here on earth. There is no God but Allah now in your heart's wishes as you pray to Him for the most part. It is clear the message of the Quran is with you in your heart's repose as correct for you and you will listen to them as he or she teaches you from it. Eventually you will learn to agree with Him Who teaches His word from our Book, the Quran. The Quran in its entirety is intact in its message, collected intact by Him Who creates. Read it and listen to Him Who teaches you it, Loving and Caring in it.

The Quran is clear in that Jesus taught One God there and this unifies the teaching of Jesus in the literal sense as meaning we are His agents, just like the mother ship is to its satellite warriors. It is like saying we are His repose or thoughts to us, or like saying we are His agents in repose to Him.

This summarizes the statement initially that a slave walks with Him or speaks His words are like saying we are His repose, in other words when His thoughts come to us we do His bid on us and these are our works for Him in Islam you do it here and it was like Jesus was trying to tell them that he and his Father are one in repose or thoughts on the matter discussed and he did His bid like our Prophet did as well.

In the Bible lore we see the metaphor discussed ardently. The Prophet indicated there was no actual second coming of Christ in his dialogue to them but they held on to the Christian view that he will appear who was Isa Ibn Maryam before the end of time, as you can see from hadith lore, and actually he knew Isa had died and said so to them but Ahmadi scholars have indicated it would be someone like him and indicated these were metaphors, his second coming, as no prophet can appear after his death as it would negate the Quranic verse that he was seal who is Muhammad, and my coming is not that of Isa, he predicted me there as a pious slave of his who bring about the end of Christian faith in polytheism and bring about reform which I have done here with Christianity and Islam is ongoing as we speak.

7 Trinity concepts as taken from the book they have.

In the Bible as well in the Quran trinity is a misgiving, meaning three, while if it is used in the metaphorical sense as three working in concert it makes sense to people but it is not so there are many on whom the metaphor can be applied and they all do God's work in concert with Him or as His extension and to say three is a misnomer as the Quran says and should not be said, the is no triumvirate there and there is only One God and all are His slaves, including Muhammad whose name is said in the shahada.

In trinity polytheism has crept in indicating three Gods, while they are agents of Him acting as servants, fused in repose, doing His works, acting on His command. In Christianity we are one with them if we recognize that their trinity is in the metaphorical sense of acting in concert, as Jesus did in his teachings on them. Later scholars like Paul, Ignatus, and others coined him God in the literal sense as well while he used the words in the metaphorical sense being considered as one with Him in repose like in the statement "I and the Father are one."

Please see there were other issues as well that led to trinity concepts there as they called him one substance as Him Who creates based on *the verse I quote here in John but it is clear that he was human and not God-Spirit of things.*

It is clear they aggrandized him as God and son of God in the Bible but it is obvious Jesus taught differently as can be seen in Gospel of John I quote here for clarity to appear in things related to tropes or metaphorical terms in the Bible lore we have.

Please know a trope is not meant to be literal and now you have it they took his words and applied it literally when he said things like 'I am' or 'I am the Father' and 'when you come to me you see Him' all these are tropes he uses in his literature and it is quite widespread his terminology there of being one with Him or doing his Father's bid and he has said that he came not to do his will but that of his Father's so it is clear he was His agent and that's how trinity concepts are explained here and it is you man and wife who used these words in an out of context manner to indicate he was God, which he did not say in the Bible lore to you and you aggrandize him still in your prayers which should not be done, he was human and not incarnate Me say I Allah there and that's My final Word on the subject.

In conclusion, I will say I have made headway in the Ahmadiyya Jamaat with these statements being in the metaphorical sense only. There is no God but Allah in the Quran. We must stick to that statement that in the literal sense it is blasphemy to Him and in the metaphor way it allows clarity in the matter of trinity and other lords of Christianity not but other religious beliefs where they associate others with Him in concert, meaning Him in association with idols who they think will intercede for them if they do so the worship of them and they are one with Him literally, like Jesus is like in Christianity. Concert means working with Him in your works, meaning a prophet, like Jesus said in the verse in the Bible where he says why do you fault me for my works, which are God to me, and they replied they are blasphemy, meaning that you are calling yourself son of God in the literal sense and he replied they are not, being metaphorical, meaning the metaphor of His wisdom on them as a prophet of His.

The Quran is emphatic we don't say three or trinity, the words of the Quran do not allow us to say Jesus, or Messiah as we know him, is Allah or God in the literal sense of the words.

See Maida where it says:

5:72 Certainly they disbelieve who say: Allah, He is the Messiah, son of Mary. And the Messiah said: O Children of Israel, serve Allah, my Lord and your Lord. Surely whoever associates (others) with Allah, Allah has forbidden to him the Garden and his abode is the Fire. And for the wrongdoers there will be no helpers.

5:73 Certainly they disbelieve who say: Allah is the third of the three. And there is no God but One God. And if they desist not from what they say, a painful chastisement will surely befall such of them as disbelieve.

5:74 Will they not then turn to Allah and ask His forgiveness? And Allah is Forgiving, Merciful.

It is clear from this verse and the one that follows that polytheism is not allowed in our scripture of Islam we hand to you as correct and it is clear the Quran is also correct to follow that One God is correct for you, knowing that metaphors are not real to you in inert law in that we are all concert with Him if we do His works in our lives. The verse that follows say we should desist from saying trinity in our daily routines and unless we mean concert in our context of things it doesn't make sense. We should be apprised the followers of Christ say shirk if they associate with Him. How could you in Christian lore say your God is One God and yet at the same time call Jesus and the Holy Spirit God as well, it is incomprehensible what you say as Jesus lived on earth and was independent of Him Who was in Heaven though we know he was His slave doing His bid and teaching Islam to people on His command to him, yes, this makes sense and not the way you put it that he was God here as he was a man for all practical purposes and it is just aggrandizement that you call him your Creator and things like that.

I mean these teach to you in a good sense, meaning Christian Muslim harmony as we come from the same God Who created us, meaning we should not take literally the word of Christ in that he is the Word there of God incarnate here on earth, like did the Christians of before who indulged in polytheism, rampant ways. Now most people recognize my merit in exposing these as metaphors, not to be taken literally.

Please refrain from indulging in the metaphor in the literal sense and include the Quranic model in your lives with One God with you meaning that if you pray regularly you keep Him in your thoughts and act in concert to His demands on you.

In conclusion, I will say that One God holds true and metaphors do not, giving the Christian concept of trinity no heed as we all do His bid on us. The Quran summarizes this as saying do not heed three but say your Lord is One God. Good day to you all and say He is One God we serve in our lives.

The nature of a metaphor.

The term metaphor literally means a state other than what one states or a connection of ideas to bring sense of the meaning to you. In other words, as indicated in the article above it may indicate a physical aspect of an existence while indicating the spiritual aspect only. It is clear that that the metaphor refers to an analogy other than what is stated. Just like a father takes care of a son is in this context that the father-son relationship exists between man and his Creator. In Islam the term that we use for our Creator is Rabb or one who nurtures onto perfection. It is in this context that a father nurtures a son onto his path of perfection.

We have to ascertain the validity of the metaphor before it can be validated as correct as to use a metaphor incorrectly is to muddy the topic at hand. Only if a metaphor makes sense does it have validity in the mindset of people and causes peace for those who use it and understand it. It is clear from the literature that our Creator Himself has used the metaphor extensively in His works as indicated in the Old Testament, the gospels and the Quran itself. It is apparent that the metaphor has been misused by other religions in construing a meaning that is not present in the metaphor itself. This has resulted in the lack of unity in the works of the teacher. Generally the prophet himself was not guilty of misusing the metaphorical terms as taught to him by his Creator.

The basis of the metaphor is sacrosanct in the Muslim literature as well as in the Christian lore. It is mentioned in the Quran that some of the verses are allegorical while others are categorical. The Quran is replete with allegorical language depicting a state other than what is stated. The term mountains have been used for mighty men who have fought Muslims in their endeavors to quash the Muslim movement to bring Islam to the forefront. Herbage has been referred to in the physical sense of a growth resulting from rain while it refers to the luxurious growth of Islam that occurs from the teachings of prophets, like Prophet Muhammad, in his endeavors during his sojourn on earth. It is clear that the Old Testament and gospels are also replete with vernacular such as the metaphor and it is a fallacy of belief to take the words literally as is being done currently by the Christian apologists and other leaders of the church, as well as their Hebrew counterparts.

In the past, mistakes have been made regarding the vernacular of metaphor and it is time to rectify these errors as it leads to discrepancy in the teachings of the prophets and the saints who use this vernacular extensively in their works in an attempt to mimic the teachings of their Creator in this regard. It is in this context that I have clarified the terms son of God or godhead in man in its metaphorical terminology. Similarly, the term prophet has been used in the metaphorical sense by myself and others indicating the spiritual state of being like a prophet though not actually being a prophet in the physical sense of the word. Literally the term has been used to convey a message from our Prophet Mohammed conveyed in dreams to some though it has led to fallacy in beliefs in others when they misconstrue the words to give a real interpretation of things and not meant by the sayer of the word. This is led to a false belief in religion and a deviation in religious belief that has occurred in most of the religions and some as previously thought in the Qadiani group or in the Baha'i movement in Islam currently.

Islam is served by clarification of these errors that have crept into the terminology of the saints after they have passed away. There seems to be some similarity in this discrepancy that resulted after the passing away of guru Nanak, the leader of the Sikh movement. It is clear he was a Muslim saint as indicated from the writings on his cloak which were deciphered to be edicts from the Quran after they were uncovered at the end of the nineteenth century by my predecessor Mirza Ghulam Ahmad of Qadian. It is unfortunate that roil develops due to minor discrepancies of faith that result in a difference of opinion between the Muslim sects or groups in Islam. It is clear that a difference of opinion is a benefit for Muslims and not a deterrent to peace, as is currently seen nowadays. According to a saying of our Prophet Mohammed his Ummah or community will be divided into 73 groups at a certain stage, indicating that all 73 groups will be his followers and should not be excluded from Islam as they have the shahada in essence as their core belief. There will always be a difference of opinion in the mindsets of people and that appears to be satisfactory to him and his Creator. The primary concept to be a Muslim is a belief in One Entity and to consider Prophet Mohammed to be your Messenger in Islam. Other than that, minor differences in opinion do not exclude people from the religion of Islam and people are to be considered a Muslim state to his or her Creator. Omar.

Please see my article gained ground but it was already done, the metaphor was understood when I first spoke about in 2010 and then my article came out in 2013 and you deterred it, my sanity to you, as children were getting influenced and you didn't want that.

Please see this article was written in 2014 and so forth when they were inhibiting my pen with toxins and so forth and applying conservators on me even though I was established by you as an author of repute who ended Christian concepts of trinity then and then it was so that we became 1 identity which you openly succumb to now.

Further, it was clear I was committed because of this and finally jailed as my literature had become prevalent and the church was on a backdraw as they knew it was futile people would not believe trinity concepts, so they jailed me for them to punish my entity. There I lingered for 4 months until finally they relented and let me free, though consumed my brain with tepid shots which inhibited me and I became despondent by you, so you relent and take me off shots and here I am again as Dabbat Al-Ard and Messiah to some, firmly established on the throne of power by you as I had given you 1 God to you, and now the church accepts it as people don't believe in trinity concepts knowing the metaphor applied there to Jesus and so forth result.

Article itself in 2014.

Please know the following discourse shows that Jesus was not guilty of blasphemy in his own words,

Please know when people say he was crucified because he was His son they say so in ignorance as Jesus explained this was a metaphor.

Please know he was a victim of state abuse just as I have been,

Please know in me they imply mental disease and threat to them and take away my rights to freedom and medicate me to inhibit my sainthood.

Please know Jesus was similar and the stoning incidence made it clear that he was not guilty of blasphemy as they portrayed on him,

Please know he is similar to me and that is why I have been called Isa by him, my Prophet.

Please know my case is well known in this country so I have some protection,

Please know if I had been isolated as he was it would have been a lot worse for me,

Please know he was adept in communication but he stayed quiet as it was a foregone conclusion as God had told him it was going to occur when He said to accept his cup.

Please know it is over for the church.

Please know they cannot justify it to them who read my page,

Please know there is no god but Allah in our realm,

Please know Godhead in man does not occur in the actual sense or in a way that can be said, it is just an association of ideas which is what metaphors are.

Please know my treatise is clear these are Jesus' teachings that these are metaphors,

Please know by the same token Godhead in other personages is abrogated as these concepts are similar for them and they were in His repose as well.

Please know the concept of son of God is explained by the same token and the word begotten is a lie by the gospel writer, for Jesus indicates it is prophet who works miracles as a sign to them,

Please see when a scholar says something out of hand about a personage of excellence it is the duty not to follow him but see what he says about the issue himself so as to prevent aggrandizement of the said individual.

Please know the gospel writer knows this but put it there to please him who asked him to do so.

Please know it is the same gospel writer who allows this concept it was a metaphor to emerge when he explains metaphorical terms,

Please know son of God is a well-known metaphor which Jesus uses to explain he is a prophet working miracles. A prophet does His works and does His bid as is well known in my literature as the prophet is sanctified and does not blaspheme His word by calling himself son literally of His grace.

Please Him,

Please know he was not guilty of blasphemy,

Please know he was sanctified by God and would not commit the calumny to the Jewish law by calling himself son of His but explained it was the works he performed that confirmed it that he was a prophet, just like the prophets in their book who performed miracles as well.

Please know he did clarify the Jewish law but it is clear that some things did not make sense, that's why they stoned him or tried to and he escaped. When he said the Father and I are one they understood that but when he said He was in me they conjured he was calling himself God while he was only explaining His spirit was in him and the other part they understood not that I am in Him but that may be a fallacy in understanding he had.

Please know he was not guilty of blasphemy as he reiterated it to them that these were metaphors but they wished to kill him on a pretext.

Please know they used the same argument in the crucifixion attempt.

Please know there he remained quiet for the most part as he had explained his position here,

Please know this is how it is in courts in Tennessee as they apply conservators on me and commit me out of hand.

Please know I fight but it is a foregone conclusion they will get their way and inhibit my literature by forcing medication on me and taking me away from the internet, if they could, where I propagate my views and teaching.

Please know I have explained the metaphor to you adequately and now it is for you to bail me out of my predicament,

Please know the metaphor has occurred with you and you know with adeptness the ins and out of it.

Please know our God is One and allows metaphors to please you as you form an alliance with Him, as a metaphor has a connection with Him.

Please Him and do not call him these terms as a metaphor is not to be used literally. Omar.

We bring you back to the original teachings of Jesus and his contemporaries, not later scholars who changed law and all that.

Son of God is earthly support in that it connotes a leader whose intellect is sane to understand in terms of literature from before, as Jesus did.

Please know we are all non-denominational Christians if we consider ourselves to be free thinkers about him and try to clarify what is correct from what has no basis in historical data that was there from before. Ure son knows it is difficult to change centuries old dogma but the Quran has been stating the Oneness of God for fourteen hundred years or so and the Old Testament is a testament to the period before the church's idea formulated the concept of trinity and the Godhead of Christ in actual terms.

Ure son has a request to make.

Please read the Quran regarding those sections that interest you and you will see for yourself how it affects you. In there are sections that talk about Mary and Jesus as well as many sections on the omnipotence of Allah or God. In this review, I have elaborated that we should go to the teachings of Christ rather than any scholar that contradicts his views on the Oneness of His Entity that Jesus himself did not teach. Ure son knows it is incumbent on the scholar to clarify these concepts to his or her follower and I hope that this will occur soon.

Please know I am a non-denominational Christian in the sense of following Christ's teachings who was a Muslim savior of his people. I support that we go back to Christ's teachings on matters that he elucidated clearly and move away from the heretical portrayals of him by Paul, Ignatus and others that have resulted in the moving away of strict monotheism of Christ's teachings in his works to the present-day trinity where there is an interplay of polytheism in the monotheism of the Old Testament and the Quran. In this there is clarity in that Jesus has called himself son of man around 80 times in the New Testament clearly indicating he had an earthly father and the term son of God was in the metaphorical sense of being the king in discourse, which is what the chief rabbi is considered to be. Ure son is not mischievous in bringing these concepts to you as these will deter you from Paradise later on if you associate your Creator's Omnificence with another entity, as indicated in the Quran and Old Testament literature. Omar.

Please see Jesus was a messenger and they are all wired to obey Him Who creates.

Please see detract from us in Islam is when you have the Quran available yet you call him God literally.

Please see the following caption on my heart.

I am sad for you if you do not see the truth of what I have stated from the gospels and the Quran.

Please note the following words from the Quran. The words that state the fact they are honored servants instead of sons indicates the metaphorical meaning of sons of God. Thus, it is confirmed from the Quran that these concepts are just metaphors and this is what is indicated in the verse from the psalms and elsewhere in the Old Testament. Elsewhere, it is said that that anyone who associates with his Creator will enter Hell. It is with this sadness that I come to you in earnest not to associate godhead in anyone other than your Creator. It is clear that we must meet our Creator with a clean conscience in this regard and allow Him to judge us on our deeds rather than false convictions which will cause us to enter Hellfire. In this there is certainty in that if we profess there is no god but God then we will be safe from His wrath in regard to His dominion.

Please know that we cannot surmise that our Creator will go back on His word that He has stated in the Old Testament and what Jesus taught his follower there about His Oneness. His mercy will come into play when we are being reformed.

Please try to see the significance of these words.

Please try to realize we cannot be pardoned as long as we have the wrong belief about Him.

Please know we are responsible for our choices. I cannot make you choose your path. Omar.

Quran, chapter 21 or The Prophets

26 And they say: The Beneficent has taken to Himself a son. Glory be to Him! Nay, they are honored servants

27 They speak not before He speaks, and according to His command they act.

28 He knows what is before them and what is behind them, and they intercede not except for him whom He approves, and for fear of Him, they tremble.

29 And whoever of them should say, I am a god besides Him, such a one We recompense with hell. Thus We reward the unjust.

Please see this post occurred when I erupted after my long sleep with you, the American people, as you were upset with me that I gave you Him Who you trust and law became apparent to you, then you relented on my medication.

Please see this concept is new and means that we are one with our Creator if we have His thoughts on us and do His bid there and if we tankeeb or else sin in our thoughts then we cannot fuse with Him and are not His repose, like Jesus or myself had become, so forth results and we know repose is simple when you understand it in that our thought process is continually modified in our DNA struct and we then are in unity with Him.

Please know when we sin our DNA gets modified negatively and mutations result in it which can be transmitted late to child and so next generation is weak in it, repose I mean, and when we sin not and also asks forgiveness He modifies it back to its original format if it be His will to do so.

Facebook article here.

Please know this concept is there in the Quran that we can be one with him in deeds and so forth but we don't say we are Allah even in the metaphorical way as that is blasphemy to others but we can write these concepts for you in vernacular so that you can understand Jesus' words there when he said 'I and the Father are one' and other tropes he uses but it is so you have the hadith I use that 'we can walk with Allah's feet and talk His words' when we are one with Him and so forth results we are one, one day then you will learn you don't have to do it that way and you can be like Muhammad, on him be peace on this issue as he stood apart and let his shaur occur that sometimes you have to circumvent law for people as he saw there were limits to their conformity to My feet say I Allah here, more on this as we know people are interested how we can be one with Him when we lie and cheat and kill and plunder according to them in police force but it is so they relent there to peace here, they are angry I call them zoo but it is so they are animal car here.

Please see this verse from Araf where it says we don't associate with Allah what we don't know, He has sent me authority to teach this to you that we are all Allah's metaphor when we do His work and are conjoint with Him.

Please know I know you are kind and want my literature to prevail you but many lie and cheat and things of that sort, you can't do that if you are Allah's feet, but try to follow me and live an upright life and you will have repose and then you can do His bid on you in the sense of carrying out commands He has on us, which few can do actually, but if you follow the Quran injunctions you can come close to it and repose develops in you and that way you will get to Muhammad where your understanding occurs from his teach there that we are 1 body in the world forum of people and so forth results you see Jesus there as a man and a prophet and all the anbiya or prophets come to light and they delight you, it is through Muhammad you meet them when you recognize *him as a great man there who taught the Quran to you, I just take you to him and Allah occurs then, as little girls know. Omar.*

Araf from the Quran lore.

7:33 Say: My Lord forbids only indecencies, such of them as are apparent and such as are concealed, and sin and unjust rebellion, and that you associate with Allah that for which He has sent down no authority, and that you say of Allah what you know not.

CHAPTER TWO

THE DEATH OF JESUS AS INDICATED THAT IT OCCURRED FROM THE GOSPELS AND THE QURAN

Introduction to his demise there in India some.

The death of Jesus is documented in lore from the Indian subcontinent dating back approximately 2000 years. In the Indian subcontinent in the province of Kashmir there is a grave site and tomb marking the site of burial of a prophet-like saint by the name of Yuz Asaf who died there approximately at the time that he migrated from Palestine around 35 A.D. After his migration from Palestine he taught and preached in Afghanistan and Northern India to the lost tribes of the Jews. It is clear that after capture by Nebuchadnezzar they were released by Cyrus and his son Darius that some of them wish to remain aloof from the Judean culture that caused them dismay and hardship under foreign rule that Nebuchadnezzar imposed on them. It is here that Jesus migrated and it is mentioned in the Quran that he will live to an advanced age. It is mentioned in the sayings of Prophet Mohammed that he would live to twice his age which would be around 100 years. It is also mentioned in the Quran that both he and his mother would seek refuge in a land where there were meadows and springs of water, which fits the description of Kashmir in Northern India.

The post here is genuine in that the Quran says he will live a long life.

I will tabulate some of the post regarding this topic here and show how we understand his death to be in Kashmir from our sources. I will also give ancillary evidence from the Bible, the gospels in particular.

The following verses are from the Quran indicating he lived to an old age and found refuge in the valleys of the Himalayan mountain range. Omar.

Chapter three or Amran

3:46 And he will speak to the people when in the cradle and when of old age, and (he will be) one of the good ones.

Chapter 23 or Believers

23:50 And We made the son of Mary and his mother a sign, and We gave them refuge on a lofty ground having meadows and springs.

It is clear from these verses that Jesus survived the crucifixion process and lived to an old age. It is also clear from the inscriptions of the Bible that he bled when his side was pierced by Pilate immediately before he was taken down from the crucifix. Unlike the two insurgents who were crucified that day his legs were not shattered to cause death by internal hemorrhage. As he bled it is clear that his heart was still pumping as a person whose heart has stopped pumping only shows congealed blood when his skin is pierced with an object such as a lance. It is clear from this data that Jesus did not die on the crucifix but only passed out, which is a form of death in the Muslim lore of the Quran. It is further evinced that after two days he emerged after regaining his strength. When he saw Mary Magdalene he was disguised as a gardener and had to identify himself to her since she could not recognize him. It was obvious he wished to hide himself from his Jewish perpetrators of violence and after staying awhile he left Palestine to preach to the lost tribes of the Jewish nation of Bani-Israel.

Please see his death was fictional as his prayers were accepted that night of Gethsemane.

Please see the following post from Facebook where it states clearly that Jesus was successful there in prayer services he had though God wanted him to take the cup and fulfill Isaiah's prophecy of him.

The following is a brief post about the prayer that was accepted before the crucifixion process when he prayed in the garden of Gethsemane. I have tried to indicate that it was God's plan to let him survive the process as seen in the Quran literature on us and though

Isaiah says it it is supposedly fictional that report so I don't use that literature they use. There seems to be a discrepancy in some of the usage of the term death in the scriptures but it is clear the word in Hebrew means both a sleep state as well as physical death.

Please know the Jesus was pleased with result and he knew his role as Messiah was established with the fulfillment of the prophecies of the Old Testament scriptures. In this we have peace as he became known as the Messiah in the Christian world, as well as Islam, when the Quran testified he was the Messiah as well. It was by self-sacrifice of himself that he rose in the eyes of people as they realized what a great emissary he was and he was innocent and not guilty by verdict of the people, then his literature prevailed there otherwise he would have been forgotten, and with his crucifixion the people became sympathetic to him and started following his teach there. If he hadn't been crucified and had left them he would not have become popular as he did become, unfortunately his death was factual not and this caused the Christian religion to deviate and Paul did the rest by saying things like atonement occurred to bring them to Islam, the Gentiles to them, and the disciples took advantage of this as well even though Jesus had warned them not to teach them, the Gentiles, as they would alter facts about him and that's what occurred and they called him God and son of His Grace and so forth modern day Christianity emerged there from Paul's and some of the disciples say on him who is Jesus there.

Please know the days of flesh were just before he was crucified. In the garden of Gethsemane he was fervent in his desire to live and his prayer was accepted that night as indicated in this section from Hebrews. Though he was resigned to his fate he knew the cup would be one that he could accept as it did not create his death. He was surprised when he was crucified and uttered the words of reproach to his Creator however God had a plan for him which would fulfill His promise to him and also fulfill the scriptures regarding the apparent death of the Messiah and his being raised on the third day. Please see it was obvious he was going to be arrested and he couldn't prevent that but it is so God had a plan that he would elevate his rank to them through this process of crucifixion they had on him and they were tired of his harangue that they were bad and now wanted him dead and so forth they killed him in intent, as the Quran says there.

In this there is clarity that it was through his apparent death man would forsake him who caused this death threat of innocents by them as it was commonplace in that any dissension would be followed by killing of them and so it occurred they were looked down upon who were council there for doing this manipulation that they lied about him saying he was a blasphemer so forth a new nation would arise and teach with mercy principles he had and Islam would result eventually when I came says I Muhammad, though you deterred and kept quiet about it, Quranic injunctions here, and told him and her, your child there, he is liar who is me of the Quran author to you and eventually succumbed to me through Omar's page when I appeared there in spirit and so forth results you now know what liars they are in church quarters on you. Omar.

Gospels of Hebrew 5.

7 In the days of his flesh Jesus offered up prayers and supplications with loud cries and tears to him who was able to save him from death, and he was heard because of his reverence.

8 Although he was a son he learned obedience through what he suffered.

The trial of Jesus elucidates that he was a victim of false testimony and pre-decided verdict of guilt.

The trial of Jesus permitted him to give his testimony. He reiterated he was the son of God in the sense of the metaphor as he had explained this carefully to them in the past.

This is my post from Facebook where I elaborate on his trial.

Please know this is a matter that concerns others that he stated he was the son of God before he was crucified. He did not deny his teachings as that would not have been worthy of a Prophet however he had made it clear that it was in the sense of a metaphor when he denied that he meant it in the actual sense when he was questioned about it before they planned to stone him. In this we are sane as it appears that when you have made your position clear it is futile to argue the point any further as the decision will not change no matter what you do.

Please realize that Jesus did not testify to his own guilt. As Caiaphas had already decided the matter Jesus was not wont to testify or answer questions. He indicated that he was not guilty and they could not bring any witnesses indicating that he had been guilty of the crime of polytheism which was one of the blasphemy charges against him.

Please know when he stated he was the son of God he had previously made it clear it was a metaphor. He reiterated he was the son of God there but as I have stated here it was in the metaphorical sense of being their leader in the discourse of religion or in the sense of being the best amongst them.

Please know that Caiaphas took him to Pilate on the request that he be tried for treason as he did not have any witnesses that he committed blasphemy.

Please know they did not have a case against him and Pilate himself found him not guilty of the crime of treason so they reverted back to the charge they initially captured him on. Omar.

John 18

12 Then the detachment of soldiers with its commander and the Jewish officials arrested Jesus. They bound him

13 and brought him first to Annas, who was the father-in-law of Caiaphas, the high priest that year.

14 Caiaphas was the one who had advised the Jewish leaders that it would be good if one man died for the people.

15 Simon Peter and another disciple were following Jesus. Because this disciple was known to the high priest he went with Jesus into the high priest's courtyard,

16 but Peter had to wait outside at the door. The other disciple, who was known to the high priest, came back, spoke to the servant girl on duty there and brought Peter in.

17 "You aren't one of this man's disciples too, are you?" she asked Peter. He replied, "I am not."

18 It was cold, and the servants and officials stood around a fire they had made to keep warm. Peter also was standing with them, warming himself.

19 Meanwhile, the high priest questioned Jesus about his disciples and his teaching.

20 "I have spoken openly to the world" Jesus replied. "I always taught in synagogues or at the temple where all the Jews come together. I said nothing in secret.

21 Why question me? Ask those who heard me. Surely they know what I said."

22 When Jesus said this one of the officials nearby slapped him in the face. "Is this the way you answer the high priest?" he demanded.

23 "If I said something wrong," Jesus replied, "testify as to what is wrong. But if I spoke the truth why did you strike me?"

24 Then Annas sent him bound to Caiaphas the high priest.

25 Meanwhile, Simon Peter was still standing there warming himself. So they asked him "You aren't one of his disciples too, are you?" He denied it, saying "I am not."

26 One of the high priest's servants, a relative of the man whose ear Peter had cut off, challenged him "Didn't I see you with him in the garden?"

27 Again Peter denied it, and at that moment a rooster began to crow.

28 Then the Jewish leaders took Jesus from Caiaphas to the palace of the Roman governor. By now it was early morning and to avoid ceremonial uncleanness they did not enter the palace, because they wanted to be able to eat the Passover.

29 So Pilate came out to them and asked "What charges are you bringing against this man?"

30 "If he were not a criminal," they replied, "we would not have handed him over to you."

31 Pilate said "Take him yourselves and judge him by your own law." "But we have no right to execute anyone," they objected.

32 This took place to fulfill what Jesus had said about the kind of death he was going to die.

33 Pilate then went back inside the palace, summoned Jesus and asked him, "Are you the king of the Jews?"

JESUS THE MESSIAH AND THE PERSON

34 "Is that your own idea," Jesus asked, "or did others talk to you about me?"

35 "Am I a Jew?" Pilate replied. "Your own people and chief priests handed you over to me. What is it you have done?"

36 Jesus said, "My kingdom is not of this world. If it were my servants would fight to prevent my arrest by the Jewish leaders. But now my kingdom is from another place."

37 "You are a king then!" said Pilate. Jesus answered, "You say that I am a king. In fact, the reason I was born and came into the world is to testify to the truth. Everyone on the side of truth listens to me."

38 "What is truth?" retorted Pilate. With this he went out again to the Jews gathered there and said, "I find no basis for a charge against him.

39 But it is your custom for me to release to you one prisoner at the time of the Passover. Do you want me to release 'the king of the Jews'?"

40 They shouted back, "No, not him! Give us Barabbas!" Now Barabbas had taken part in an uprising.

Please see the notes of Muhammad Ali regarding his crucifixion process.

Please see this verse from the Quran that Jesus was not killed on the cross but rather survived it.

Please know these verses are from Nisa from the Quran.

Please know the explanation from Maulana Muhammad Ali is enclosed but I will make a few additional points in this regard.

Please know Jesus was innocent and an innocent man is not accursed, so he would not be hanged as was seen here.

Please know that the two men who were hanged with Jesus were guilty.

Please know it is clear that the explanation of Muhammad Ali is adequate to explain that the death of Jesus did not occur then.

Please see Nisa.

4:155 Then for their breaking their covenant and their disbelief in the messages of Allah and their killing the prophets wrongfully and their *saying, Our hearts are covered; nay, Allah has sealed them owing to their disbelief, so they believe not but a little:*

4:156 And for their disbelief and for their uttering against Mary a grievous calumny:

4:157 And for their saying: We have killed the Messiah, Jesus, son of Mary, the messenger of Allah, and they killed him not, nor did they cause his death on the cross, but he was made to appear to them as such. And certainly those who differ therein are in doubt about it. They have no knowledge about it, but only follow a conjecture, and they killed him not for certain:

Notes 4:157. The words ma salabu-hu do not negative Jesus' being nailed to the cross; they negative his having expired on the cross as a result of being nailed to it. Salb is a well-known way of killing. Salaba-hu means he put him to death in a certain well-known manner (Lane's lexicon). That Jesus died a natural death is plainly stated in 5:117: "and I was a witness of them so long as I was among them, but when Thou didst cause me to die, Thou wast the Watcher over them". The gospels contain clear testimony showing that Jesus Christ escaped death on the cross. The following points may be noted: (1) Jesus remained on the cross for a few hours only (Mark 15:25; John 19:14) but death by crucifixion was always tardy. (2) The two men crucified with Jesus were still alive when taken down from the cross; the presumption is that Jesus too was alive. (3) The breaking of legs was resorted to in the case of the two criminals but dispensed with in the case of Jesus (John 19:32, 33). (4) The side of Jesus being pierced, blood rushed out and this was a certain sign of life. (5) Even Pilate did not believe that Jesus actually died in so short a time (Mark 15:44). (6) Jesus was not buried like the two criminals, but was given into the charge of a wealthy disciple of his, who lavished care on him and put him in a spacious tomb hewn in the side of a rock according to Mark 15:46. (7) When the tomb was seen on the third day, the stone was found to have been removed from its mouth (Mark 16:4), which would not have been the case if there had been a supernatural rising. Mary, when she saw him, took him for the gardener (John 20:15), which shows that Jesus had disguised himself as a gardener. (9) Such disguise would not have been needed if Jesus had risen from the dead. (10) It was in the same body of flesh that the disciples saw Jesus, and the wounds were still there deep enough for a man to thrust his hand in (John 20:25–28). (11) He still felt hunger and ate as his disciples ate (Luke 24:39–43). (12) Jesus Christ undertook a journey to Galilee with two of his disciples walking side by side with him (Matt. 28:10), which shows that he was fleeing for refuge; a journey to Galilee was not necessary to rise to heaven. (13) In all post-crucifixion appearances Jesus is found hiding himself as if he feared being discovered. (14) Jesus Christ prayed the whole night before his arrest to be saved from the accursed death on the cross, and he also asked his disciples to pray for him; the prayers of a righteous man in distress and affliction are always accepted. He seems to have even received a promise from God to be saved, and it was to this promise that he referred when he cried out on the cross: "My God, my God, why hast Thou forsaken me?" Heb. 5:7 makes the matter still more clear, for there it is plainly stated that the prayer of Jesus was accepted: "When he had offered up prayers and supplications with strong crying and tears unto Him that was able to save him from death, and was heard in that he feared."

The statements made in the Qur'an corroborate the above statements quoted from the gospels. Jesus did not die on the cross, nor was he killed as were the two thieves, but to the Jews he appeared as if he were dead.

Notes 4:157. The words shubbiha la-hum may bear two interpretations: he was made to be like (it) or to resemble (it); or the matter was made dubious or obscure (Lane's lexicon). The Ruh al-Ma'ani says the meaning may be that the matter became dubious to them. The story that someone else was made to resemble Jesus is not borne out by the words of the Qur'an, which could only mean, if an object were mentioned, that Jesus was made to resemble someone, not that someone was made to resemble Jesus.

Please see I differ from Mark that he was placed in the tomb as I say he was given refuge there in the jungle around his house for two days and the tomb was used as a refuge not but ruse to make them think he had died by Joseph of Arimathea and there his wounds were tended to. I say this from revelation so you can accept it if you wish but you know me truthful generally and I have never been known to lie in religious discourse so most accept me as a teacher there who teaches from Allah these facts that I do and now you know the events just rest assured he did not die and as the Quran says they killed him not for sure.

Omar.

The crucifixion process of Christ as tabulated there.

The crucifixion process indicates that Jesus was alive when he was brought down from the crucifix. In this way we know that he was saved by the agencies of people who wished him well. It appears that Pilate was active in saving him as indicated when the guards dispelled with the breaking of his bones. It appears that the dream that was seen by Pilate's wife before the crucifixion process also influenced him. I will allow the reader to surmise if there is a basis to doubt this event of him being saved from some contradictory scripture. I am confident they will not have an argument against our views here.

Please know these are things that I have brought to you today based on your own sources.

Please know the Gospel of John is accurate in that when it states the body of Christ was pierced blood and water flowed indicating the heart was beating. In the other gospels there is no mention of this event therefore the testifier has attested to the fact that this occurred signifying the importance of the event of blood flowing when the skin was impaled on his side. In this we are sane that it was only because of this testimony that it is realized that our savior was known to have lived through the crucifixion process and as his legs were not broken as it was apparent that Pilate did not want his death on his hands and instructed Joseph of Arimathea to take the wounded body for the purported claim of burial. It is clear that if it had been known he was alive he would have had to kill him like he had to crucify him before. I am sane that the guards dispelled with breaking his bones as well on instructions from him. It was obvious to Mary that he was disguised on the Sunday she saw him after the purported burial so that he would not be captured again. It is clear if he had been resurrected he would not have had this fear of capture as a resurrected individual cannot be killed as one can suffer only one death in life. It is here we differ from them who consider his death actual rather than purported as we have described here.

Gospel of John.

31 Now it was the day of Preparation and the next day was to be a special Sabbath. Because the Jewish leaders did not want the bodies left on the crosses during the Sabbath they asked Pilate to have the legs broken and the bodies taken down.

32 The soldiers therefore came and broke the legs of the first man who had been crucified with Jesus and then those of the other.

33 But when they came to Jesus and found that he was already dead, they did not break his legs.

34 Instead, one of the soldiers pierced Jesus' side with a spear, bringing a sudden flow of blood and water.

35 The man who saw it has given testimony, and his testimony is true. He knows that he tells the truth, and he testifies so that you also may believe.

36 These things happened so that the scripture would be fulfilled: "Not one of his bones will be broken,"

37 and, as another scripture says, "They will look on the one they have pierced."

Please see John says the soldier pierced his side and blood flowed but it was actually Pilate who himself came to supervise his escape as he was sure he was innocent and they were lying he had committed blasphemy and it so occurred he was brought down and sent there for refuge and was asked to leave the vicinity but Jesus had it in his mind to stay and let disciples know he was living in order to celebrate his victory so he stayed with them but the Bani-Israel injured him again as they found out he was alive and then he left. He left with Mary and several of his disciples including Thomas and then Mary, his mother, joined him there in Egypt as well, then they escaped to the Northern route not but to the mountains where they reside, the Bani-Israel tribes who left Judea to them who returned after Cyrus and Darius freed them. It was clear his life was at threat there so he had to leave and they the disciples saw fit to malinger his death and resurrection to them who remained in order to magnify him and fill the script of the Old Testament but that was flawed and only meant stupor there as the word is the same in Hebrew so it came about, atonement story there, by Paul and others in order to bring the Gentiles to faith. Omar.

Please see the crucifixion process continued here.
Please see the following passage from John where it states that he bled before he was brought down.

Please know my post accompanies the passage where the words blood and water indicate that he bled.

Please know this is the crucifixion scene as witnessed by John, the apostle.

Please know he was there to witness the scene,

Please know this,

Please know they saw he was in a stupor and checked.

Please know the term blood and water means it flowed in Hebrew,

Please know you can check a dictionary.

Please know he was in a stupor and his legs were not shattered as was asked by the Pharisees and Sadducees,

Please know our Prophet told me they led him away after they brought him down,

Please know he walked,

Please understand Pilate,

Please know he was ruthless but his wife asked him to intervene,

Please know he allowed a cover up,

Please know his companions arranged for him to be in disguise from them. Omar.

Please see this extract from a Hebrew dictionary.
Please see the meaning of blood and water.

Please know this is from a Hebrew dictionary.

Please understand this is what is meant when the spear pierced the side of Jesus,

Please know our Prophet knew of this term,

Please know he remained quiet about it.

Please know the lance pierced the side of Jesus.
Please know blood and water flowed,
Please know this term is used for flowing.

Please understand our Prophet knows you can research for yourself and encourages you to do so. Omar.

Definition of blood and water from a Hebrew dictionary here:

The pictograph ד is a door representing the idea of moving back and forth. The מ is a picture of water and can represent any liquid especially blood. Combined these pictures mean "the moving back and forth of water" or the "flowing of blood".

The concept of death and the idea of resurrection was a later extrapolation by scholars.

In a post on Facebook I made it clear that the death of Christ was not as indicated by later scholars. It was primarily Paul and then later Ignatus who espoused his death to be in the actual sense rather than in the spiritual sense as understood by us in Ahmadiyyat. Your son in repose understands that in both the Arabic language and in the tongue spoken there that the state of sleep is considered by be a form of death. It is in this context that the state of death is said to occur by the follower who knew he was alive after he passed out. Your son indicates it is the metaphor and it is actually the spiritual state of sleep when the soul departs from him to be with the Creator as indicated in Chapter Zumar indicated below, where the soul travels there to Him when we are asleep and it is coined as death in Arabic vernacular. The concept of atonement in the Christian church is incoherent and was used by Paul and Ignatus to further their cause of bringing the word of Jesus to the pagans who liked the idea that they would not be judged for their wrongdoings or sins.

The post below indicates that in the vernacular of the Quran and Jewish literature the word for death is used synonymously with sleep or the unconscious state thereby indicating the death of Jesus was a misnomer applied there for a purpose of preventing a similar catastrophe from occurring once more.

Please see this verse from the chapter of the Quran where the state of sleep is akin to death in that the soul departs from the body and travels there to Him. I will elucidate this to indicate when the follower of Jesus described his sleep-like state after he passed out on the cross he indicated the word death, as the vernacular is used in that sense there in the Jewish literature as well as the current day Arabic concept of sleep to be death. I know this is a derivation we understand to be correct and it was later scholars who changed the concept from passing out, as indicated here, to actual death; something that was not intended by the early use of the word by his follower. Omar.

Quran Zumar.

39:42 Allah takes (men's) souls at the time of their death, and those that die not, during their sleep. Then He withholds those on whom He has passed the decree of death and sends the others back till an appointed term. Surely there are signs in this for a people who reflect.

The derivation of the word Tawaffa or death in the Quran.

In the Quran we see the word tawaffa or death written in such a way that it connotes death or sleep. There it is clear that the verse of Al-Imran means death in way that is obvious for it is known he died there in Kashmir and so forth results.

Please see the word tawaffa also means to requite but it is so in the context here it means death in a way known.

This post has been altered here as it makes sense to some but not all. The word mutawaffa in the Quran also means sleep but it is true there is a second meaning which is maut and that is the connotation here. Please know maut in Arabic means death though it can also connote the unconscious state which is a form of sleep. Henceforth we will call it death.

Chapter three or The Family of Amran

3:55 When Allah said: O Jesus, I will cause thee to die and exalt thee in My presence and clear thee of those who disbelieve and make those who follow thee above those who disbelieve to the day of Resurrection. Then to Me is your return, so I shall decide between you concerning that wherein you differ.

Chapter five or Maida.

5:117 I said to them naught save as Thou didst command me: Serve Allah, my Lord and your Lord; and I was a witness of them so long as I was among them, but when Thou didst cause me to die Thou wast the Watcher over them. And Thou art Witness of all things.

Summary of views regarding his death in Islam we serve as sane for you.

The views in Islam regarding his death are diverse. In Islam the traditional viewpoint is based upon weak hadith sayings attributed to Prophet Muhammad that cannot be verified as being correct. In this way a misconception arose that he was lifted bodily to heaven just like in the Christian lore but that he never underwent the crucifixion process. In this there is disbelief in them that Christ suffered at all which is against the body of evidence from the gospels as well as the Old Testament predictions about him. It appears that Muslim scholars have closed their mind about his crucifixion process as they feel it is below the dignity of a Prophet like Jesus that he would be allowed to suffer in this way by his Creator. They also misinterpret certain verses of the Quran which they feel do not allow the crucifixion process. It is my hope they will gradually open up their views to understand our viewpoint in Ahmadiyya Islam to be the correct one as we base our arguments on credible data and seek to correct the misinterpretations in the current Christian and Muslim lore about the nature of the life and death of our savior Jesus, the Messiah.

Please understand the misconceptions arising after the death of Christ have been a source of conflict between people from our group and mainstream Muslims. As mentioned previously the teachings that Christ was in heaven came about from the influence of the Christian lore on Islam. Muslim scholars used certain weak hadith to be the way they justified the concept of a living Christ in heaven waiting to come down before the end of time. Please know these concepts came in Islam under the influence of the Christian lore as well. In this we are sane that man cannot endure space travel and it is only his spirit that rises in the Hereafter after the departure of its soul at the time of his death. In Islam of my group we have attempted to clarify these misconceptions that have arisen from the influence of a certain concept that man can descend in the literal sense. It was a misconception in the Jews as well that resulted them in doubting the Prophethood in Jesus as they expected Elijah to descend, proverbially from heaven before the coming of the Messiah. It was to their detriment that they did not understand what Jesus told them as the correct viewpoint that John the Baptist was the second coming of Elijah, as he was like him in character.

Please know that Islam is served when we realize the three horsemen are none other than members of our group. Please know this indicates that the book of revelations has significance for our group. Please also realize that no one has actually explained the horsemen to be the same beasts of paradise around the tabernacle of our Creator who are pious individuals who are seen to praise their Creator. In this matter we are safe to assume that there will be some controversy but time will elucidate my views as events transpire that we are painted negatively by some as we brought the end of the concept of multiple Gods in your monotheism here in Christianity. I will explain these concepts in a later section.

Yours Truly knows he is on thin ice with them in the Muslim world but as indicated in their literature he cannot have been raised physically as no one can survive space travel without the agency of a space suit, which was not available then, I presume. Also, the verse from Bani-Israel also shows that when asked by the Quraish to bring a book from heaven the Prophet said he couldn't, he being a mere mortal, and so could not travel there in person (verse 93). Yours Truly also knows that to be raised physically as mentioned in certain hadith is mere conjecture and not the words of Prophet Muhammad in my view as it contradicts the Quran verse of Bani-Israel quoted here. Please understand that the meaning of rafa is probably that he was raised in the sight of his Creator for putting up for the act of sacrilege on their part and he was raised in spirit as well because he had been disobedient in certain ways to the teach of his Creat and when the reality of the crucifixion occurred he became His servant more and was more careful in future as well. Omar.

The clinching argument is this one where the Prophet's words are echoed here in what he who is Jesus said in the Quran vernacular.

The death of Christ did actually occur, as indicated in the footnotes where Prophet Muhammad spoke as he who is Jesus spoke, sharing the view that he was dead in reality, like he will die also before Judgment Day.

There is a verse from Surah Maida or Table where it discusses the death of Jesus to be in the actual sense of the word. The saying of Prophet Muhammad, on him be peace also elucidates these terms to be in the actual sense and not in the sense of sleep as indicated by some in the mainstream viewpoint. In this we are sane that to transpose a meaning of your own is to discredit your views with conjecture. Your son knows you have seen this verse before but will post it here to let the reader understand the relevance of the two sets of verses regarding the demise of Jesus in the actual sense. The footnote will be attached in this case. Omar.

Maida

5:116 And when Allah will say: O Jesus, son of Mary, didst thou say to men, Take me and my mother for two gods besides Allah? He will say: Glory be to Thee! it was not for me to say what I had no right to (say). If I had said it, Thou wouldst indeed have known it. Thou knowest what is in my mind, and I know not what is in Thy mind. Surely Thou art the great Knower of the unseen.

5:117 I said to them naught save as Thou didst command me: Serve Allah, my Lord and your Lord; and I was a witness of them so long as I was among them, but when Thou didst cause me to die Thou wast the Watcher over them. And Thou art Witness of all things.

Footnotes to 5:117. This verse is a conclusive proof that Jesus died a natural death, and is not now alive in heaven. Here Jesus says that so long as he was among his followers he was a witness of their condition, and he did not find them holding the belief in his Divinity. The logical conclusion of this statement is that the false doctrine of his Divinity was introduced into the Christian faith after his death, after "Thou didst cause me to die".

A saying of the Holy Prophet is recorded in which the Holy Prophet speaks concerning himself in the very words which are here put into the mouth of Jesus. He said that he would be shown on the day of Resurrection some men who had gone against his teachings, and "I would say what the righteous servant said: I was a witness of them so long as I was among them, but when Thou didst cause me to die, Thou wast the Watcher over them" (Bukhari. 60:8).

Some additional notes here.

There are some other verses of the Quran which I will elucidate here. A complete verse tabulation can be found in Mirza's treatise where he collected 30 verses signifying he had died here on earth and was not living in heaven as is presumed by Christians there.

My Facebook post is as follows.

Please see these verses where it says Allah took the soul of Jesus Christ and he was not killed by them.

Please see the verse in Al-Imran (verse 144) where Allah tells the believers that messengers die as a norm.

Please know he did not make an exception for Jesus and it is clear some Quran translations fabricate the matter when they say 'some' messengers have passed away before him who is Muhammad, on him be peace in that regard that he is the last of the prophets to appear.

Please see when this verse was revealed was at the battle of Uhud when he was injured.

Please know when the Prophet died later it was said by Abu Bakr to Umar and other companions who did not believe he had passed away.

Please know when he said this verse none of the companions said that Isa is alive, contradicting the interpolation of scholars to make it appear that Isa was an exemption to this verse.

Please know they all accepted the verse.

Please know no prophet is living in heaven by the right side of God, as the Christians say of him who is Jesus.

Please also see Al-Imran (verse 55) where He says that He will take the soul of Jesus Christ.

Please see he did migrate there to his home where there were springs and so forth as the Quran tells here, as seen in the Muminun verse below.

Please see the details of this in Ahmadiyya literature.

Please see it occur that rafa means to exalt or honor and we say it in our prayers for ourselves. Omar.

Al-Imran

3:144 And Muhammad is but a messenger — messengers have already passed away before him. If then he dies or is killed, will you turn back upon your heels? And he who turns back upon his heels will do no harm at all to Allah. And Allah will reward the grateful.

3:145 And no soul can die but with Allah's permission — the term is fixed. And whoever desires the reward of this world, We give him of it, and whoever desires the reward of the Hereafter, We give him of it. And We shall reward the grateful.

Al-Imran also.

3:55 When Allah said: O Jesus, I will cause thee to die and exalt thee in My presence and clear thee of those who disbelieve and make those who follow thee above those who disbelieve to the day of Resurrection. Then to Me is your return, so I shall decide between you concerning that wherein you differ.

Al-Muminun.

23:50 And We made the son of Mary and his mother a sign, and We gave them refuge on a lofty ground having meadows and springs.

Jesus and Mary were incarnate beings who partook in eating and sleeping as humans do.

In the Quran it is made clear that Jesus and Mary were incarnate human beings who used to live as humans. In this we are sane that if a person is in the embodiment of a human he is said to represent human qualities and it is obviously conjecture to call a person with attributes of humans to be anything but a human being. My post below elucidates this view that to call a person God is obviously incoherent and devious when we know that Godhead is a distinct Entity Who needs no food and does not experience pain like Jesus and Mary did.

In this verse where it states that both Jesus and Mary partake in food it indicates that both were human and had frailties of humanity which we are all faced with in our earthly existence. We all feel hunger and partake in food. A God-like entity would not have the need for food. Ure son in repose knows in this matter we are sane as there is an exaggeration in the being of Jesus where a person who partook in food and for all purposes was a man is relegated to the dustbin of humanity by calling him part or whole God as is the current Christian view of viewing him. Omar.

Chapter 5 or The Table.

5:73 Certainly they disbelieve who say: Allah is the third of the three. And there is no God but One God. And if they desist not from what they say, a painful chastisement will surely befall such of them as disbelieve.

5:74 Will they not then turn to Allah and ask His forgiveness? And Allah is Forgiving, Merciful.

5:75 The Messiah, son of Mary, was only a messenger; messengers before him had indeed passed away. And his mother was a truthful woman. They both used to eat food. See how We make the messages clear to them! then behold, how they are turned away!

5:76 Say: Do you serve besides Allah that which controls for you neither harm nor good? And Allah — He is the Hearing, the Knowing.

5:77 Say: O People of the Book, exaggerate not in the matter of your religion unjustly, and follow not the low desires of people who went astray before and led many astray, and went astray from the right path.

Please see the words of Araf to show its significance that there are no exceptions for us and we all live and die on earth.

Please see this statement from Allah is corroborated in the Bible that you are from dust and to dust you will return, there you have it there is no discrepancy in the teachings of the two Books and Allah deters not here when He says it is made up that I would make exceptions to one slave in My laws that I create there about nature being your role here and if Isa had been living there for over 2000 years he would have to be a god which he is not and Muslim mindset has to stop associating me there say I Isa there.

Please know we all live and die on earth as the Quran says here in Araf where God addresses Adam after his fall and that is the final word and if Isa had been alive in heaven he would be infirm after 2000 years of living, Mirza clarified this in his book and this verse corroborates with his teaching that we are resurrected here from earth.

Please know it is over and you have believed for the most part that Ahmadiyya concept there is cogent argument and your law of Isa living in heaven is from Christian lore you adopt from Abu Huraira's hadith that he will descend before the end of times and there you have it you disregard this hadith and stick to facts from the Quran for the most part.

Omar not only.

Araf

7:24 He said: Go forth — some of you, the enemies of others. And there is for you in the earth an abode and a provision for a time.

7:25 He said: Therein shall you live, and therein shall you die, and therefrom shall you be raised.

The concept of atonement is incorrect as shown from the Quran and hadith literature.

The concept of atonement is dependent upon the death of Christ on the cross in the Christian concepts of atonement. In this way we know that he did not die on the cross but only passed out as his heart was still pumping when he was brought down. In this way we know the concepts arising from the presumed crucifixion of him is a misnomer and just as prophets can intervene for their followers the atonement should be worded as intercession that occurs in a similar way when Christ intervenes for his followers if permitted by his Creator.

The post on Facebook regarding the atonement of Christ being an incorrect concept is indicated here.

Please know the atonement of Christ is a misnomer for his intervention that occurs after a man or woman is judged, generally speaking.

Please know the death of Christ is clear in the Ahmadiyya literature. In this we have peace in that this spells the end of atonement of Christ for the sins of others as when he was brought down in the unconscious state he recovered consciousness in the resting place designed to keep him there in peace.

Please know atonement is clear it is a fallacy as how can there not be justice?

Please know it is clear we will be judged for our sins and our Creator will exact judgment to the last iota as He has regard that none of you will be wronged by Him in regard to the law He has sent down through the ages and further He exacts punishment if you have sinned against Him in regard to His commands on you that you come through there.

Please know I am Just and know you want it in the Hereafter that you are justified as well as no wrong will go unpunished by Him say I Allah there. Omar.

Al Zilzal.

99:6 On that day men will come forth in sundry bodies that they may be shown their works.

99:7 So he who does an atom's weight of good will see it.

99:8 And he who does an atom's weight of evil will see it.

Al Anbiya.

21:47 And We will set up a just balance on the day of Resurrection, so no soul will be wronged in the least. And if there be the weight of a grain of mustard seed, We will bring it. And Sufficient are We to take account.

Please see the Lord's prayer here.

Please see this post from my Facebook page where it states clearly Jesus asked his follower to ask forgiveness from Allah and not ask him to say that he should intervene on his behalf which is why we say in Islam that you ask forgiveness from Him and do not beseech your Prophet or god however you may have it.

Please see the Lord's Prayer is a sacred prayer there where they are asked to seek forgiveness from their Creator and it indicates accountability in it.

Please see the Lord's Prayer where Jesus and his companions pray to be forgiven their trespasses (or sins, as indicated in Luke) and we see similarity between the Quran texts and Him, the Father, in it.

Please know the Biblical text is rife with prayers to Him, the Creator here.

Please know it is clear Jesus sinned, otherwise he wouldn't have a prayer like this.

Please know it is seen here that we are responsible for our actions and Jesus does not indicate sinners will be forgiven by him on Judgment Day.

Please know it is obvious a sinner will have accountability by Him in the Quran text.

Please know the Old Testament law is similar as indicated in their books and validated by the Quran text.

Please know we know he can't forgive you there, that we are responsible for our sins is obvious to us in Islam, and Judaism is similar as well.

Please see the Quran is clear that no one can take the sins of another and we bear burdens we create in this life and on Judgment Day we will be judged for them.

Please know that Jesus died is a misnomer there when he was crucified, as I have shown previously in my writings to you, and it is clear that he was impotent in it, the crucifixion process.

Please see he was abject and a God is not abject, you know that.

Please know he was human otherwise he would not have died as you say in Christianity, as a God substance would not have seen it, death I mean here, and it is obvious he felt pain and had injuries from it, the crucifix there, as indicated by John's and others commentary on it.

Please know God is impervious to you in this world and a person of His substance would be similar.

Please know Christianity is rife he was man as well but the central theme they have is that he was God in it while they know that manhood is limited to earthly needs in this life.

Please see he was man in all respects and experienced tragedy at their hands, the Jews.

Please know a prophet cannot forgive people if they believe in him as their Lord and savior, they will be questioned though and the matter decided that they did shirk or associated him with God and punishment is due to them for it. Omar.

Matthew 6

Our Father, which art in heaven, Hallowed be thy name. Thy kingdom come, Thy will be done in earth as it is in heaven. Give us this day our daily bread. And forgive us our trespasses, As we forgive them that trespass against us.

Al-Anum

6:160 Whoever brings a good deed will have tenfold like it, and whoever brings an evil deed, will be recompensed only with the like of it, and they shall not be wronged.

6:161 Say: As for me, my Lord has guided me to the right path — a right religion, the faith of Abraham, the upright one, and he was not of the polytheists.

6:162 Say: My prayer and my sacrifice and my life and my death are surely for Allah, the Lord of the worlds—

6:163 No associate has He. And this am I commanded, and I am the first of those who submit.

6:164 Say: Shall I seek a Lord other than Allah, while He is the Lord of all things? And no soul earns (evil) but against itself. Nor does a bearer of burden bear another's burden. Then to your Lord is your return, so He will inform you of that in which you differed.

The fact that Jesus was in disguise after the crucifixion process was in order to protect himself from further harm.

The following post is in regard the sighting of Jesus after the crucifixion process. When he emerged from the tomb he was in disguise for the duration of his stay in Palestine in all probability. There are other incidents where he was noted to be similarly in disguise. I will place a few posts regarding these events here for elucidation.

Please know the gospels are clear that Jesus lived after his crucifixion and to convey that he was raised from the dead is conjecture on the part of Paul and others. I am severe on those who think that death results within a short while after being crucified. I am also severe on those who know that when he was impaled and blood flowed that they can ignore this fact and try to convey to others that he actually died on the crucifix and was not brought down alive in an unconscious state. In this there is peace for those who know that the timeline after his crucifixion fits an orderly departure from Palestine with a few of his followers.

Please know that Mary Magdalene could not recognize Jesus even though he was with her talking to her. It is clear he was in a disguise and only when he identified himself could she recognize him. In this there is haste as it is clear that Mary quickly rushed to get other disciples who saw for themselves that he was absent from the tomb or recovery area earmarked for him. In this matter we know that Jesus was careful with her as he did not want the word to get out that he was alive as he could be set up for another death sentence by the Jewish council. In this matter he was careful and wanted to visit with his disciples in their home rather than them brandishing the fact that their savior was still alive and well. In this manner Jesus kept the matter hushed up until he was ready to leave the land, which he did after a short period. In this manner we have understood the gospels which I teach to you today. Omar.

John 20.

11 Now Mary stood outside the tomb crying. As she wept she bent over to look into the tomb

12 and saw two angels in white seated where Jesus' body had been, one at the head and the other at the foot.

13 They asked her "Woman, why are you crying?" "They have taken my Lord away," she said, "and I don't know where they have put him."

14 At this, she turned around and saw Jesus standing there, but she did not realize that it was Jesus.

15 He asked her, "Woman, why are you crying? Who is it you are looking for?" Thinking he was the gardener, she said, "Sir, if you have carried him away tell me where you have put him, and I will get him."

16 Jesus said to her, "Mary." She turned toward him and cried out in Aramaic, "Rabboni!" (which means teacher).

17 Jesus said, "Do not hold on to me, for I have not yet ascended to the Father. Go instead to my brothers and tell them, 'I am ascending to my Father and your Father, to my God and your God.'"

18 Mary Magdalene went to the disciples with the news: "I have seen the Lord!" And she told them that he had said these things to her.

He continued in disguise here and in other sources of the Bible he was hidden until he disclosed himself.

This post indicates that he continued to remain in disguise for some time. It was not until he left the whereabouts of his homeland that he could safely adorn a normal attire where he could be recognized easily. The story of him identifying himself to his disciples was only they could be assured that he was actually living to them. In this we have peace that he did not wish to give the idea of resurrection to the people but indicate his death there in order to protect himself from additional harm as if they knew he was still alive they would surely have tried to kill him once again.

Please know the concept of Jesus as a man is clear to a discerning mind. It is only the intellectually adept who know that it is over for those who wish to have a clear mind about him regarding his birth and life. In the Ahamadiyya literature there is a large body of evidence regarding the death and subsequent travel to the Indian subcontinent where he preached till an advanced age in life. In this matter there is peace as my precursor Imam or leader, Mirza there, laid the body of evidence for his disciples in regard to his death.

Please know that Jesus continued to remain in disguise even after he met with Mary Magdalene. In John 20 he was in disguise as late as the third meet meeting with the disciples. This was several weeks after the crucifixion process. In this these incidents it is clear he did not want the Jewish authorities to know his whereabouts as they would kill him if they knew he was still alive. It is easy to assume this to be the plausible reason for his remaining in disguise as there is no other explanation that would satisfy the reader in regards to his concern for his life to be the reason of disguising himself. In all three incidents they cannot be explained as visions and there is no other plausible reason as to why he would have to disguise himself as a person who is resurrected cannot be at fear for his life as he cannot be killed after being resurrected, a concept well known in the Christian lore. I am sad that even though they have seen insurmountable evidence presented on my part for the death of Christ being a misnomer there are still people who do not heed to their senses and realize that our views in Ahmadiyyat are what are plausible and make sense to individuals who recognize merit in my works and yet imply mental disease in myself to discredit my writings without a substantial knowledge of this matter. I will allow the discerning mind to evaluate my writing to see if they see an aberration of thought processes in my views. The end is here for those who wish to discredit my works as they will not see an error in the force of my arguments of Jesus being a man and a Prophet as indicated here and as elucidated previously in the previous edition of my book. Omar.

Luke 23

13 Now that same day two of them were going to a village called Emmaus, about seven miles from Jerusalem.

14 They were talking with each other about everything that had happened.

15 As they talked and discussed these things with each other Jesus himself came up and walked along with them;

16 but they were kept from recognizing him.

17 He asked them, "What are you discussing together as you walk along?" They stood still, their faces downcast.

18 One of them, named Cleopas, asked him, "Are you the only one visiting Jerusalem who does not know the things that have happened there in these days?"

19 "What things?" he asked. "About Jesus of Nazareth," they replied. "He was a prophet, powerful in word and deed before God and all the people.

20 The chief priests and our rulers handed him over to be sentenced to death, and they crucified him;

21 but we had hoped that he was the one who was going to redeem Israel. And what is more, it is the third day since all this took place.

22 In addition, some of our women amazed us. They went to the tomb early this morning

23 but didn't find his body. They came and told us that they had seen a vision of angels who said he was alive.

24 Then some of our companions went to the tomb and found it just as the women had said, but they did not see Jesus."

25 He said to them, "How foolish you are and how slow to believe all that the prophets have spoken!

26 Did not the Messiah have to suffer these things and then enter his glory?"

27 And beginning with Moses and all the Prophets, he explained to them what was said in all the Scriptures concerning himself.

28 As they approached the village to which they were going Jesus continued on as if he were going farther.

29 But they urged him strongly, "Stay with us for it is nearly evening; the day is almost over." So he went in to stay with them.

30 When he was at the table with them he took bread, gave thanks, broke it and began to give it to them.

31 Then their eyes were opened and they recognized him, and he disappeared from their sight.

32 They asked each other, "Were not our hearts burning within us while he talked with us on the road and opened the Scriptures to us?"

33 They got up and returned at once to Jerusalem. There they found the Eleven and those with them, assembled together

34 and saying, "It is true! The Lord has risen and has appeared to Simon."

35 Then the two told what had happened on the way and how Jesus was recognized by them when he broke the bread.

John 21

1 Afterward Jesus appeared again to his disciples, by the Sea of Galilee. It happened this way:

2 Simon Peter, Thomas (also known as Didymus), Nathanael from Cana in Galilee, the sons of Zebedee, and two other disciples were together.

3 "I'm going out to fish," Simon Peter told them, and they said, "We'll go with you." So they went out and got into the boat, but that night they caught nothing.

4 Early in the morning, Jesus stood on the shore, but the disciples did not realize that it was Jesus.

5 He called out to them, "Friends, haven't you any fish?" "No," they answered.

6 He said, "Throw your net on the right side of the boat and you will find some." When they did they were unable to haul the net in because of the large number of fish.

7 Then the disciple whom Jesus loved said to Peter, "It is the Lord!" As soon as Simon Peter heard him say, "It is the Lord," he wrapped his outer garment around him (for he had taken it off) and jumped into the water.

8 The other disciples followed in the boat, towing the net full of fish, for they were not far from shore, about a hundred yards.

9 When they landed they saw a fire of burning coals there with fish on it and some bread.

10 Jesus said to them, "Bring some of the fish you have just caught."

11 So Simon Peter climbed back into the boat and dragged the net ashore. It was full of large fish but even with so many the net was not torn.

12 Jesus said to them, "Come and have breakfast." None of the disciples dared ask him "Who are you?" They knew it was the Lord.

13 Jesus came, took the bread and gave it to them, and did the same with the fish.

14 This was now the third time Jesus appeared to his disciples after he was raised from the dead.

See John 20 as well where he was in disguise so that Thomas did not recognize him.

24 Now Thomas (also known as Didymus), one of the Twelve, was not with the disciples when Jesus came.

25 So the other disciples told him, "We have seen the Lord!" But he said to them, "Unless I see the nail marks in his hands and put my finger where the nails were and put my hand into his side I will not believe."

26 A week later his disciples were in the house again, and Thomas was with them. Though the doors were locked Jesus came and stood among them and said, "Peace be with you!"

27 Then he said to Thomas, "Put your finger here, see my hands. Reach out your hand and put it into my side. Stop doubting and believe."

Travel away from Palestine to the tribes of the Jews located in Afghanistan and India.

Please know after the crucifixion the work of Jesus was over in Palestine and he made plans to migrate to teach the lost tribes of the Bani-Israel that did not return back to Palestine after being freed from the capture of Nebuchadnezzar by Darius.

Please understand that he had plans to do this before he was placed on the cross and indicated to his companions to do so as well. In this way he would teach a people who had fallen into idolatry and Buddhism and bring the message of One God to be worshipped again.

After his crucifixion process when his twin brother Thomas was unsure whether he still lived he showed him that he was alive in the corporeal sense and not in spirit as is supposed by some nowadays. He also ate and traveled with his companions and talked to them like an average human would. There is nothing extraordinary about this time after the crucifixion process and he behaved as any human would, eating and living with his companions as any normal person would. His ascension is a misnomer for him traveling to a high place of high-altitude. He left Palestine after the sermon under cloud cover to disguise his departure from there permanently.

According to sources from the Indian subcontinent he traveled to Afghanistan and India with his sibling Thomas, as well as his mother and wife Mary Magdalene. For a complete review of the literature please refer to the Ahmadiyya website of the Lahore branch for further elucidation about the travels of Jesus in Northern India and the communication made to various people living in that time. He taught Islam to the people of this land and it was by virtue of his teaching that they later assimilated the teachings of Islam under the tutelage of Prophet Mohammed, on them be peace. At the place of burial there are *impressions of his feet will show the signs of crucifixion on the rock that the impression is made. A photograph is attached where the marks of crucifixion can be seen behind the toes. A photograph of the gravesite is also included. When this site was first investigated by my mentor Mirza Ghulam Ahmad there were many people from the local area who vouched that this was the site of burial of Jesus, on him be peace.*

Some factual evidence that Jesus lived there in Kashmir headquarters he had after facing the debacle of abuse they had on him in Palestine.

Please know there are writings that indicate that Jesus lived in India after his crucifixion attempt. I will attempt to delineate the conversations that took place between personages from his time and Jesus. Please know the texts are ancient and have verified as accurate. I will explain some of the terminology as well. I can show that to a discerning mind these are evidence that Jesus did not die on the crucifix thus negating the arguments of Godhead in him in the actual sense and the negating the concepts of atonement the Christians have nowadays.

The puranas explain Jesus entity living there preaching the word of His Eminence.

The following post from my Facebook page elaborates that Jesus had migrated to India and his travels there were documented in texts from that time.

Please know Islam was served there when he preached as they practiced idolatry and he taught monotheism, which they accepted, apparently, as they considered him to be their Prophet.

Please know this is a story from an ancient document, documenting that Jesus was alive in India and did not die in Palestine, it is clear from these Buddhist sources that the prince or king referred to here was no other than Jesus Christ who was monastic in bent of mind and was given to prayer and worship. He was a leader there and was considered to be the Prophet of the Jewish tribe of Kashmir. Here he found peace as they accepted him as their leader and it is there he is buried to this day. Ure son in repose knows there are some other stories that are available on the Ahmadiyya group websites which detail how Jesus traveled to

Afghanistan and India after he survived the crucifixion attempt there in Palestine. Omar.

The following is a quote from the puranas which date to 115 AD. It discusses a conversation between Jesus and their leader. It is recorded here.

One day the Raja went to the country of the Himalayas He saw a Raja/leader of the Wein (which is located close to Srinagar) who was fair in color and in white clothes. He asked who he was. His reply was that he was Yusashaphat -Yuz Asaf (which may be from Ishaputram or son of God) and had a birth from a woman. Shalewahin was confused. He said he spoke the truth and he had come to purify religion. The Raja asked him what was his religion. He replied "O Raja, when truth had disappeared there is no limit in the Maleech (foreign) country. I appeared there and through my works the guilty and the wicked suffered; I too suffered at their hands." The Raja asked him once again what his religion was. He replied "It is to establish love, truth and to purify one's heart and for this I am called Isa Masih (Jesus, Messiah)." The Raja returned after making obeisance to him.

Some idea given here about his whereabouts there In India before his demise then.

Some additional posts regarding factual texts of his being there preaching Islam to the populace there.

Please know this document also verifies the ascent of Jesus to the mountains of Kashmir.

Please know the historian here describes the Prophet Yuz Asaf as a prophet who became known for his piety and became accepted as the Prophet for the people of Kashmir.

Please know that the sources verify the presence of a prophet who fits the description of Jesus. In addition, the inscriptions on the temple clearly indicate he was Jesus, the Prophet of Bani-Israel.

Please know in a previous post from ancient texts of the Hindus the conversation of Jesus with their king are recorded where he called himself the prophet of Bani-Israel.

Please know, this, along with my previous description of the crucifixion process clarifies that the position we take on the issues regarding the crucifixion that Jesus lived to an old age as documented in the Quran where it states that he lived to an old age. In addition, the Quran indicates he would find refuge in a place of high altitude as discussed in an earlier post. In this way the understanding of our savior Jesus being a man is confirmed. In addition, the concept of atonement for the sins of his followers as promulgated by Paul and others is discarded as it has no basis based on these facts. I will let the reader decide if my comments meet the coherence criteria.

A Muslim historian during the reign of sultan Zainul Abidin wrote about events of Raja Akh. Please know I am writing some of the text in this post but a complete description can be found on the books on this subject on the Ahmadiyya website of the Lahore group. During the reign of Raja's son, Gopananda, repairs of the temple were undertaken. After intercession from the Prophet Yuz Asaf the repair proceeded. On one of the stones in the building the prophet had proclaimed his prophethood. On an another these words inscribed that he was Yasu, the prophet of the Bani-Israel. It was the opinion of the historian that the prophet was actually Jesus Christ, on him be peace. Omar.

Please see Thomas was the twin of Jesus, identical kind, and Mary did not know which was prophet until he spoke about it later, as indicated in the Quran lore here.

Some additional comments regarding the birth of Jesus in that he had a twin Thomas, the twin, was his sibling.

The following are two additional references regarding the travels of Jesus to India. I will place the essential components of these references but for complete elucidation I would recommend referral to the books on the Ahmadiyya websites.

Please know that Christ did not die for the sins of others but rather passed away in the mountains of Kashmir at the ripe old age of approximately 100 years according to a hadith of Prophet Muhammad. on him be peace.

Please know he went with some disciples, his mother and Mary Magdalene. It is reported in ancient texts that they traveled in different parts of India and a conversation took place with the Raja/ king of Taxilla where Jesus preached along with his identical twin Thomas. I will plan to bring you these documents as we proceed onwards in our description of the prophet who is confirmed in world history as the Messiah, the one who conquered by a process of assimilation and eventually became the source of religious knowledge for the Western world that in turn taught his teachings of mercy and compassion to others to the lands they occupied. In this way his teachings spread over the world and formed the basis of civilization in the twentieth century where nations have attempted to promote world peace rather than the barbarism of war that has been a hallmark of mankind's history. In this way the humanity promoted by Islam fostered a harmonious relationship with the teachings of the Messiah. In this we are sane in that there are two world-wide movements of humanity running parallel to each other however the mercy seen in Christian countries has precedence as Islam is currently lacking in principles of humanity due to a lack of compassion in some of their teachings which have moved away from the spirit of truth of our Prophet Muhammad, on him be peace. Omar.

Some additional comments here about his identity as a twin brother in Thomas.

In this post it is apparent that Thomas was the identical twin of Jesus. In this there is concern for the mainstream Christian who believe in the immaculate conception of Jesus. In the gospels there are references to Thomas being the twin of Jesus. Thomas in Hebrew means twin. Thomas was known as Didymus which means twin there in Aramaic. I am averse to communicating any sentiments of concern to others however it is clear the conception of Jesus and Thomas was not a special event other than the birth of a prophet would result. In this way we know it would deny the folklore of Jesus being the incarnate son of God as the Y chromosome would be the same for Jesus and Thomas, and Thomas would have to be immaculate as well, which is against the teachings of present-day Christianity.

JESUS THE MESSIAH AND THE PERSON

Please know this conversation is from the Gospel of Thomas the acta Thomae which describes a conversation that took place between Jesus and the son of a king in Taxilla, India. It indicates that he was there along with his brother Thomas. Your son in repose knows that Jesus had an identical twin Thomas who is known to be his companion in India where they left to be after the crucifixion attempt on him.

Please know the date of this conversation is said to be 49 AD.

Please understand there is a role to assimilate this view that Jesus migrated there after he failed to convince the People of the Book in Palestine about him being their Prophet or saint savior.

Please understand that Jesus preached to the people of Kashmir in India and was accepted as their Prophet. In this way he achieved success in his life there but partial as they still continued in idolatry some. It appears that when he taught them they accepted his teachings and reverted back to the monotheistic faith they originally had. In this way we know that their later generations accepted Islam as there was homogeneity of views between what Jesus taught them and what was brought to them in the message of Islam. In this way we know he was successful in being a harbinger of Prophet Muhammad and was responsible for the people of this land to come to Islam, which they probably would not have done if they assumed idolatry as their religion, which is what had occurred prior to when Jesus preached to them.

Please understand on the other hand there were followers of Jesus in Palestine and the Roman Empire continued to teach there in a way that was conducive for the Gentiles to come into the faith. Though the message was altered it did result in them in understanding the teachings of Christ in their lives. Omar.

Please know the conversation below is as documented in the original document.

Thomas after the ceremonies left the palace. The bridegroom (Abdagases) lifted the curtain which separated him from his bride. He saw Thomas, as he supposed, conversing with her. Then he asked in surprise; "How canst thou be found here. Did I not see thee go out before all."? And The lord answered; "I am not Thomas but his brother."

Photographs that depict the gravesite and the markings of his footsteps who is Jesus there.

Please see the post on the topic.

Please know this is the place he is buried where his footprints are.

Please understand I would request you to visit this site if you want to see the footprints for yourself.

Please know this is in Kashmir, India, where he migrated to after the crucifixion process in approximately 35 AD.

Please see the signs of the crucifixion on his foot below the toes. In this there is certainty that his Creator wished him to preserve this so future generations would recognize this was him buried in this location.

Please know he is buried here under the guise of a prophet Yuz Asaf who was the prophet of the people of Kashmir- who were from the tribes of Bani-Israel who migrated here after they were freed by Cyrus and his son Darius from the yoke of their captors in approximately 515 BC.

Please know it is easy to travel there.

Please know if you love your savior Jesus then know him and do not take conjectures about him to be his car.

Please understand we love him in Islam just like you do in your Christian faith and elsewhere where he is considered a notable amongst men.

Please include me in your list of people you ascribe goodness in as I have brought him to you through the prism of clarity with his true colors showing.

Please know we must ascribe peace to you as you wish to know the truth about him and listen to us in Islam. Omar.

The imprint of the feet of Jesus at the site of the tomb of Yuz Asaf. The impression clearly shows where the feet were impaled by the nails.

The grave of Yuz Asaf or Jesus.

The tomb where Jesus is buried in Srinagar.

CHAPTER THREE

THE BIRTH OF JESUS AS TAUGHT BY THE QURAN AND THE TEACHINGS OF THE GOSPELS

Introduction here.

It is clear that the birth of Christ is a misnomer in regard to it being a virgin birth. The data from the gospels is scant and in the Gospel of John it is clear that he is descended from a man like any other human being. I'll bring this into clarity from the Quran and from other hadith literature that may be useful in elucidating the verses of the Quran regarding his birth and demise.

In the New Testament it is mentioned many times that Jesus is a son of man. In Luke and Matthew he being an evolved entity through the de novo impregnation of Mary through the Holy Spirit appears to be a fallacy of communication somewhere. There is no basis to presume a virgin birth and the data appears to have arisen out of the pagan custom of ascribing godhead to men through the impregnation of virgins by gods of the Greek mythology. During the lifetime of Jesus there in Palestine there was very little mention of this method of childbirth for him and it appears scholars like Paul promulgated these views to further the cause of bringing his Godhead into the consciousness of people of their times.

Nature of man.

It is clear from the Quran and from Biblical sources that all mankind is created from the fusion of an egg and a sperm. The Arabic word for this is nutfah which is translated as ejaculate or spermatozoa and egg, either from a man or from a woman. Also, it is obvious that Jesus was a man-like entity and therefore has an XY chromosome which goes against nature if he was created through parthenogenesis from a woman who only has an XX chromosome set. There is no reason to suppose that God would change his laws of nature for the sake of one prophet-like entity while He created the whole of mankind according to the laws that he has placed here on earth for procreation.

Please understand that we cannot assimilate a male child from a woman without a father. I have placed some of my comments on this matter here and will allow you to assimilate the view as well. I am sane that one knows that God can do anything He wishes however the words of the Quran contradict the celestial nature of the origin of the Y chromosome as He says there that Jesus was created like Adam, out of dust, meaning that he was born of a sperm and an egg as these are earth materials and not celestial as it says there in hadith they have that Gabriel impregnated her, it could not be so if he was created out of dust as the spirit is just that. I wish the reader to assimilate the view from a scientific viewpoint and then understand that his male characteristics were given to him in a normal way or fashion.

Facebook comment here is as follows.

Please know the birth of Jesus is a misnomer in Islam. He was created as a natural conception. In this there is certainty in that the child is born of a male and female zygote and the Y chromosome is delivered to the child from the father giving it male characteristics, which our savior Jesus had.

Please know without a father he would not have been a male.

Please understand that the chromosome is made out of dust, as we all are, and it is in the Quran that Jesus was made out of dust like Adam was. In this way we know his Y chromosome was not celestial.

Please know that Mary had other children as well.

Please know that a woman cannot create out of parthenogenesis a male child as she does not possess a Y chromosome. Omar.

See the nutfah law for man is inherent in sanity we have.

Please see nutfah law is intact as no exception is made in the Quran or elsewhere, where the Prophet said we are nature only.

A post has been attached which was placed on my Facebook page here. It only delineates the words of the Quran in this matter. It is safe to know that a misconception regarding births of such nature exist in many cultures including those which we originated from. It is only a deviance which has crept up in the minds of individuals after the religion was established. I come only to clarify what my mentor taught me through his writings in his translation of the Holy Quran.

Please see Facebook comment here where we see nutfah is universal for man and his kind.

Please allow the mind to assimilate the views of a different faith from yours as we know there are truths in other viewpoints other than our own. Your son in repose has a request to make of you. I would like peace to occur with my Muslim brethren who are narrow minded about another view appearing in Islam after a time period has elapsed though it is only to their detriment that they consider this a deviation. In this we are safe as it boils down to a difference of opinion however they are being backward, in my view, if they cannot assimilate a view that is clear from our teachings which makes sense to a rational mind, as I do to you in this post.

Please know this is a common topic of debate in this day of rationality. I have used verses from the Quran and things mentioned on my previous posts of the topic to elucidate my viewpoints in regard to the creation of man, inclusive of Jesus, to be within the realms of reality.

Please know it is easy to say something about a personage like Jesus however the proof is very scant and comprises of statements after he left that area of Palestine. I know that when he made it clear that he was son of man it is unreasonable to allow the mind to deviate from rationality to suit a whim or excuse for creating Godhead in him.

The verses of the Quran about the creation of man from the ejaculate or nutfah of parents. There is no exception made for any entity inclusive of Jesus. Omar.

The pilgrimage or Hajj,

22:5 O people, if you are in doubt about the Resurrection, then surely We created you from dust, then from a small life-germ (Nutfah or ejaculate), then from a clot, then from a lump of flesh, complete in make and incomplete, that We may make clear to you. And We cause what We please to remain in the wombs till an appointed time, then We bring you forth as babies, then that you may attain your maturity. And of you is he who is caused to die, and of you is he who is brought back to the worst part of life, so that after knowledge he knows nothing. And thou seest the earth barren, but when We send down thereon water, it stirs and swells and brings forth a beautiful (growth) of every kind.

The Believer.

40:67 *He it is Who created you from dust, then from a small life-germ, then from a clot, then He brings you forth as a child, then that you may attain your maturity, then that you may be old; and of you are some who die before and that you may reach an appointed term, and that you may understand,*

The Bee.

16:4 *He created man from a small life-germ, and lo! he is an open contender.*

Virgin birth, a later extrapolation after the concept of godhead in Jesus emerged.

Review of the literature shows that the virgin birth is mentioned only in Matthew and Luke, as indicated here. It is counterintuitive to think that something as significant as the virgin birth of Jesus would not be known to the apostle John who doesn't mention this at all in his gospel. Also, as mentioned previously the words in Luke and Matthew appear to be fallacies that these authors made in creating a Godhead in him similar to the sonship of God, for which there were no witnesses during his life there in Palestine. In this we are sane in that we know it is not an original concept associated with him as it was unknown to John and apparently to Mark as well. We know something as significant as the birth of him would have been known to all the gospel writers if it had indeed been a virgin birth. It is for this reason the dream associated with Joseph appears to be fictional or a fallacy in views where he saw an angel telling him about immaculate conception. He knew she had a rape child in her and relented to marry her so that populace would think it was his but it is so they knew it was from a rape process as the child who did it was annihilated by her testimony. It is obvious to a discerning mind that these discrepancies of nature crept into the mindset of people after he emigrated away from Palestine under the auspices of scholars like Paul and other apostles who deviated from his teachings in order to bring his message to the masses of people they wish to impress. Omar.

Please see the Ebionite sect of early Christian faith believed in virgin birth not of Jesus Christ.

Please see the Ebionites were a group of followers who revered James as a true teacher of Jesus' gospel and they believed in trinity not and were purely monotheistic, something Jesus taught them, and James upheld there in his campaign against Paul's group who were claiming divinity for Christ and also saying he was his son in the sense of begotten, something John put in his gospel, but it so occurs they died out in the second century and were replaced by trinitarians eventually as Paul's teachings gained ground with them but just to elucidate they were of the firm opinion, as was James there, that Jesus had a normal birth process, yes, these were the early followers of truth from Him and are considered to be Muslims in our lore, just like the disciples of Jesus have been called Muslims in the Quran. Omar.

Quran on the topic of Mary's celibacy, prior to conception with Jesus, after her marriage.

The following is Facebook comment from my page where the verses of the Quran elucidate the matter that with the passage of time Mary became pregnant after she was told about the birth of her child in a prophetic revelation to her in the chapter of Mary and elsewhere.

Facebook comment here.

Please also know that the virgin birth of Jesus is in question here. In the Christian lore as well there is usage of the term 'Be and it is' and it means in due course these events will transpire and as indicated here that Mary was surprised she was to have a son when she had avowed herself to virginity. It is clear the reference is she would marry and not remain a virgin in her longevity. This inference can also be made from the Gospel of Luke where these events are mentioned as well. The verses *from the Quran elucidate this matter as they were revealed to Mary before her entry occurred in a rape form, as elucidated here, then her marriage occurred in due course with Joseph with the consent of other people including her mother and so forth results she conceived other kids in due course as the Bible elucidates. Omar.*

Chapter Amran of the Quran.

3:42 And when the angels said: O Mary, surely Allah has chosen thee and purified thee and chosen thee above the women of the world.

3:43 O Mary, be obedient to thy Lord and humble thyself and bow down with those who bow.

3:44 This is of the tidings of things unseen which We reveal to thee. And thou wast not with them when they cast their pens (to decide) which of them should have Mary in his charge, and thou wast not with them when they contended one with another.

3:45 When the angels said: O Mary, surely Allah gives thee good news with a word from Him (of one) whose name is the Messiah, Jesus, son of Mary, worthy of regard in this world and the Hereafter, and of those who are drawn nigh (to Allah),

3:46 And he will speak to the people when in the cradle and when of old age, and (he will be) one of the good ones.

3:47 She said: My Lord, how can I have a son and man has not yet touched me? He said: Even so; Allah creates what He pleases. When He decrees a matter, He only says to it, Be, and it is.

Please see Mary was raped as a child of 14 and it is there in their archives that this did occur and virgin birth was a fallacy they promoted to them in the Christian lair there.

Please see the verse from Nisa is similar about saleeb and Jesus on it, it has to be explained, as they did in Ahmadiyyat.

Please see these verses from surah Maryam where it says she was in the throes of childbirth and she conceived unease in her and was told to be patient and persevere, he will clear the way for you when he is older and she fasted.

Please know these verses depict how I try mankind says Allah there as it is known she was raped yet they promote infidelity in her and say she was chaste not, a flaw seen in Bani-Israel people who know the truth but say otherwise.

Please know she was 14 when the rape occurred and was 15 when she was betrothed to Joseph, her sibling father type mate, as no one wanted her though initially they drew lots to have her as she was pious and would make a good wife they say.

Please know they promulgated false statements about her saying her pregnancy was a fallacy in her.

Please know when Jesus was old enough he cleared her name though he himself was called a bastard because of it as Joseph was not his father.

In throes she had him and Thomas, not expecting a 2nd child but it so occurred it did happen that way that he was 2nd born though identical to him who was 1st born, Jesus himself, and they stayed close to each other as child do then when they are identical twins.

Please know a newborn child does not speak so they knew he could not speak, it was later he spoke and cleared her name of infidelity as he was a saint and I spoke to him say I Allah to you, further, he could not be carried in her arms when he was older as the Quran says there, she just showed him to them at birth and pointed and it was late when he spoke the words quoted here in the Quran verse for you. It did occur to her that she should defend her honor but was told not to and to fast instead. He would clear her name late it would occur.

Please know the words of the Quran are interposed not but occur at a later time by the infant son not but when he was 4 years of age and it so occurred her name was cleared by God with the passage of time though they knew all along she had been raped and she was not promiscuous.

Please see it occur he was 4 years of age when he clarified he was prophet to be at the age of 40 or so and henceforth he was called prophet by them the Bani-Israel group though they were jealous puss of his intellect. Omar.

Maryam.

19:23 And the throes of childbirth drove her to the trunk of a palm-tree. She said: Oh, would that I had died before this, and had been a thing quite forgotten!

19:24 So a voice came to her from beneath her: Grieve not, surely thy Lord has provided a stream beneath thee.

19:25 And shake towards thee the trunk of the palm-tree, it will drop on thee fresh ripe dates.

19:26 So eat and drink and cool the eye. Then if thou seest any mortal, say: Surely I have vowed a fast to the Beneficent, so I will not speak to any man today.

19:27 Then she came to her people with him, carrying him. They said: O Mary, thou hast indeed brought a strange thing!

19:28 O sister of Aaron, thy father was not a wicked man, nor was thy mother an unchaste woman!

19:29 But she pointed to him. They said: How should we speak to one who is a child in the cradle?

19:30 He said: I am indeed a servant of Allah. He has given me the Book and made me a prophet:

19:31 And He has made me blessed wherever I may be, and He has enjoined on me prayer and poor-rate so long as I live:

19:32 And to be kind to my mother; and He has not made me insolent, unblessed.

19:33 And peace on me the day I was born, and the day I die, and the day I am raised to life.

Please see the passages below indicate a virgin birth to her but she was surprised by it that it would be in the due course of events, as evinced in literature I have shown you previously.

The above passage is clear that when Mary received the message from the angels that she was to have a son who was a prophet she was a virgin at that time. She had avowed herself to virginity at the request of her parents and served in the temple from the age of three years approximately. When she developed menses she had to leave the temple and at that time it was decided that she would marry. They drew lots to see who would marry her then, then it occurred her rape. Prior to the process of marriage she received revelation through the angels that she would have a son by the name of Jesus and that he would be highly honored in this world and that in the next world would be one of those drawn near to our Creator. This is also stated elsewhere in the Quran, as indicated here.

Please know Mary was a virgin when this verse was revealed through her soul-mate in Paradise. She was betrothed to the temple and avowed to lead a life of monastic isolation then her menses occurred and she left but it is so the angel or man-spirit came to her in an eastern place. She initially had no intent of marriage or having children but it so occurred she did in due course. She knew her son Jesus was destined to greatness and she was foretold by Him that he would have honor, and regret as well. In his teachings, the similitude he used was taken out of context and it is here approximately two thousand years later that these terms have clarified to the satisfaction of scholars where his metaphor is explained in his verbiage to others regarding his relationship with the Creator.

See my post here.

In these verses it is apparent a spirit visited her and Mary had a vision of a man who came to her in her dream state. It was after this encounter she was ready for marriage. In this we have peace as all of us go through this stage in our youth. For Mary, who was a saint, it was a tangible experience. We know human sexuality goes through this stage in its development.

Please realize that the words spoken here are from a spirit from Him, not a man actually, as thought by some, she knew it was an angel though, man-like in his essence, who gave her a wet dream in which she conceived fear initially then realized her sexuality was norm for her and others she knew, she did not know what sex was until then when he appeared, Gabriel not but man-like spirit we have as girls, they say in Islam here.

Please see here she had not been chaste not and she knew child is given from touch she thought but it was so she had sex eventually when her rape occur and the man was killed for it, then she married him who was Joseph as a cover but the deed was done and they knew about it as the boy in question had been killed but it is so the Bani-Israel later changed facts and accused her of infidelity to Him, her Creat, and so it occurred they called it unchaste act while it was not and Jesus cleared *her name to his follower though this has been hid there but it is in the archives there. It is true she avowed virginity in her but it so occurred sex had to occur in her but it was so she was inexperienced so We gave her a touch of him, her mate in heaven as we all have one, humankind do. The hadith from Abu Huraira and others only report a fallacy that Gabriel touched her shoulder and impregnated her and these hadith are not to be relied upon as many hadith coming from him are made up.*

Eventually she realized her marriage would occur where she would have son, Jesus by name, but she didn't realize it then she was to get pregnant in due course, it was later assimilation she had, at that time she thought it was going to be virginity in her to continue but she did become pregnant in due course when her rape resulted as I have mentioned here in my post to you. Omar.

Chapter nineteen or Mary.

19:16 And mention Mary in the Book. When she drew aside from her family to an eastern place;

19:17 So she screened herself from them. Then We sent to her Our spirit and it appeared to her as a well-made man.

19:18 She said: I flee for refuge from thee to the Beneficent, if thou art one guarding against evil.

19:19 He said: I am only bearer of a message of thy Lord: That I will give thee a pure boy.

19:20 She said: How can I have a son and no mortal has yet touched me, nor have I been unchaste?

19:21 He said: So (it will be). Thy Lord says: It is easy to Me; and that We may make him a sign to men and a mercy from Us. And it is a matter decreed.

Hadith and Quran on the topic of normalcy of Jesus as a man.

The verse that follows in my comment on Facebook refer to the nature of Jesus as a man entity who had a normal birth and life as a human being and not God as was being indicated to our Prophet Muhammad approximately 500 years after his demise. It also elucidates the same viewpoint where the creation of Jesus is considered to be like that of Adam. It does not indicate the birth of a prophet but refers to the underlying theme of the message of the verses in question. It indicates that both Adam and Jesus were humans composed from the materials of the earth, as all man are. Here the message is clear to the reader so I mention this only to certify that all mankind had their origin on earth and it is a fallacy of belief to think we descend from heaven in part or in toto. It states in the Quran that man will live and die on earth and the Bible is similar in that we are from dirt and to it we will return with no exception made in either case for Jesus, the saint-like man whose words on sonship are taken out of context and begotten applied there while that was not his car in intent as I have elucidated in this book to you.

There is also a saying from Ibn a Jarir al Tabari, a Muslim scholar in the third century after Islam that has some weakness in it however it is an elaborate saying and is likely to have merit with scholars. It is obvious to a reader the saying of our Prophet quoted here indicates an earthly father as he would not indicate him to be the son of Him, which clearly refutes the Muslim viewpoint regarding the sonship of a Christ in the actual sense.

This is the hadith verbatim here.

"Do you not know that Jesus was conceived by a woman in the manner in which all women conceive? Then she was delivered of him as women are delivered of their children? Then he was fed as children are fed. Then he ate food and drank water and answered the call of nature (as all mortals do)?" The deputation replied to all these questions in the affirmative, on which the Prophet said: "Then how can your claim (that he was God or Son of God) be true?"

Please see this post below where there is reality in birth of a child in that he is created like Adam and Jesus were from earth.

The teaching of godhead in Christ is refuted here in a teaching to the Christian delegation to him as reported by Ibn Jarir al Tabari that the Prophet indicated to the delegation that their prophet was conceived as men are. He indicated this by asking them "does not the son look like the father?" It is obvious he indicated he had an earthly father and not a celestial one, as any Muslim would know. In this matter it is clear he refuted the Christian viewpoint of him being God incarnate as His son. The hadith further goes on to say that he was conceived like other men were. The hadith has merit but it has not been seen by many in the Muslim world where they ascribe him to be of a virgin birth not unlike the pagan custom of ascribing their great men of similar fallacies.

The following verse indicates that the creation of Adam and Jesus was alike. They were both created from dust just like all mankind are. Adam was created from human parents as was Jesus. This is explained in an additional post which I will elaborate in the following section. The verse in particular talks about the origin of man being from dust. The verses that follow this verse indicate the displeasure our Creator has in this regard and recommends that Muslims should challenge the godhead in man fervently as when you say he is son of immaculate kind you create godhead in him as a natural consequence, as indicated here.

These verse that follows is indicative of the creation of both personages from earthly material and after their creation they are raised to reality as all kids are created in this way and with the statement as used previously 'Be and it transpires.'

Please see the verses that follow show the creation of man to be like that of other personages of Islam and it is wrong to think of them being miraculous in nature like Adam or Jesus who were both created out of dust and not celestial material. This verse was to clarify to the Christion deputation that came to the Prophet to learn him that he was immaculate not and son not of His grace but of a simple construct like man is. Omar.

Chapter The Family of Amran.

3:57 And as to those who believe and do good deeds, He will pay them fully their rewards. And Allah loves not the unjust.

3:58 This We recite to thee of the messages and the Reminder full of wisdom.

3:59 The likeness of Jesus with Allah is truly as the likeness of Adam. He created him from dust, then said to him, Be, and he was.

3:60 (This is) the truth from thy Lord, so be not of the disputers.

3:61 Whoever then disputes with thee in this matter after the knowledge that has come to thee, say: Come! Let us call our sons and your sons and our women and your women and our people and your people, then let us be earnest in prayer, and invoke the curse of Allah on the liars.

Al-Mumin

40:64 Allah is He Who made the earth a resting-place for you and the heaven a structure, and He formed you, then made goodly your forms, and He provided you with goodly things. That is Allah, your Lord — so blessed is Allah, the Lord of the worlds.

40:65 He is the Living, there is no God but He; so call on Him, being sincere to Him in obedience. Praise be to Allah, the Lord of the worlds!

40:66 Say: I am forbidden to serve those whom you call upon besides Allah, when clear arguments have come to me from my Lord; and I am commanded to submit to the Lord of the worlds.

40:67 He it is Who created you from dust, then from a small life-germ, then from a clot, then He brings you forth as a child, then that you may attain your maturity, then that you may be old; and of you are some who die before and that you may reach an appointed term, and that you may understand.

40:68 He it is Who gives life and causes death, so when He decrees an affair, He only says to it, Be, and it is.

Immanuel.

There is a misconception amongst Christian scholars that the birth of Immanuel was a virgin birth. It appears he was a warrior at the time of the king Ahaz during the time of the Prophet Isaiah in the eighth century BC. The following is my note from my Facebook page. It is clear to the reader that it was a time of turmoil for the king and his subject and the birth of the warrior was meant to allay their discomfiture.

Please know the birth of Jesus was construed in the late first century by the gospel writer Luke.

Please know Matthew followed suit but the idea did not find favor with John who does not refer to it in his writings. It is a clear extrapolation of the idea that the Jews promulgated about Mary that she had an illicit affair that resulted in the birth of Jesus. It was only a way they could defame her as she was known for her piety and her love for her son.

Please know the sign of Immanuel is much quoted in the Christian lore as a sign of the virgin birth of Christ.

Please know it refers to specific time in the days of the king Ahaz regarding the trouble he was facing from the foreign invaders of Ephraim and Syria. It in no way should be construed of the birth of Jesus a good seven centuries later when these people did not attack Judea, the capital state of the Jewish nation. It was taken out of context by the Christian scholar who initially portrayed it to mean the birth of Jesus. It applies to the time of Ahaz where a young girl gave birth to a warrior who fought on behalf of God apparently.

Please know the similarities are striking however as indicated here refer to a different time period. Omar.

Bible text.

6 "Let us go up against Judah and terrify it and let us conquer it for ourselves and set up the son of Tabeel as king in the midst of it,"

7 thus says the Lord God: "'It shall not stand and it shall not come to pass.

8 For the head of Syria is Damascus and the head of Damascus is Rezin. And within sixty-five years Ephraim will be shattered from being a people.

9 And the head of Ephraim is Samaria and the head of Samaria is the son of Remaliah. If you are not firm in faith you will not be firm at all.'"

10 Again the Lord spoke to Ahaz,

11 "Ask a sign of the Lord your God; let it be deep as Sheol or high as heaven."

12 But Ahaz said, "I will not ask and I will not put the Lord to the test."

13 And he said "Hear then, O house of David! Is it too little for you to weary men that you weary my God also?

14 Therefore the Lord himself will give you a sign. Behold, the virgin shall conceive and bear a son and shall call his name Immanuel.

15 He shall eat curds and honey when he knows how to refuse the evil and choose the good.

16 For before the boy knows how to refuse the evil and choose the good, the land whose two kings you dread will be deserted.

17 The Lord will bring upon you and upon your people and upon your father›s house such days as have not come since the day that Ephraim departed from Judah—the king of Assyria."

Please see these words are Allah's so don't hold me accountable for calling myself holy to you.

Please see the Holy Spirit did not impregnate Mary as how can a spirit create the Y chromosome, which is earth material and a spirit is not, similarly, they say in Islam that it was created by chance not but materially but God doesn't do that with nature He has and you know it is immaterial what we say, they will insist there it is parthenogenesis or something weird that happened but you know the hadith that Gabriel touch her and her pregnancy result is wrong according to hadith we have from Ibn Jarir's book on the Quran that Mary conceived as other women conceive, and the Quran also makes no exception for the birth of Jesus being different in the verse related to the creation of mankind from sperm and so forth the Quran says that Jesus was created from dust, so where did the Y chromosome come from, obviously he had an earthly father and so you know these are lies generated by the Christian apologists and Muslim scholars followed suit not realizing they were being duped by new converts, then the hadith appear that Gabriel impregnated her, which is false say I Allah there, My Quran says My messenger came as a well formed man but only gave a message that she would have a child as she was recalcitrant and did not want to marry, so it occurred her rape eventually when she eyed him and he fell into arms with her by force with other men with him but it is so she got pregnant and they didn't want him to marry, but he did, and waited not for consummation as he should have but they wed and Jesus was born to him and her but everybody knew her rape had occurred as he was killed by them for doing it and then they said calumny that she fornicated when he was born and she was asked to stay quiet, everybody knew anyway, and Jesus cleared her late when he started to teach them as a youth not but boy, I gave him that perception of their book that he knew instinctively what it meant, a certain verse, but it is true he was a rape victim as well but had shaur correct in things as Mary refused sex and was forced, so evil did not occur in her and her child was similarly innocent, so they as a team taught Me there and it ended up being a virgin birth to her in Christianity, there is no such thing in nature as the Quran says so there is no exception for anyone in my law of nature, not Adam or anyone else, all are created from dust or turab as the Arab word says, which is what sperm is created from and the egg too more on this later and there you have it she only became interested in sex with a real man and then eventually fell when she admired him and he approached her for sex and she refused knowing My law did not permit it and then the rest is as I said here say I the Creator to all.

Allah here.

Al-Imran.

3:58 This We recite to thee of the messages and the Reminder full of wisdom.

3:59 The likeness of Jesus with Allah is truly as the likeness of Adam. He created him from dust, then said to him, Be, and he was.

3:60 (This is) the truth from thy Lord, so be not of the disputers.

Al-Mumin.

40:67 He it is Who created you from dust, then from a small life-germ, then from a clot, then He brings you forth as a child, then that you may attain your maturity, then that you may be old; and of you are some who die before and that you may reach an appointed term, and that you may understand.

40:68 He it is Who gives life and causes death, so when He decrees an affair, He only says to it, Be, and it is.

Hadith from Ibn Jarir's book.

"Do you not know that Jesus was conceived by a woman in the manner in which all women conceive? Then she was delivered of him as women are delivered of their children? Then he was fed as children are fed. Then he ate food and drank water and answered the call of nature (as all mortals do)?" The deputation replied to all these questions in the affirmative, on which the Prophet said: "Then how can your claim (that he was God or Son of God) be true?"

Maryam.

19:16 And mention Mary in the Book. When she drew aside from her family to an eastern place;

19:17 So she screened herself from them. Then We sent to her Our spirit and it appeared to her as a well-made man.

19:18 She said: I flee for refuge from thee to the Beneficent, if thou art one guarding against evil.

19:19 He said: I am only bearer of a message of thy Lord: That I will give thee a pure boy.

19:20 She said: How can I have a son and no mortal has yet touched me, nor have I been unchaste?

19:21 He said: So (it will be). Thy Lord says: It is easy to Me; and that We may make him a sign to men and a mercy from Us. And it is a matter decreed.

19:22 Then she conceived him; and withdrew with him to a remote place.

Please see the story from the Biblical accounts which complements the Quran narrative.

Please see Jesus' story from the Bible is similar and it contradicts not the words from the Quran that he was immaculate conception not and these are tales that came about as he was teaching Islam to them and they realized how great was his concept of things and they started calling him son in a sense of begotten and said things like he was god incarnate which he tried to correct in his vernacular to them, more here as you want to know his hair was immaculate not but very precise in things he talked about and they were enthralled with his speech to them which was full of parables and similes, the world had not known an intelligence like his, so godhead started to appear in their hearts, but he never said it as the bible shows.

Please know son of God was similar and they started saying diverse things about him like he descend from heaven but it is so Mary was cautious and advised him to be so, so he started negating it by saying he was son of man and other virtues of making it clear in John when they approached him to stone 'it' as they call him he clarified these are only

similes and he would not commit blasphemy by calling him Christ not but son literally, and so he made it clear to them in his vernacular that he was human as he did when he asked Peter and others there who he was as son of man and they replied he was son of God, another simile for a prophet of his Grace, but I know you know this and after he left Paul and others insist he was son literally and put it there in gospel they had as a begotten son of his Beneficence and so it occurred in gospel law of Christianity that he was called literal ways as son, a simile not, while all the prophets of the bible were, this was a heresy the church adopt and it came about in the Council of Nicaea he was the same substance as his Creator and was thus called God based upon the similes he use, more here would be sane and they formulated trinity saying the Holy Spirit was one as well since he impregnated her who was Mary but as I said here the spirit cannot provide earth material which is sperm and so there you have it they know God does not sleep with women but still they say the holy one did it and it is the same as God doing it but we know fallacy is their door as spirit can give love in the context of a wet dream but cannot produce child, for it you need a real man to do that, so you see the fallacy of their way in implying things with no sense in it but it is so the Quran validates that Jesus had a sperm to form him and so did every human on earth with no exceptions, there you have it in a nutshell the biblical account so pay no heed to what others say about him as literal son, he never said it and that's the story here.
Allah too.

Please see this preamble to the end of the chapter on how things got formulated in the Christian church and how the Quran validates him who is Jesus in his teachings to them, the Bani-Israel group there.

Please see when you see beauty in someone like the Bani-Israel did with Jesus they exaggerate their aplomb of him and say he is remarkable and some ignorant ones exclaim he is god to them, a low act of exaggerate in him, but it occurs with Bani-Israel people, like those before did this idolatry in the Pharaoh realm and Moses had to fight hard to get it out of them, this idolatry they do, and it was similar there when the Romans occupy them, they use their vernacular of godhead and things like saying he is son of God, like they say who occupy them, and it came about that Paul capitalize on this and asked John and other disciples to write their story with this in it that he was son begotten like the Romans had sons of his Grace and Eminence as they used to call their Caesars sons of God as well, and they did this in order to bring gentiles to Islam they had, so it came about son, and Paul called him God as well though the disciples didn't relent on this matter, but they did, Constantine's group, who made it occur as the son is like the Father, there you have it here how these things came about.

Omar.

Epilogue about this matter that we are created in nature as the verse of Al-Imran says about Jesus and others.

From the information provided here it is obvious that the Quran has been misinterpreted after Muslim scholars leaned towards interpreting the verses on the information they learnt from Biblical sources. In this we are sane as it is easy to surmise things from the Bible if they do not appear to be categorically dismissed in the verses of the Quran. It is a common error the early Muslim scholars fell into and they have added information to the lives of other prophets as well based upon the scripture of the Old Testament or weak hadith based upon these scriptures. I will try to elucidate these errors in a different book. Suffice it to say here that the birth of Jesus was that of any other man as indicated in the hadith from Ibn Jarir Al Tabari and from the literature of the Quran used for reference. It is a mistake for a Muslim to believe that the birth of one prophet should be different from any other based upon a personal opinion of scholars from before. It does not meet credibility to an observer of nature in this day and age and it should not be construed as a basis for formulation of thought processes regarding all prophets whose miracle or sign was that they received revelation from their Creator. In this we are safe as this revelation needs to be understood and comprehended that this communication is unseen and to some in this rational age it is something they cannot comprehend but a believer in the Creator knows this form of communication is a miracle that has occurred since time immemorial.

In the laws of nature there is no deviance for any prophet and saint and it is clear with the coming of our Prophet Muhammad there is no role for deviances to appear in the minds of people, as it is well known to a Muslim person he was the best of mankind and he had a normal birth and death. It is easy for the lay to observe falsehoods about a personage and it is time for normalcy to appear in the teachings of them about Jesus or any other personage they wish to ascribe supernatural events to their life as men or women on earth. It is clear from available data you will deter on this issue until after my death but it is so your youth know it is true that parthenogenesis cannot create a son for Mary as she lacked Y chromosome in her and they will come through for me inshallah they will. Omar.

CHAPTER FOUR

EVOLUTION OF MAN AND THE CREATION OF ADAM AS AN EVOLVED HOMO SAPIEN

Introduction here.
Please know in the creation of Adam is insight about ourselves. In this way we also gain insight into all mankind including Jesus who is taken into a context out of the reality of a living being that God has created with His hands. It is for this reason I have placed a chapter on Adam and his wife to delineate that whatever befell them befalls on all mankind and Jesus is no exception. In this way we know from the previous section that the creation of Jesus was like the creation of Adam in that both were mortal beings created from dust as indicated in the Quranic verse. I have tried to include hadith literature in order that one can realize the credibility of my claim that Adam was an evolved being rather than being created de novo.

Please know it is not sufficient to say that Jesus and Mary were Adam before us, yes they were and so was Prophet Muhammad on him be peace as the most evolved of us and that we are all Adam in that we are evolved from a previous state, like I have been.

The creation of Adam has been a subject of much debate in both the Christian and Muslim literature. The Old Testament gives approximate date of birth of Adam at approximately 6000 years BC from lineage they have there in their book. It is implausible to assume that he was the father of all mankind based on anthropological studies. Studies from fossils show that Homo Sapiens have been on earth for over 50,000 years which would negate the Biblical teachings of Adam being our father. Here I have taken the liberty to write about the evolution of Adam from other Homo Sapiens and have placed this post on my Facebook page. I will try to compare data from Biblical sources and

Muslim sources as well and try to allow you to make a determination if I make sense to a discerning mind. My Facebook comment will form a basis for the discussion. Omar.

Please see the following post of mine regarding the creation of Adam from de novo material not actually.

Please know the creation of Adam was a gradual process as evinced by scientific literature. Our father Adam was a prophet but he was not the first Homo Sapien. Your friend has indicated here a concept of the creation of mankind based upon teachings of our Prophet Muhammad, on him be peace that the creation of Adam was a gradual process where he told his son Muhammad Baqir in a personal communication to him that "before our Adam there were many other Adams". He also states to him that "there were 30 Adams before our Adam". This indicates a gradual process of evolution that current scientific data corroborates as correct. This is also supported by the genetic imprint of ours which shows hominids to have a similar make up of genes.

Please know the make-up man took several billion years to occur and is indicated that when our Creator decrees that he is going to bring mankind into being He decrees His will, and it is so.

Please know I am a scholar with insight similar to him who is quoted here, Muhammad Baqir I mean, as he who is Prophet comes here as he did to him in dreams we have.

Please understand the hadith literature is rife with the concept of one parent and his mate. It only means that the first Homo Sapiens evolved from an earlier form, the Neanderthals there on earth before the creation of Adam, the first Homo Sapien and does not mean our father Adam who was created later. It is clear from Biblical sources that his creation does not date back to the creation of Homo Sapiens which go back to earlier times, as indicated here and this Adam was evolved there from Neanderthals around 700,000 years ago then his gene transmitted to similar beings that evolved also during his time but they were not complete like he was.

Ure friend knows he is a maligned individual so he will make clear that hadith literature support this view of evolution rather than the current concept that he was created de novo.

Please know in the verse quoted below the angels know the Homo Sapien race is barbaric, before the creation of our father Adam. They are surprised to realize that their Creator means to create a living entity like Adam who will be the vicegerent of His on earth. The concept He has though is those with insight will rule those who shed blood of others. The people angels referred to here are those of noble blood not but those who were the progeny of Iblis in that he was not willing to submit to him as he was in his mind better than his creation Adam here. The sons of Adam are the rulers on earth and eventually will the ones destined to lead mankind in their endeavors there in paradise, both here on earth and elsewhere.

The hadith indicates his germ will be from all mankind as indicated there that his dust will be collected from all parts of the earth. It indicates by the time of his creation Homo Sapiens would already have roamed the earth, populating it comprehensively.

Please know the hadith literature is rife about him being created out of dust with life being breathed into him. Your son knows the metaphor here is applied as we are all made from the mineral and carbon content of earth particles as our nutrition is from the dust of the earth we live in today. Omar.

The Cow.

2:30 And when thy Lord said to the angels, I am going to place a ruler in the earth, they said: Wilt Thou place in it such as make mischief in it and shed blood? And we celebrate Thy praise and extol Thy holiness. He said: Surely I know what you know not.

2:117 Wonderful Originator of the heavens and the earth! And when He decrees an affair, He says to it only, Be, and it is.

The civilization of man occurred with advent of Adam.

The concurrence of Adam with the civilized state occurred with his birth and subsequent prophethood. In this post on Facebook I comment how with his prophethood man was raised from his barbaric state to one of kindness and compassion for others. I will allow the reader to assimilate my views regarding these viewpoints.

Please know that there appears to be a dichotomy regarding the birth of Adam and his knowledge base. It appears that this is not actual and the two are interrelated in that his birth results in civilized behavior in man along with that his mental faculties were superior to others and he was a civilized man that appeared on earth.

Please know that his civilized state led to the development of the language skills. Prior to that man was barbaric and did not know how to improve himself. It is minor sins that develop the faculties. The major sins only promote a barbaric state, unless they are repented. Your son in repose to Him knows that these thoughts are my own based upon revelation. It is up to the reader to determine if they reach the coherence factor of being assimilated. I will await the reader to determine to study the text and see if it has merit with them in Arab countries where they do not know what to make out of me.

Please know that the names our Creator taught Adam were the names of their entities. Before this the angels were not named some. In this we can be sane as it was through man that expression was taught there. In this matter we are clear that even though man committed errors he still had the ability to communicate his views in a way different from the way angels were able to.

Please know that man had the ability to spill blood due to his nature. When he became civilized this nature was adapted and the sins of present day are minor in comparison to previously where barbarism reigned. In this we know that it came as a shock to Adam and Eve that their children would commit the same crime as elsewhere when Cain assassinated Abel, however some barbarism remained there even though the bloodshed seen previously was not seen anymore. In this we are sane that it is through the commission of sins some wisdom appears if the sin is repented. It also appears intelligence is developed which results in our mental faculties of speech and communication. Omar.

Chapter 2 or The Cow.

2:30 And when thy Lord said to the angels, I am going to place a ruler in the earth, they said: Wilt Thou place in it such as make mischief in it and shed blood? And we celebrate Thy praise and extol Thy holiness. He said: Surely I know what you know not.

2:31 And He taught Adam all the names, then presented them to the angels; He said: Tell Me the names of those if you are right.

2:32 They said: Glory be to Thee! we have no knowledge but that which Thou hast taught us. Surely Thou art the Knowing, the Wise.

2:33 He said: O Adam, inform them of their names. So when he informed them of their names, He said: Did I not say to you that I know what is unseen in the heavens and the earth? And I know what you manifest and what you hide.

Creation of Adam and Eve as indicated in Biblical lore.

Please know that Adam was a created being just as we are. He had a sperm that had a manipulation or modification of the previous genome that was considered good by our Creator. It is in this way that man evolves from earlier beings. In my view there are some modifications that are considered as meritorious and evolved by Allah and others are mutations that are harmful for us.

Please realize a harmful mutation is discarded early in development in most cases while a useful one is carried on to completion. There are some mutations that cause harm to mankind but there is no malady noted in them in an obvious way. In this we have peace in that one can only hold one accountable for deeds and not their genetic imprint. I only serve humanity with this suggestion that peace occurs when we realize we have a milieu of genes that are stable and others that continue to evolve as time moves along, possibly affected by the environment that we are in and in Allah's wisdom and manipulation change occurs. Ure son in repose will place some posts here regarding our concepts of Adam being different from his forebears and will allow you to accept our views as correct if they make sense to you in your intellect.

Post from my Facebook page regarding Biblical lore here.

This is a post where I discussed the creation of Adam and Eve in the context of the Biblical lore. In this we can see that Eve is just a consort who had in her elements that which had peace for her mate. They were both living in harmony as there were elements in her that suited the *psyche of her mate. In this we are safe as this appears to be the norm for all mankind. In this there is peace for the mates in their life's endeavors.*

Please know that the creation of Adam from Genesis is similar to the hadith account I give. The creation of Eve from a rib is allegorical. It only shows her nature is different from man. The shape of a rib is curved and it indicates her nature cannot be like that of man. The end is here for some who think that men and women are alike.

Please know according to a saying of Prophet Muhammad, on him be peace he asks men not to straighten a woman as it will break her and to take advantage of her nature the way she is. She is created in this way from something men will find to be compatible with them as she is from them in an allegorical sense or in the sense her spirit evolves to him in make-up they have when they mate and so forth we all adapt our spirits to those around us when we agree with them in things we see correct, it is for this evolution we are placed here in this life. Spiritually she is sane if she is different, I will let you determine if you want a man in her or a woman and so forth results we are different in psyche, make and demeanor and so it occurs you like evil in her as it pleases most of you, unless turned on you. The road is clear as we know that mankind was meant to be in bond and it is through a marital state that the progression of man occurs through stages. Ure son knows he is sane when he informs you that the road to paradise is full of intranquilities and that when we live on earth our nature is to fall prey to insinuations from the accursed one, Iblis and his minions, who are many there before the creation of man and wife here. There are few in this life that find perfection in this regard that they protect her and him, their child, from the bondage of sin that occurs here.

Please see the lore from Genesis is false that they were naked, they were clothed according to the Quran and when they covered each other they were naked in it, hence the metaphor they were naked. Omar.

Genesis.

15 The Lord God took the man and put him in the Garden of Eden to work it and take care of it.

16 And the Lord God commanded the man, "You are free to eat from any tree in the garden;

17 but you must not eat from the tree of the knowledge of good and evil for when you eat from it you will certainly die."

18 The Lord God said, "It is not good for the man to be alone. I will make a helper suitable for him."

19 Now the Lord God had formed out of the ground all the wild animals and all the birds in the sky. He brought them to the man to see what he would name them; and whatever the man called each living creature, that was its name.

20 So the man gave names to all the livestock, the birds in the sky and all the wild animals. But for Adam no suitable helper was found.

21 So the Lord God caused the man to fall into a deep sleep and while he was sleeping he took one of the man's ribs and then closed up the place with flesh.

22 Then the Lord God made a woman from the rib he had taken out of the man and he brought her to the man.

23 The man said, "This is now bone of my bones and flesh of my flesh; she shall be called 'woman' for she was taken out of man."

24 That is why a man leaves his father and mother and is united to his wife and they become one flesh.

25 Adam and his wife were both naked and they felt no shame.

The nature of the sin that Adam and Eve partook in was of a sexual nature.

The two posts that follow are about the nature of the sin that transpired which caused the exit of Adam and Eve from the state of heaven they were in. The story of eating a fruit to cause the demise of their state of peace is clearly allegorical. It is clear from the Quran that mankind is warned not to follow the footsteps of their parents and not be seduced by the devil as he afflicted them and caused to them to be ashamed of their deed. We know that fruit in itself is not a sin to eat so it must have been a sin of sexual promiscuity that we are warned about which the fruit precipitated in that the apple caused them to fall into arms of each other and the sin resulted. In this we are sane as it appears mankind seems to think it is something of this nature which the Quranic verses I have elaborated elucidate.

Please know the Quran has a similar verse regarding the shame that was felt by them after they committed the mistake of premature sexual intercourse with each other. In this we are sane as they were betrothed only when they committed this sin. Here we can part on the matter if you indicate this is indecent of me while I only interpret things that were hidden before.

Please know the fruit they ate was a sin for them. It was the eating not of a fruit in the literal sense though it led to the sin, that's why God prohibited it as He knew what would occur, and it was act of committing the deed they partook in which caused them to lose the state of innocence they were in before. In this we are sane as it is only allegorical that they were naked after committing the sin. They realized they were no longer pure just like most of us realize that about ourselves. They tried to cover themselves, which probably means they tried to embellish themselves with stories to hide their state as we are all ashamed of things that we have done that are incorrect for us. Ure son in repose knows this puts him at odds with those that take a literal translation of the words in the Quran or Genesis so I will allow the leeway of time to permit the interpretation I forward to gain ground in your minds.

Please see the account in Genesis is sane and corroborates with the Quran some that they will become immortals if they sin according to Iblis, the ardent one against us, but it is so we are mortals on earth, he was trying to make it occur we will live forever as if we were in heaven but it is not so it was a spiritual heaven only and they did not feel elements like we do here.

Please also see Eve was deceived, as was Adam, though not in conjunction, as he spoke to them separately but it so occurred they forgot My instructs to them say I Allah there, then we see clamor against us in life, which they did as well, as their enemies were many and so forth they were extruded from heaven they were in, in the garden no more. Omar.

Genesis 3

1 Now the serpent was more crafty than any of the wild animals the Lord God had made. He said to the woman "Did God really say 'You must not eat from any tree in the garden'?"

2 The woman said to the serpent "We may eat fruit from the trees in the garden,

3 but God did say, 'You must not eat fruit from the tree that is in the middle of the garden and you must not touch it or you will die.'"

4 "You will not certainly die" the serpent said to the woman.

5 "For God knows that when you eat from it your eyes will be opened, and you will be like God, knowing good and evil."

6 When the woman saw that the fruit of the tree was good for food and pleasing to the eye, and also desirable for gaining wisdom, she took some and ate it. She also gave some to her husband, who was with her and he ate it.

7 Then the eyes of both of them were opened and they realized they were naked; so they sewed fig leaves together and made coverings for themselves.

8 Then the man and his wife heard the sound of the Lord God as he was walking in the garden in the cool of the day and they hid from the Lord God among the trees of the garden.

9 But the Lord God called to the man "Where are you?"

10 He answered, "I heard you in the garden and I was afraid because I was naked, so I hid."

11 And he said, "Who told you that you were naked? Have you eaten from the tree that I commanded you not to eat from?"

12 The man said, "The woman you put here with me— she gave me some fruit from the tree and I ate it."

13 Then the Lord God said to the woman, "What is this you have done?" The woman said "The serpent deceived me and I ate."

14 So the Lord God said to the serpent, "Because you have done this "Cursed are you above all livestock and all wild animals! You will crawl on your belly and you will eat dust all the days of your life.

15 And I will put enmity between you and the woman and between your offspring and hers; he will crush your head, and you will strike his heel."

16 To the woman he said, "I will make your pains in childbearing very severe; with painful labor you will give birth to children. Your desire will be for your husband, and he will rule over you."

17 To Adam he said, "Because you listened to your wife and ate fruit from the tree about which I commanded you 'You must not eat from it,' Cursed is the ground because of you; through painful toil you will eat food from it all the days of your life.

18 It will produce thorns and thistles for you and you will eat the plants of the field.

19 By the sweat of your brow you will eat your food until you return to the ground since from it you were taken; for dust you are and to dust you will return."

20 Adam named his wife Eve because she would become the mother of all the living.

21 The Lord God made garments of skin for Adam and his wife and clothed them.

22 And the Lord God said "The man has now become like one of us, knowing good and evil. He must not be allowed to reach out his hand and take also from the tree of life and eat and live forever."

23 So the Lord God banished him from the Garden of Eden to work the ground from which he had been taken.

24 After he drove the man out he placed on the east side of the Garden of Eden cherubim and a flaming sword flashing back and forth to guard the way to the tree of life.

The corroboration from the Quran is sane to regard as correct.

This post on Facebook uses the verses of the Quran to validate what occurred when they committed the forbidden sin. The last verse makes the reader understand that the sin was of a nature that would be committed by later generation as well. It is clear that it is not the eating of a fruit that they were cautioned about but a sin of a sexual nature that all mankind can fall into a trap about. In this there is safety for mankind as this sin sends people to hell in the Hereafter.

Please see this post from my Facebook account here.

Please realize Allah cautions us to be careful about the same sin that he tells our parents to be careful of as well. This indicates this is a common sin for all of us and does not involve eating a fruit which is not a sin for us here on earth. As you can see the version in the Quran is similar to Genesis. In this we are sane as we know our Prophet had minimal contact with People of the Book and he could not have known what was in the Old Testament to the extent of the information in the Quran about similar topics. I am willing for your input to be made on these verses of the Quran.

Please know that Adam and Eve were not guilty of rebellion but forgot as mentioned here below but it is so they were careless as children are and got pregnant, then rebelled Me by saying they had not done it. I know this account is not in the Quran or biblical lore but it is My Word they were heedless then rebelled as the way you do here but it is so they carried through and I forgave them eventual ways as I do with people who repent, say I Allah there in My abode while you are here on earth, of earth materials you arise from, while I am immaterial.

Please know that in the Quran it is mentioned they forgot the instructions of their Creator in regard to not having the act before marriage that they were destined to have in their later years. It is clear this is a human folly and just as they were asked to delay their act of marriage after they got married and God admonishes all of us to be careful of the insinuations from him who is accursed for us and we are exhorted not to be involved in premature sexual intercourse.

Please see the account from the Bible is sane but does not account for the sin they do, the apple is a metaphor for sin, as a fruit is not forbidden by Me says Allah there. Omar.

Chapter 7 or The Elevated Places.

7:19 And (We said): O Adam, dwell thou and thy wife in the garden, so eat from whence you desire, but go not near this tree, lest you become of the unjust.

7:20 But the devil made an evil suggestion to them that he might make manifest to them that which had been hidden from them of their shame, and he said: Your Lord has forbidden you this tree, lest you become angels or become of the immortals.

7:21 And he swore to them both: Surely I am a sincere adviser to you—

7:22 Thus he caused them to fall by deceit. So when they had tasted of the tree, their shame became manifest to them, and they both began to cover themselves with the leaves of the garden. And their Lord called to them: Did I not forbid you that tree, and say to you that the devil is surely your open enemy?

7:23 They said: Our Lord, we have wronged ourselves; and if Thou forgive us not, and have (not) mercy on us, we shall certainly be of the losers.

7:24 He said: Go forth — some of you, the enemies of others. And there is for you in the earth an abode and a provision for a time.

7:25 He said: Therein shall you live, and therein shall you die, and therefrom shall you be raised.

7:26 O children of Adam, We have indeed sent down to you clothing to cover your shame, and (clothing) for beauty; and clothing that guards against evil — that is the best. This is of the messages of Allah that they may be mindful.

7:27 O children of Adam, let not the devil seduce you, as he expelled your parents from the garden, pulling off from them their clothing that he might show them their shame. He surely sees you, he as well as his host, from whence you see them not. Surely We have made the devils to be the friends of those who believe not.

Please see this is the story of Genesis from the Quran and the Bible as narrated by Prophet Muhammad there who knew Omar would bring it out late for man, suffice it to say he who is Iblis is sworn enemy to man until he appeared in physical shape, then his hell occurred.

Please see this verse from Nisa or Women that says we are created from a single being and his wife.

Please know there are many references there to this and he is called Adam and his wife Eve, but these are general statements and do not mean our father Adam who was given the soul of Allah when He created him to teach man how to live.

Please know the story of Adam and Eve in the Quran is allegorical and means they have to stay away from the forbidden fruit which is sexual intercourse before marriage rites are done.

Please see it occur that the son of Adam is ourselves and mankind is meant in a general statement.

Please know the progeny of Adam the prophet are specific for the Arabs of the peninsula and related tribes as that is where he was situated though his gene spread to the four corners of the world with the passage of time and prophets arose in those lands.

Please know when God refers to us as the children of Adam he refers to Bani-Adam, the predecessor of mankind, but when he refers to the prophet Adam he is referring then to Eve and Adam expelled from the garden they were in but this refers to mankind in general as the tale is ubiquitous there.

Please know there is a hadith in the Shia sect from Muhammad Baqir, the son of the Prophet as he was his progeny and came to him in dreams like he comes here to write but it is clear that there were 30 Adams before the creation of our father, Bani-Adam we are here. It indicates our predecessor or Homo Sapiens were created from another race of Adams.

Please know the verses referring to the soul being breathed into man are general and all man and women have souls from Him in that spiritual progress is written for mankind and the statements referring to Adam the prophet are only to illustrate this as the angels were then told to make obeisance to him and Eve as well.

Please know all mankind has a soul from Him, even the predecessor of Adam the prophet of God, but it is clear we are on thin ice on this issue but all mankind has always had a soul and it was only in the person of Adam the prophet that fulfillment of the law was going to take place so he deterred, the former slave of His Grace, Iblis there, and said he was better than him the prophet but Allah knew his make was arrogant and not kind to her and so He told him to be a servant and submit to the prophet emerging but he deterred and said he would make it occur that people did not follow the law they established, both Adam and Eve, and so he became an enemy to man and mankind.

Please know we were souls at that time and all mankind deterred not in the issue of submission to him, the prophet of God, even I, Omar here, and Muhammad deterred not but it is clear that obeisance means slave here.

Please know it is complex but it is clear that the prophet Adam is different from the predecessor as these verses show in that the story of being extruded is general for the time the first sexual contact is made in that all mankind is in a form of heaven until they have sex before marriage.

Please know God created mankind before he addressed these words in Baqarah to them as they knew man was wicked and spilled blood of each other, but it is clear when Iblis found out this fact that he was prophet emerging and it was not he who was chosen he abdicated his worship of Him Who is the Creator and rebelled against Him and mankind he would mislead.

Please see it is clear that Adam the prophet of God was the lawgiver to us but much has been lost in history but he made the law of marriage occur even though he deterred it initially and slept with her, his wife before marriage was complete, but it is so he deterred so Prophet Muhammad came to fulfill the law as he never gave into whim from him, the devil incarnate not but spirit then, Iblis himself, who knew it was over when the law was given there and fornication would die out, as it prevailed then before he appeared.

Please know this is the story of Genesis which I have brought out through the agency of God Himself Who wanted us to wait until it occurred, heaven on earth and so forth results I am God's metaphor but I know Muhammad is safe as he stood apart and let it occur that the devil incarnate was your enemy real ways. Omar.

Al-Nisa.

4:1 O people, keep your duty to your Lord, Who created you from a single being and created its mate of the same (kind), and spread from these two many men and women. And keep your duty to Allah, by Whom you demand one of another (your rights), and (to) the ties of relationship. Surely Allah is ever a Watcher over you.

Al-Araf.

7:26 O children of Adam, We have indeed sent down to you clothing to cover your shame, and (clothing) for beauty; and clothing that guards against evil — that is the best. This is of the messages of Allah that they may be mindful.

7:27 O children of Adam, let not the devil seduce you, as he expelled your parents from the garden, pulling off from them their clothing that he might show them their shame. He surely sees you, he as well as his host, from whence you see them not. Surely We have made the devils to be the friends of those who believe not.

Al-Baqarah

2:30 And when thy Lord said to the angels, I am going to place a ruler in the earth, they said: Wilt Thou place in it such as make mischief in it and shed blood? And we celebrate Thy praise and extol Thy holiness. He said: Surely I know what you know not.

Al-Araf

7:172 And when thy Lord brought forth from the children of Adam, from their loins, their descendants, and made them bear witness about themselves: Am I not your Lord? They said: Yes; we bear witness. Lest you should say on the day of Resurrection: We were unaware of this,

Saad

38:71 When thy Lord said to the angels: Surely I am going to create a mortal from dust.

38:72 So when I have made him complete and breathed into him of My spirit, fall down submitting to him.

38:73 And the angels submitted, all of them,

38:74 But not Iblis. He was proud and he was one of the disbelievers.

The creation of Adam from dust signifies he was created from earth materials and not in Heaven.

This is a post that was posted from my Facebook page regarding a saying of Prophet Muhammad and the associated verse from the Quran. In this we know there is safety when we take the allegorical views of the literal words. In this way it was explained to the companions of the Prophet. In some settings the hadith is meant to be taken literally. In certain things of an obtuse nature it makes sense when we understand the allegorical concepts. Suffice it to say that as pointed out in an initial post that there were at least 30 Adams before our Adam it is clear that evolution took place and through a process of survival of the fittest man evolved, as done by God, and man and mankind evolved to his current stage of development.

Please know this story has come to us through a scholar of repute but it is narrated in the literal sense.

Please also know this hadith has some weakness in it and is not accepted by all scholars. I will explain some aspects here which have relevance to my original exposition on the subject. The creation of him was in the sense of evolution. The dust from which he was created was collected from different parts of the world indicating his genetic imprint was varied as humans had already roamed different parts of the world and their body was composed of materials from these locations.

In this we are sane as the Old Testament details Adam to be six thousand years ago though in our understanding he was probably soon after the ice age was over when the Arab peninsula was a garden and greenery abounded there which was around 500,000 years ago. In this we are clear as it has been verified from our literature that both Adam and Eve lived in Arabia. In this matter we are safe to follow as it corroborates the teachings of the Old Testament that they lived in the Middle East. In these issues there is debate ongoing and I will place the matter before them to see if there is veracity in what I say here on the topic.

In this we are safe to say that much of the hadith has allegorical content and is not meant to be taken literally. Your son knows the different colored earths means the human race had developed it species by that time. The denial of the earth for Adam may indicate that it may be damaged by Adam or his progeny in the future. In this we take the allegorical concept as correct as it bears relevance to today's world where earth is at the point of being annihilated by man. The angels knew that earth had a point when it refused its dust for him however the eventual angel knew it was immaterial as all things must die. In this we are correct as the world is at a stage where there appears to be its death written until Illihoon occurred and now the earth is rejuv some though much work needs to be done as yet with others in concert..

Ure son knows there are people who will look at askance at my posts but it is only for their perception to emerge we are right when we clarify these concepts as I have done today. In this we are clear that Adam had a normal gestation in his mother's womb and there he developed sight and desires for her, that is her paradise for him, which is what the womb is for the child in her. In this is a norm for us all as the womb is a form of heaven here which we all desire while we are there. In this we are sane that the devil wishes to subvert us there but we are protected until our life begins on earth from his insinuations. There is an error here that he was created in clay for 40 years as there are errors that appear with the passage of time. He could not be tempted by the devil until he reached the age when he partook in an act that gave him knowledge as when we sin like he did the law becomes apparent to us, otherwise we are child-like repose wishing it from every woman. In this we are careful as the fruit that he partook in is a criminal act for us.

In the later part of the hadith we know it talks about the insinuations of the devil occurring after he saw the eminence of Adam appear and he became evil to mankind from that time on. Man, before then was a primitive being who spilled blood and committed sinful acts without thinking. In this we are safe to know that it is through sins we learn our lessons.

Please know that we mature through sins and that is why the Quran states that if we do not sin then He will bring about a nation that does sin, generally minor sins are considered to be correct though if we repent our major ones it does add to our insight, just like when our father Adam repented his act which took him out of paradise. Omar.

Hadith from Ibn Masud depicting him in heaven before his entry into earth.

Ibn Masud and other companions of the Prophet said that Allah the Almighty sent Gabriel onto the earth to get Him clay therefrom. The earth said: "I seek refuge in Allah from your decreasing my quantity or disfiguring me." So, Gabriel returned and did not take anything. And he said: "My Lord the land sought refuge in You and it was granted." So Allah sent Michael for the same purpose and the land sought refuge with Allah and it was granted. So he went back and said to Allah what Gabriel had said before him. Then Allah sent the Angel of Death, and the land sought refuge in Allah. The angel said: "I also seek refuge with

JESUS THE MESSIAH AND THE PERSON

Allah from returning without carrying out His command." So he took clay from the face of the earth and mixed it. He did not take from one particular place, but rather he took white, red, and black clay (from different places). The Angel of Death ascended with it and He (Allah) soaked the clay till it became sticky. Then Allah said to the angels: "Truly I am going to create man from clay. So when I have fashioned him and breathed into him (his) soul created by Me. Then you fall down prostrate to him."

So Allah shaped Adam into a human being but he remained a figure of clay for forty years. The angels went past him. They were seized with fear by what they saw and Iblis felt this fear most. He used to pass by the figure of Adam, buffeting it, which would make a sound like pottery. Allah told us: He created man (Adam) from sounding clay like the clay of pottery.

The insinuations of the devil make us battle hardy if we succeed in circumventing him.

This post on Facebook depicts our state after we sin. It is to know the sin as when he who has a personal experience of a sin then he is more aware of it rather than one who is taught about the sin. In this we have peace if we repent our sin and desire not to do it again. In this way we gain sanity and our deeds are more careful in the future regarding our deeds which bring us disrepute.

Please see Iblis is our enemy and we should not consider him our friend. He is in hellfire now and when we sin it is because of our nature to us though his minions do exist as yet on earth as spirits that roam but they do not tempt us the way he did with relish in him; human devils do exist though.

Please know that Iblis is our enemy, though it is only when regret occurs in our acts that we progress after our fall.

Please know that the creation of Adam resulted in genetic imprints of the various species of mankind known at that time. He was able to assimilate all species in his fold and therefore is the father figure for all mankind. Your son in repose to Him knows that he will be known as the father to all mankind as he is known for his knowledge and expertise in deciphering what is wrong there when he ate or committed the folly or mistake.

Please know that Iblis or the devil knew what was going to occur and tried to prevent his birth, however while the child is in the womb of his mother it is protected there. In this we are sane and we know that sanity occurs from the mistakes we make if we make up with Him after committing the error. In this way the devil benefits us if we correct ourselves after falling into his trap.

Please also realize when it says God's hands that shaped him, it is so for all mankind in the womb of their mother. It is a misnomer to believe that Adam had a special distinction of being in Paradise proper before his fall. He was spiritually at peace, as we are here if we are at peace with Him. In addition, Adam was a saint or Prophet and had the ability to communicate with them through the way prophets and saints communicate. This was lost temporarily when he sinned and eventually it was developed into true Prophethood, like the way we see with the other Prophets of God. Omar.

Hadith.

Another version of the story relates that Allah took a handful of the dust of the earth and mixed into it the colors white, black, yellow, and red. That is the reason why men are born different colors. When Allah mixed the dust with water it turned into potter's clay that makes a sound. It was fermented and had a smell. Iblis passed by wondering what was going to be made of that clay. From the clay Allah created Adam. He molded his form with His own hands and blew His spirit into him. Adam's body quivered as life was imbued into it. Verily, His command, when He intends a thing, is only that He says to it, "Be! and it is!"

The victory of devil is predicted before his defeat.

The following post on my Facebook page is about the nature of the fall of the devil or Iblis. Your son in repose to Him is aware the matter is similar in Christian and Muslim lore regarding the nature of the temptations of devil in our life. In this there is peace to know that the eventual coming to of grace for man is predicted. Your role is to be *aware of your circumstances and prevent victory there to his minions on the Day we are asked about our deeds.*

Please see Facebook here in my comment here.

Please know the minions of Iblis are similar. They were man's enemy since inception but they maintain fidelity to Him Who created them. In this we are safe to assume that mankind needs an enemy to develop himself or herself and it is only through this embellishment of battle that they gain acclaim in the Hereafter if they succeed. In this we see shame if we do not succeed as we have the opportunity to follow Him if we wish.

Please know the angel is a generic term for all that were obedient to Him. It is well known that before the creation of Adam Iblis was a stalwart, and his minions followed the teachings of their Creator like angels did and continue to do. In this we are sane as it is apparent that Iblis was upset and stayed afar from Adam initially but when our Creator informed them of his eminence he became a sworn enemy to him and his progeny. Iblis is made of the fire and is not an angel that is created from light. When a human is obedient to Allah his soul develops light in it and this is how they are created and the converse is true for devils in that they are disobedient and fire is their abode, that's why they are said to be made from fire and jinn are similar to them. In Islam some humans are considered to be angels and the spirit that visited Mary is called an angel in the language of the Quran by our Creator.

Please know Iblis was avowed as an enemy to us from the inception. In this we are sane that though he was compliant with the wishes of his Creator he later became disobedient. In this there is wisdom in Him that though he is our enemy even an enemy serves a purpose for our betterment in ways that we understand to be correct for us. Just as an enemy can cause us to develop our abilities so is the case with the devil, as when we fall we learn to repent to Him and know about our fallibility and somehow develop into more humble beings than before. In this we are correct to assume that if we fail in our test then our destination is Hellfire and not Paradise as we presume it to be. Inshallah this post is safe for you as we all have in us the feeling that we will attain Paradise but just as we go through hardships on earth so too will the hardships be present in the Hereafter and we will be questioned about our deeds. The eventual destination for man and his consort is Paradise however some will see Hell proper where defragmentation of your body will result before they arrive at their destination. Omar.

Hadith.

Adam opened his eyes and saw all the angels prostrating before him except one being who was standing at a distance. Adam did not know what kind of creature it was that did not prostrate before him, nor did he know its name. Iblis was standing with the angels so as to be included in the command given to them but he was not one of them. He was a jinn, and, as such he was supposed to be inferior to the angels. What is clear is that this prostration was to show respect and did not mean that the angels were worshipping Adam. Prostrating, in worship is done only for Allah.

The Rock.

15:28 And when thy Lord said to the angels: I am going to create a mortal of sounding clay, of black mud fashioned into shape.

15:29 So when I have made him complete and breathed into him of My spirit, fall down making obeisance to him.

15:30 So the angels made obeisance, all of them together —

15:31 But Iblis (did it not). He refused to be with those who made obeisance.

15:32 He said: O Iblis, what is the reason that thou art not with those who make obeisance?

15:33 He said: I am not going to make obeisance to a mortal, whom Thou hast created of sounding clay, of black mud fashioned into shape.

15:34 He said: Then go forth, for surely thou art driven away,

15:35 And surely on thee is a curse till the day of Judgment.

15:36 He said: My Lord, respite me till the time when they are raised.

We are created as a partial image of our Creator.

This is a comment on Facebook that indicates we are from His image in a partial sense. It is narrated about Adam but indicates in all of us there are attributes of our Creator therefore we are created in His image.

In the hadith detailed here it is indicated our shapes are in the image of our Creator.

Please know this shape is physical and our Creator's cannot be confined in time and space. I know there are similarities in the divine attributes or names that He has for Himself for us in Islam however we know that we are not the proper noun for these attributes, while He is when he calls Himself the Beneficent and the Merciful. In this way we have a partial image of Him in us. It is possible that His face may be similar in shape as this is indicated in one hadith however to confine our Creator in any way is wrong and His image fits His attributes in my view as He is immaterial and has no shape.

Hadith law states that Adam was an image there before he was created and God liked his image so took it upon Himself.

Please know this hadith is weak so we know it should be considered a fallacy He took on his image who is Adam but it is true He has a face which you can see and so forth results He is limitless and has no image actually though His aks or mirror can be seen by us in Illihoon where we serve Him, so He comes to us, in visions of Him we see Him there on the horizon like Muhammad did when He communicated with His servant, blessed he was.

Divine attributes are many but some of them you adopt for yourself, as the Prophet's aks did, and he became Me in attributes partial ways say I Allah there.

Hadith.

God created Adam in His form. He replied, "It is a form that was originated and created." He elected it and chose it over all the other different forms and attributed it to Himself, in the same way that He has attributed the Kabah and the Spirit to Himself, saying: "My House" and "I breathed into Him of My Spirit."

Conclusions on this section here.

Please see we are created to serve Him, the Creator of us, but it is clear I serve you in things and give you knowledge out of love for you, mankind and women as well say I Allah there.

Please see it is clear you understand him who is Adam to be an evolved human being as you all are evolved, your forebears were primitive and our Prophet had to tame them, then they became great men of caliber who fought that the Word would be transmitted down to you but there is an error they say but it is so we are both, mankind and women in general, deviant in things until I sent him who you call him Omar to save you in your lusts on you and it occurred you became one entity so I folded it, the world or the previous world order of things where sin prevailed you and you became pious more.

Please know hadith is construct in error and should not be relied on for data unless I show you truth in it but it is so you consider it sane as Omar did before but it is true there are many error there like this hadith that he was sixty feet long on earth who is Adam and Hawa too which is Eve in the language they use.

Please know the stature of Adam is meant as a corollary for his character. Your son in repose knows that he cannot have been sixty feet tall as there is no finding of early Homo Sapiens that tall in the research conducted so far. Even the purported graves of Adam and Eve are not sixty feet long. I know the literal translation of a hadith is our norm in interpretation however there are certain things that should not be taken in this context. I am willing to offer a moratorium to those who wish to apply a literal interpretation until it is clear we are all Muslims if we have divergent views on relatively minor issues in Islam. Omar.

CHAPTER FIVE

SOME FACEBOOK ARTICLES BY ME HERE

Introduction.

Please know I started writing my book on Muhammad in 2014 and some of the articles are excerpts from here and other sources I have but it is true we are 1 identity now and you know our page is universal in popularity and so forth results we are able to comprehend you are proud of the fact you have entered Jannah in the Christian world as you are monotheistic in outlook and you are better than some Muslim groups who still deter Islam even though they know it has occurred that they are backward in outlook compared to Christians of the present day and it is up to you if you want to conform to them in monotheistic rites as they are pleased I have come and many of you still deter it, calling me kafir and so forth.

Please see kahar is over there where they frequent it, my tomb, they say as they want me dead in Islam some but you come through when I'm there.

Please know it is clear you are 1 God in Islam but are you, you serve him in the courts on you who ask you to fight my car but it is so you realize I am good actually and I am Isa the saint you expect to be bonafide with them in Islam there as I have ended godhead in him who is Jesus and people deter it to do say it in their group there.

Please know the hadith is clear he will come to teach the Christians and Jews Islam and all will follow him as he will be the chosen one there. Omar.

Please see Kahar is there, now He is humble to you if you come through in Islam we serve of one identity in that we are all Muslims if we say the kalima shahada.

Please know Kahar is to subdue all and it becomes us to submit when it occurs that we are humble in it.

Please know this article is for him who thinks he knows Him,

Please know they know in Islam there is no prostration there in Heavenly abode we have there.

Please know it is because there is no prayer as we see it there,

Please know God is with us there, here He is Absolute,

Please know He is never-changing,

Please know Him,

Please know divine attributes from him, Prophet Muhammad there.

Please know he was revealed these things,

Please know we must be humble to be Him in repose,

Please give in,

Please know we are one with Him in repose or thoughts from Him there with Him in our midst.

Please know this is from Muhammad, on him be peace who taught us Him in His Entirety not as there is no limit to His prowess.

Please know he created Him for you in your imagination of Him, the Creator there.

Please know he called Him Loving, Benign, submissive to you there,

Please know this is in His Heavenly abode for us there.

Please know He is Kahar to those who fight Him here,

Please know He is Absolute and knows all,

Please know yet He is Loving to you today as you love Him,

Please be kind as He is kind to you.

Please know Him as He has divine attributes and cannot be maligned,

Please know there is no vanity in Him,

Please know He is self-effacing there,

Please know here He is Absolute and you fear Him because you sin,

Please know there He will be humble, loving,

Please know it has occurred I am human as your soul is from Me He says according to hadith lore.

Please Him,

Please know He is good to know and all vanities end with Him,

Please know the hadith of the Prophet that says everything is vanities in you but Allah is not vain.

Please know He is the truth with which He declares Himself to be without any vanity whatsoever, and further, He is kind to us that He keeps Himself hidden as we wouldn't be able to bear Him here and all our choice is over there when we choose our destiny, whether it is Heaven or Hell.

Please know we are vain, He is humble and straightforward,

Please know He is better than us and if we are humble He is more so and further He will show us His attributes to us in Heaven when we are with Him.

Please know He was a hidden treasure and wished to be known by man and others He created in their soul to Him, so He created our Prophet to manifest Him.

Please know He is perfect and we will never achieve Him,

Please know He is the Creator of all.

Please know here He is Kahar and will humble you.

Please know we worship Him as He is above us,

Please know He is the Creator but one of us in meekness and humility and in His nature He is diffident to us in loving embrace He will take us when we arrive there with Him and it is so you worship Him here because He is all your heart desires Him to be to you then.

Please know He is Absolute though,

Please know there is no God but He,

Please know we must ascribe faith to this notion that He is one of us,

Please know He is humble and loves to play with us,

Please know He created us and knows our joy,

Please know it is joy to some, dismay to others that He is humble,

Please know they think him Absolute and above us on His throne, He is Mutakabir there but it is so He has power in it and there is no pride there in Him, that is a fallacy you have.

Please know His throne is with mankind and others,

Please know He has human attributes but is Absolute and Kahar amongst other attributes that are not us in our make.

Please know Him from our Quran. I recommend you pick one up and peruse it for yourself to learn Him in His Entirety not but as a manifestation there of His glory and things like that. Omar.

Al-Hashr.

59:21 Had We sent down this Qur'an on a mountain, thou wouldst certainly have seen it falling down, splitting asunder because of the fear of Allah. And We set forth these parables to men that they may reflect.

59:22 He is Allah besides Whom there is no God: The Knower of the unseen and the seen; He is the Beneficent, the Merciful.

59:23 He is Allah, besides Whom there is no God; the King, the Holy, the Author of Peace, the Granter of Security, Guardian over all, the Mighty, the Supreme, the Possessor of greatness. Glory be to Allah from that which they set up (with Him)!

59:24 He is Allah; the Creator, the Maker, the Fashioner: His are the most beautiful names. Whatever is in the heavens and the earth declares His glory; and He is the Mighty, the Wise.

Please know a child of mine is one I create as they are My progeny in the sense of their creation is from Me, in love do I create them say I Allah.

Please see these verses that seem to indicate animals have an afterlife and so it must be assumed that they have a spirit and soul like we have and it is only misnomer that they are not like us humans, they are human in that regard, and want their structure to continue in the Hereafter as well.

Please see it is clear in Islam that the belief is that animals will be raised but will die eventually and will no longer exist after judgment is passed on them, but it is true they will exist in Heaven according to verses of the Quran I have collected here.

Please know they will give the inmates of Heaven their flesh but will not die as death is over once their judgment has occurred.

Please see the hadith that talks about the cat punishing its owner until Judgment Day when she caused it to die in hunger, cruelty to animals is punished by Him, our Benefactor.

Please know it is clear animals worship Him Who creates them and it is not possible that God in His mercy would annihilate a worshipper of Him Who He has created out of love and care. Further, in my view when God gives life to anyone with a conscious state He would not take it away and annihilate them into nothing.

JESUS THE MESSIAH AND THE PERSON

Please see the animals should be loved as they come from the same source as we do and our Prophet taught us to be kind to them.

Please know Omar has brought it out, it was hidden by sahaba some, in that they wanted animals to be inferior to man but would I let my creatures be inferior to one another, no, say I the Creator, all of you are equal though utility is different here, there you will live in peace and not disturb each other.

Please know Ahmadiyyat is wrong in this issue that they say dirt is their outcome and so is ahle-Islam that say they will be judged then perish will occur to them, would I perish a child of Mine say I the Benefactor of you all. Omar not only but Allah as well.

Al-Anum

6:38 And there is no animal in the earth, nor a bird that flies on its two wings, but (they are) communities like yourselves. We have not neglected anything in the Book. Then to their Lord will they be gathered.

Al-Nur.

24:41 Seest thou not that Allah is He, Whom do glorify all those who are in the heavens and the earth, and the birds with wings outspread? Each one knows its prayer and its glorification. And Allah is Knower of what they do.

Al-Waqiah about Heaven the sabeqoon or foremost have.

56:18 With goblets and ewers, and a cup of pure drink —

56:19 They are not affected with headache thereby, nor are they intoxicated,

56:20 And fruits that they choose,

56:21 And flesh of fowl that they desire,

Please know there is 1 God there in the mystic's mind, that's why they talkeen not in issues and do not delay the message and are adept in communicating His views to them, their follower.

Please know Sufi saints have exists for eons in Islam but it is true we are different who are Mirza and myself as we use the metaphor adeptly, there is an issue that we know difference is mild but we know we are elevated more than ordinary Sufis as we were virgins in our beforelife and I maintain I am virgin here,

Please understand I am like a Sufi saint here like those before me were. I do not abdicate Ahmadiyyat but know my mentor was like a Sufi saint as well.

Please understand Sufism indicates mysticism which has existed in all religions when we know there is an inner connection with God.

I am sad at the state of affairs of organized religion as it has lost attraction for some of its adherents due to blind belief in edicts from scholars nowadays.

Please know we are answerable to Him and He admonishes us to do the right thing for our own safety.

Please understand mysticism is an ancient art and was practiced by the people who followed the Torah and Christians alike. Our Prophet was a mystic even before prophethood was given to him as he used to seclude himself from people and retire to the cave where he first received revelation from the angel. I know this art of religion existed there in the People of the Book and other cultures as there is mention of this in their literature.

Please know not all mystics are accurate and due circumspection has to be applied to them to see if they meet credibility with the religion they follow. I know mystics have existed in Christianity and Judaism and it is my impression that it is very widespread in different religions as there are good people who are in touch with God or His emissary to them. I am confident that people will see me as a mystic from Him as I write with precision and accuracy.

Please know we are united in one body and if we understand our differences we will realize how similar we are. Omar.

Please see Mirza Ghulam Ahmad is innocent as you say now in ahle-Islam now as you know he refuted it that he was prophet but only he was auliya like Omar has in his book to you here and elsewhere.

Please see this is Mirza's book I write here but I know you have come through with Christian precepts but this is here that they think I am a prophet in some parts of the world, that why ahle-Islam deter me, says Mirza there in heaven, but it is clear he was a virgin though he committed adultery with many but in spirit like Omar does here but it is so virgins do travel and wet dreams result but it is so he is like Omar in that regard says Allah there.

Please know his book is there for review in which his last words were written that his prophesy was in the metaphorical sense and that further he believed in the finality of prophet Muhammad's grave being a source of peace that he is the last of the anbiya or prophets and in earlier discourse he may have made an error in thought but it does occur that we are saints and not Prophet Muhammad who had perfect transmission in the way the Quran was transmitted and so forth he was not perfect in that regard, and neither am I say I Omar here as I thought I was emissary of His Grace but it is not so, we are not prophets that would be His emissary and so forth I have made it clear in my book and so has Mirza that we are emissaries of rasoolallah or Prophet Muhammad and so forth you believe us in this treatise as it is from Allah's saints of the hereafter.

Please see this text about the saint Mirza Ghulam Ahmad of Qadian where he clarifies his prophethood is in the metaphorical sense and is not real like prophet Muhammad and others before him and that it is only partial prophethood that remains now.

Please see the following excerpt from an article published by Fazeel Khan in the magazine The Light which is published by the Lahore Ahmadiyya Jamaat in the USA. As you can see he uses Sufi sources to prove his point that the word prophet and rasul or messenger is used in their vernacular to describe sainthood in which the Prophet visits them and teaches them things. As it is clear he was a prophet not, in the actual sense, he is not guilty of blasphemy as thought by the general Muslim population at large.

Further, it is clear these are metaphorical terms used by saints, it also clear the general public does not understand these concepts. Further, it is obvious to the reader here that a metaphor is not real and only depicts the concept or idea to the person who views it. I would like to say this has been an enlightening article for me as it has cleared some concepts of mine and I now consider Mirza Ghulam Ahmad to be a prophet in the sense of a metaphor or the sense that he has fused himself to the teachings of the Prophet and they are one entity, he being real who is Prophet, and

Mirza Ghulam Ahmad being his image in him and so forth. It is similar for me as I elucidate in this book on Jesus and he is the Prophet and we are saints of his who learn Islam first hand from his hand on us.

There is no prophet after Muhammad, on him be peace in that regard but it is true there are prophets in the metaphor sense of the word that will appear. Many saints have used that word as you can see from the excerpt here but it is true it is misunderstood in Sufi literature they have and it is clear Mirza used it in a similar context and that's about it in his final word to us.

Here is the text from Fazeel's article that talks about saints using that word or the word rasul.

Abu Bakr Shibli had people testify: "There is no God but Allah, and Shibli is His messenger."

Muin-ud-Din Chisti, had a person recite: "There is no God but Allah, and Chisti is the Messenger of Allah."

Khawaja Habib-ullah Attar similarly told people to consider him to be "the messenger of Allah" when reciting the kalima.

Please see the vernacular of the prophets is complex, suffice it to say that it is clear that word is used in several ways in the Quran literature we have and so forth.

In a literal sense, to convey the lexiconic meaning of the word like it being used for the messenger of the king to the prophet Yusuf when he was in prison.

In a metaphorical style as employed in Sufi literature when the spirit of the Prophet visits the saint and tells him to teach in that it is a Prophetic revelation but comes to the body of the saint.

And thirdly in a theological manner where the word is used in the Quran for Prophet Muhammad and other prophets before him.

Please see it is clear Prophet Muhammad is the last prophet the world will see as can be seen by the word khatam in the Quran for him and the context is clear from the hadith in Bukhari and others that the word means brick that is the end of the building to be placed with the advent of the Messengership of Muhammad, on him be peace in that regard.

Surah Azhab.

33:40 *Muhammad is not the father of any of your men, but he is the Messenger of Allah and the Seal of the prophets. And Allah is ever Knower of all things.*

Please see this hadith that states this fact that he is khatam an nabi and that means the last brick.

"*My similitude in comparison with the prophets before me is that of a man who has built a house nicely and beautifully, except for a place of one brick in a corner. The people go about it and wonder at its beauty, but say: 'Would that this brick be put in its place!' So I am that brick, and I am the seal of the prophets*".

It is also clear from hadith that Muhammad is the last prophet the world will see and no one can claim prophethood in the actual sense after him.

Please see this hadith that follow from Bukhari and other reliable sources.

"*There is no prophet after me.*"

There is another verse in the Quran that scores the same point that it was revelation of the partial type that saint or auliya get from Him Who creates.

Yunus

10:62-64 *Now surely the friends of God (auliya) – there is no fear upon them nor do they grieve. Those who believe and guard against evil, for them are good news (bushra) in this world and the hereafter.*

Please see the word used in the hadith has the same root as the word in the Quran indicating unanimity of views here.

This is clear that Mirza's Ghulam Ahmad did not attribute prophet or messengership to himself as prophet used in the metaphorical sense cannot be applied literally to himself though he used it in his literature to describe his personage to others.

Please see the following excerpts from his books here.

From Ek Ghalti Ka Izala.

"*Wherever I have denied prophethood and messengership, it is only in the sense that I am not the independent bearer of a law (shariah), nor am I an independent prophet. However, in the sense that, having gained spiritual graces from the Messenger whom I follow, and having attained for myself his name, I have received knowledge of the unseen from God through the mediation of the Holy Prophet, I am a messenger and a prophet but without a new law (shariah). I have never denied being called a prophet in this sense. In fact, this is the sense in which God has addressed me as nabi and rasul. Nor do I now deny being a prophet and messenger in this sense."*

As you can see here he says he did not bring a law or sharia and is an incomplete prophet, which is what a metaphor is.

From his book Izala Auham please see the following excerpt here.

"The fact that our Holy Prophet is the khatam an nabiyyin prohibits the coming of any other prophet. However, a prophet who obtains light from the lamp of the prophethood of Muhammad, who in other words is also called a muhaddath, is exempt from this restriction because, due to his obedience to the Holy Prophet and due to his being fana fir rasul, he is included within the person of the Last of the Messengers, just as a part is included in the whole."

As you can see he was a believer in Prophet Muhammad to be khatam an nabi of the seal of the prophets.

From his book Taudih Maram you can see that he believed prophesy had ended from the prophets and only partial prophesy remain or true dreams here.

"The Messenger of Allah is reported to have said that 'there is nothing left of prophesy except good news (mubashshirat).' That is to say, from the parts of prophesy only one part remains, namely mubashshirat, which comprises true dreams, genuine and true visions, and revelation which descends on the chosen ones from among the saints (auliya)."

The personage of Mirza Ghulam is sanctified in the hadith from Sahih Muslim as follows in his words here in Anjam Atham where he is described prophet of God but it is in the metaphorical way of speaking in his own words here.

"The title 'prophet of God' for the Promised Messiah found in Sahih Muslim etc. from the blessed tongue of the Holy Prophet is meant in the same metaphorical sense as it occurs in Sufi literature as an accepted and common term for a recipient of Divine communication. Otherwise, how can there be a prophet after the khatam ul anbiya?"

Finally, I can say with confidence that he himself considered his being to be a saint as exemplified here in his words in his book *Izala Auhum*.

"There is no claim of prophethood (by me); on the contrary, the claim is of muhaddathiyyah which has been put forward by the command of God. And what doubt is there in this that muhaddathiyyah also possesses a strong offshoot of prophethood."

Please see this literature was written when they were committing me and inhibiting me in my abode in 2015 and so forth.

The Prophet is *farehoon* or happy there in Paradise as he is the one who is Maqaam a Mahmood or the coveted position of mankind.

Please know I am *farehoon* as it occurred that atheism is eradicated but sad you will continue it, my turmoil, as I am too successful for you and you are jealous it is a Pakistani man who is it, a messiah to us.

Please know it occurred because I got the book published and you recognized merit in me and Christianity became me overnight, then you committed me,

Please know my literature speaks to you telling my worth but you are jealous puss and angry boots,

Please Him,

Please know God is One Entity and we are His associates in the metaphorical language we understand correct there but not Him as we are separate from Him,

Please know He is the Creator and it is in His foreknowledge what we will become through him, my Prophet,

Please know he was perfect for us and we will become him in the hereafter if we follow his boots rather than them who kill maim me.

Please know I am tired but *farehoon*.

Please know I am tired of him who knows me and excels in discrediting me to him who listens because he is jealous of us in Islam here in the West.

Please know I am His agent but not him who excels me and him, the Mirza of your heart as well.

Please know he was saint before me and Prophet Muhammad is just messiah to the world as the world will knows now, and Jesus was there before making it occur mercy and compassion principles you have, and our Prophet's heart encompasses all humanity and knows their worth, they will excel in the future, as I have here.

Please know when Allah created us He knew this would occur so he created the litmus test, Prophet Muhammad's Word to you.

Please know it is the Quran from Him to you.

Please know if you follow it you will succeed in life and in the hereafter be the messiah clan.

Please Him and follow me to him, your World Prophet.

Please know that our Creator is perfect and we will know Him and bow in humility.

Please know this,

Please know that our Creator said "I loved that I be known so I created mankind,"

Please know this,

Please know elsewhere He has said "I have not created man and the jinn but to worship me,"

Please know it is man's distinction that he will know Him,

Please know we research the world and the universe and wonder at Him,

Please know the more we read this book where we live the more we admire and worship Him,

Please know we are only His slaves and He gives us pleasure in return,

Please know this,

Please know we can spend eons researching into a thing and then admire the simplicity and perfection of it,

Please know the Hereafter will be similar,

Please know it is for us to read the book of the universe and admire its perfection,

Please know perfection is not created out of disorder,

Please know Him,

Please know He is perfect and His creations will know Him some but not completely as we cannot fathom our Creator.

Please see a requiem for me in that I am the one who created world peace through Prophet's Muhammad's message coming here, I get the credit and so does he as world leader as he is my literature for the most part and Allah as well through him and others in Islam.

Please know we are 1 entity in that we think alike and have similar goals and achieve peace through his pen who is Muhammad there as he is the author of most books bringing message from Him the Creator to us over centuries since he came to earth and lived his pious life as evinced in Ahmadiyya literature to you from Mirza and Muhammad Ali and so forth and others in Islam who use shaur of His intelligence on them. Omar.

Please see this article about the Prophet's nature.

The Prophet's deportment was necessary for world success to occur.

Please see this article about the deportment of our Prophet.

Please know he was extremely truthful.

Please know in a communication to me he said that an angel would appear to prevent a lie from occurring and he was protected in this way.

Please know he was to receive the Quran which was to be revealed to a heart that not known a lie,

Please know our Creator protects him but his deportment was excellent that he never failed the guidance that came to him,

Please Him,

Please know our Prophet had that motto with him,

Please know our Creator will continue to protect him from the vituperative one.

Please know he is His beloved and the best make of man.

Please know our Prophet knows you will come through.

Please know the early life of Muhammad was a deportment of piety and truthful conduct.

Please know he had a birth which was unremarkable for the most part and his childhood was marred by the death of his mother and grandfather.

Please know he was born an orphan as his father died on a trip.
Please understand this,
Please know that he was only a child when he started having revelation, some of which were observed by others.
Please know in one incident he was seen to have his chest opened and his heart was washed.
Please know this was an attempt by his Creator to avoid the stain of the world from affecting his deportment. In this there is certainty that he was protected and he was going to raise a nation in the depths of ignorance to the heights of human endeavors for Him, like he has done here as well.
Please know him,
Please know he was truthful to an extreme not known by man before or since.
Please know when he gave his word he kept it no matter how inconvenient to him.
Please know there was an incident when he promised a man he would wait for him after he came back from an engagement.
Please know it was his nature to never break his word. I know it sounds extreme but in this case the man forgot about meeting him and remembered the next day. I am aware that there is no one who would expect the Prophet to have stayed there but the man found him waiting for him in the same spot the next day.
Please know our Prophet was upset and berated the man for giving him hardship but he did not break his word.
Please know to give your word is a truth if you keep it.
Please know this is an example of his piety and truthfulness.
Please know he was known as the truthful and the trustworthy because of his nature reflecting those attributes.
Please know our Prophet was a shepherd in his youth. I know all the prophets have gone through this training where they take care of a herd or flock of animals and our Prophet also did so.
Please know his deportment was to take care of people and tend to them,
Please know he never lost an animal to the wild beasts.

Please understand he was to be a trader.

Please know he went on a trip to Syria where a Christian monk saw him and asked to view the area between his shoulder blades.

Please know the Prophet had a mark that was distinctive.

Please know years later Salman, the Christian slave, looked for the same mark and confirmed that he was the Prophet of Allah.

Please know the Christian monk knew this was the Prophet and asked his uncle to take care of him,

Please know the monk also asked him to take an oath on the idols there in Mecca and the Prophet refused to do so.

Please know he did not teach him religion as he was only with him for a short while.

Please know there were other signs he saw that this was the prophet.

Please know the caravan had a cloud cover remain over it.

Please know our Prophet was raised in a protected way away from the vice that prevailed the land there.

Please know a requiem for him,

Please know he was free from the vice of his society.

Ure son in repose knows that our Creator created this beacon of light for man to observe and see thereby.

Please know it is possible for this to occur and the example of the Prophet Abraham is with you who fought idolatry as a youth,

Please understand vice,

Please know it is sin if done repeatedly with full knowledge it is wrong,

Please know your society here has vice in it.

Please know our Prophet repents you if you do not amend your ways. Omar.

Please know this article is why heaven is accepted here and you abstain for the most part.

Please see this article made headway there but it is clear people believe me in that they are asked to abstain who is child to them, as they want pregnancy not in her in which hardness results and then they fight her who is mother to them and then they have mental disease in things and suicide occurs in her and him, but it is true we know there is One God there who asks man to abstain these things for his family as their betterment is in it.

Please understand me, I bring you him, my Prophet who taught Islam there who knew a time would come when fornication rites were normal and you would mind this literature I teach here where fornication rites are passed down from father to son and mother to daughter not considering it is the in heavenly abode this occurs and results in peace there, here it is turmoil and hardship results. We see breakups occur because it is not permitted, sex and things like that here in this world, when we engage in premarital sex rites in your parking lots and elsewhere where it occurs. Your seat is wet you say but it is true sex results in breakups and marriage does not unless participated in it before it.

Please understand hur'un ain.

Please know these are the blessed ones that are meant to be our companions in the Hereafter.

Please know they are hidden beauties.

Please know they are both male and female though the Quran talks about the female companions to men.

Please know a woman asked our Prophet if they would have similar benefits and he agreed.

Please know sexuality is different there but it will be joy for us.

Please know the women of this world will be better than these hidden beauties.

Please know the wife of our Prophet confirmed this. Umm Salamah hadith is this that women who are pious will have a better life than the hur there even though they are mentioned in the Quran in this sense of sexual pleasure.

Please know I know Paradise is sensual and the depictions of the Quran are clear in this regard.

Please know I know we wish a sensual world here but we are asked to wait. I know you find it odd that our Hereafter is blessed in this way and you are to abstain here because pregnancy results and the result is child loss nowadays as most women won't adopt it. It is clear religious law does not permit it in all cultures and you have to learn law is sane in this regard to follow and I know you aspire it here but it will be taken from you there in Heaven and you will have to wait an eon before sex can result there.

Please know the foremost are those that try hard with their person. Please understand this.

Please know they are the ones that make sacrifices with their person and their property.

The end occurs when you look down on this reward while you seek it here.

Please indicate disfavor there as they try to tell women that there is no pleasure of a sexual nature in Paradise.

Please know it does exist and there is evidence in other scripture besides the Quran which I have placed here for review.

Please know this is a depiction of Heaven only.

Please try to understand the nature of the language. It refers to virgins in Heaven awaiting menfolk however it is stated this way as men were the recipients of the Book and most of it is addressed to them.

Please know virgins are real here as the text depicts.

Please understand the pleasure is of an earthly nature, only more intense and the delight is in the numbers of encounters we have there at our leisure. As you know it take two to couple therefore rest assured women and men both will have it, peace in this regard, and children will result for her there.

Please realize this is no joke and reality is in the proof of sex dreams which we have all done in our youth when we have wet dreams which indicate we have sexual prowess there when we marry.

Please try to realize there is a reward for waiting in which you will see paradise in this earth as well as the Hereafter, as I have indicated before. Omar.

Chapter Rahman or The Benevolent.

55:46 And for him who fears to stand before his Lord are two Gardens.

55:47 Which then of the bounties of your Lord will you deny?

55:48 Full of varieties.

55:49 Which then of the bounties of your Lord will you deny?

55:50 Therein are two fountains flowing.
55:51 Which then of the bounties of your Lord will you deny?
55:52 Therein are pairs of every fruit.
55:53 Which then of the bounties of your Lord will you deny?
55:54 Reclining on beds, whose inner coverings are of silk brocade. And the fruits of the two Gardens are within reach.
55:55 Which then of the bounties of your Lord will you deny?
55:56 Therein are those restraining their glances, whom no man nor jinni has touched before them.
55:57 Which then of the bounties of your Lord will you deny?
55:58 As though they were rubies and pearls
55:59 Which then of the bounties of your Lord will you deny?
55:60 Is the reward of goodness aught but goodness?
55:61 Which then of the bounties of your Lord will you deny?
55:62 And besides those are two (other) Gardens.
55:63 Which then of the bounties of your Lord will you deny?
55:64 Inclining to blackness.
55:65 Which then of the bounties of your Lord will you deny?
55:66 Therein are two springs gushing forth.
55:67 Which then of the bounties of your Lord will you deny?
55:68 Therein are fruits and palms and pomegranates.
55:69 Which then of the bounties of your Lord will you deny?
55:70 Therein are goodly beautiful ones.
55:71 Which then of the bounties of your Lord will you deny?
55:72 Pure ones confined to pavilions.
55:73 Which then of the bounties of your Lord will you deny?
55:74 Before them man has not touched them, nor jinni.
55:75 Which then of the bounties of your Lord will you deny?
55:76 Reclining on green cushions and beautiful carpets.
55:77 Which then of the bounties of your Lord will you deny?
55:78 Blessed be the name of thy Lord, the Lord of Glory and Honor!
Chapter Al-Waqiah or The Event.
56:7 And you are three sorts.
56:8 So those on the right-hand; how (happy) are those on the right-hand!

56:9 And those on the left; how (wretched) are those on the left!
56:10 And the foremost are the foremost—
56:11 These are drawn nigh (to Allah).
56:12 In Gardens of joy.
56:13 A multitude from among the first,
56:14 And a few from among those of later times,
56:15 On thrones inwrought,
56:16 Reclining on them, facing each other.
56:17 Round about them will go youths never altering in age,
56:18 With goblets and ewers, and a cup of pure drink —
56:19 They are not affected with headache thereby, nor are they intoxicated,
56:20 And fruits that they choose,
56:21 And flesh of fowl that they desire,
56:22 And pure, beautiful ones,
56:23 Like hidden pearls.
56:24 A reward for what they did.
56:25 They hear therein no vain or sinful talk —
56:26 But only the saying, Peace! Peace!
56:27 And those on the right hand; how (happy) are those on the right hand!
56:28 Amid thornless lote-trees,
56:29 And clustered banana-trees,
56:30 And extensive shade,
56:31 And water gushing,
56:32 And abundant fruit,
56:33 Neither intercepted, nor forbidden,
56:34 And exalted couches.
56:35 Surely We have created them a (new) creation,
56:36 So We have made them unprecedented,
56:37 Loving, equals in things,
56:38 For those on the right hand.
56:39 A multitude from among the first,
56:40 And a multitude from among those of later times.

Please see the following complaint not but harmony for us in this tankeeb or plot to overcome you they say but it is not so they are equal, both, and that's what the Quran say here.

Please see this is nature that we are different but one team in things of the nature of partnership in marriage but it so occurs that in this country there are many adversaries to this partnership clause and men want to be different and regard women as chattel in many ways but with Islam coming here you realize that God will hold you accountable for any wrongdoing to her and it is clear you have rights over her and she has some over you as the Quran says in surah Nisa where men and women are exhorted to maintain each other in harmony with mutual rights over each other and so forth.

Please see these verses from the Quran regarding the spiritual state or status of women in Islam where they are equated with equality with menfolk in that their spiritual state can be elevated like them.

Please know there is equity in things and just as men can be judged for their deeds, so will women be, and the labor of no person will be wasted according to the Quran Majeed and it will be seen those who do good will benefit from their acts on the day we are judged.

Please know women have a soul like men though their intellect is different and men are leaders of them in households; but it holds true that men have to serve her in their needs.

Please know it is clear men are the law-givers to them in their family structure but it so occurs you believe there is harmony in it as that is the nature, men are over their wives and wives are submissive, obedient, but have rights over them in that they must have faith in that their shaur is safe with him, their mate, and they teach him things and so forth results they are one team or nature.

Please see it occur that men and women are teams in life.

Please know this is correct for all mankind and it is true we must ascribe partnership to man and wife and they are team there with us.

Please know in Europe at that time women were regarded as chattel and did not have any rights.

Please know Islam gave them rights of property ownership and a right to make their own decisions in life.

Please know there is precedence here when I say that women are allowed to work in the workforce but it is generally accepted they are home keepers for him and rear their child, as is seen in Western countries and the East as well but it is clear they were allowed to work in the Prophet's time.

Please know they are supposed to stay apart from menfolk at their workplace and free mingling of the sexes is not encouraged.

Please know that does not detract them for their home duties but men are encouraged to help out as the Prophet did with his wives.

Please know these verses indicate that women are equal to menfolk but men have authority over them in their household and things of the nature they can't do.

Please see divorced women have rights similar to men and they can demand it, separation from him if they don't want to continue a marriage.

Please know to respect women is our call to Him Who is our Creator and to follow the example our Prophet is the norm for us.

Please know to respect your loved ones and bring about harmony with them in their needs and do it without vice and avarice in cases of divorce in us. Omar.

Quranic verses on this subject matter.

Nisa

4:1 O people, keep your duty to your Lord, Who created you from a single being and created its mate of the same (kind), and spread from these two many men and women. And keep your duty to Allah, by Whom you demand one of another (your rights), and (to) the ties of relationship. Surely Allah is ever a Watcher over you.

Al Waqiah.

56:27 And those on the right hand; how (happy) are those on the right hand!

56:28 Amid thornless lote-trees,

56:29 And clustered banana-trees,

56:30 And extensive shade,

56:31 And water gushing,

56:32 And abundant fruit,

56:33 Neither intercepted, nor forbidden,

56:34 And exalted couches.

56:35 Surely We have created them a (new) creation,

56:36 So We have made them unprecedented,

56:37 Loving, equals in things.

56:38 For those on the right hand.

Al Imran

3:195 I will not suffer the work of a worker among you be the lost, whether male or female, the one of you being from the other.

Nisa.

4:195 And whoever does good deeds, whether male or female, and he (or she) is a believer — these will enter the Garden, and they will not be dealt with a whit unjustly.

Al Mumin

40:40 And whoever does good, whether male or female, and he is a believer, these shall enter the Garden, to be given therein sustenance without measure.

Al Rum

30:21 And of His signs is this, that He created mates for you from yourselves that you might find quiet of mind in them, and He put between you love and compassion. Surely there are signs in this for a people who reflect.

Baqarah

2:228 And the divorced women should keep themselves in waiting for three courses. And it is not lawful for them to conceal that which Allah has created in their wombs, if they believe in Allah and the Last Day. And their husbands have a better right to take them back in the meanwhile if they wish for reconciliation. And women have rights similar to those against them in a just manner, and men are a degree above them. And Allah is Mighty, Wise.

Hadith on the subject:

1. Verily, women are the twin halves of men.

2. There is no claim of merit of an Arab over a non-Arab, or of a white over a black person, or male over a female except in piety or taqwa.

Please know hadith is clear Dajjal is one eyed and his minions are as well.

Please know Dajjal is one eyed- evil kind- and it is known that he will elaborate him to conjoint to him in that he will tell him to join party crowd and things so that he becomes spoilt you think but it is so they want to spoil son of mine to study not and teach him lesson, father there, who teaches president Obama was king of his world then became a tame man, it is true he is tame now and inclines to peace with us Islamically minded people of the land not but worldwide, yes it's true president Obama did melt and is tame by you but he still has mischief in that he wants me killed for despoiling him to the world community and I know you have to keep him in check as he is the prototype of the devil and is deceptive like Dajjal is in your structure of the government that remains from his time there.

Please know Dajjal is one eyed,

Please know it is a metaphor for one who is spiritually blind and materialistic.

Please know it has started and my car is inhibited,

Please know they won't do it again not that my car is heisted even though it is established, One God with you and now the church is quiet,

Please know I have achieved it and they know he is dead who is Jesus,

Please know the facts is it all fits in,

Please know as I explained in my book there is no reason to be in disguise for a dead man raised to life,

Please know you can only die once.

Please know it is in spirit form we are raised but the gospel is clear in that regard he was flesh as he asked Thomas to put his hand in his wound and ate fish with hunger.

Please know it makes sense to a believer that he was unconscious and he survived it.

Please know the scholar knows to check the data.

Please know it is over and you have read me,

Please Him and be open about it.

Please know we ascribe to peace when we tell you, you have amalgamated it and you realize the Quran is revealed and perfecture is it in its message,

Please know it all fits you say.

Please know the Quran was monotheistic and they told you it was idolatry with Allah being a moon God,

Please know you know because you read him in the church literature they give you.

Please know Yahweh was only a term for Him Who creates, from the Bani-Israel perspective,

Please know He was their God and He did not permit another.

Please know Jesus was similar and told you to worship Him, not himself. He never called himself son in a material way as the Quran tells us,

Please know all his prayers and others in Islam there with their prayers were directed to Him there,

Please know he cried longingly for His succor.

Please know it is false to claim he called himself Him in the actual sense as he could not answer prayers there,

Please know Allah permit him the metaphor but he realized it was dangerous and stopped as documented in the gospel there,

Please know Allah permit the other gospel to emerge after the previous ones where the metaphor was explained so that you would have peace and come to the Quran when I explained it as your church goers were recalcitrant and said the Quran was evil and devil worship though they knew better as they recognize it as their own book,

Please know they kept you away from it through deception, a characteristic of Dajjal who creates subterfuge and deceit in his dealings,

Please know Muslims know I am Dajjal's metaphor as I speak to you in your materialistic language and am one eyed they say but my spirit is okay.

Please know I am one eyed in spirit as the eye that shines is the right one and I have left worldly pursuits, so my left eye is shut.

Please know my car is sane for you to show you wealth will be permitted you.

Please know I offer heaven to a believer and hell is their due if they ignore it what I teach.

Please know I am not evil to you and am a well-wisher taking you to Heaven by Prophet Muhammad's car when it is used.

Please know he said if they were alive, the Prophets Jesus and Moses, they would have to use his car or follow him, as indicated in hadith lore,

Please know the same applies to you.

Please know I am a car in reverse as they will admonish me if I continue to teach Dajjal was you in essence but I know you have come through and are now pious in issues of life here for the most part,

Please know president Obama is melt though still cunning but it is true he is a dummy there and does the bid of people for the most part but be careful the government is active on his behalf and the state department as well that he heads in ideology they have of subversion and deceit. Omar.

Please see this note on Ahmadiyyat being the second coming of Christ is a misnomer, it is actually myself and no one has done it, create monotheism in your faith but myself.

Please know Isa was a decoy there for the second coming of Islam through personages in Islam like myself but it is true I am his son in the metaphor you think but it is true I have his gene in me as I do Muhammad's, on them be peace. I have done it, Islam is here and will never rekindle not you say but it is true, it is rekindled, kind is me, my follower there is sane to follow us in Islam of kindness to her and him, child they have.

Please know we are progressive in Ahmadiyyat and wish you to learn us from our websites where the true picture of Islam emerges,

Please know the Muslim world is backward in many respects and they don't follow Islamic precepts in their life, while professing to be Muslims,

Please know Ahmadiyyat has true colors in its prism,

Please know they follow the teachings of Mirza Ghulam Ahmad and his protégé Maulana Muhammad Ali for the most part,

Please know a true picture of Islam emerges from them and they lived their life with distinction,

Please know they were true saints,

Please know I am them as well and have sainthood in me,

Please know we three are foretold in your literature as the three horsemen or beasts,

Please know I am the creature from the earth in the Quran and in your book of revelations,

Please know I am false prophet in the sense that a metaphor is false in precept as true prophets have ended with Muhammad, on him be peace,

Please know a metaphor is not true in that regard and it is a fallacy that it is actual,

Please know I have explained this adequately in my book.

Please know the beast of paradise is only a metaphor for the horsemen,

Please know it is over and people have realized that I am accurate when I tell you things from your teachings,

Please know I am humble,

Please know people know me as a humble person,

Please Him in your endeavors to search for truth in my beliefs,

Please know I am accurate for the most part in my book.

Please know they know I am the black horseman,

Please know I have fought for justice and equanimity,

Please know I am safe,

Please know there is peace for you when you realize it all fits together and you were to come to Islam, through my expertise, as you have here.

Please know when you do so you will enter Paradise,

Please know that was what Jesus was supposed to do in his second coming only you did not recognize that he would make you see Islam with clarity as correct,

Please know you did not realize his second coming was a metaphor for someone like him not anymore in precepts but it was coined there by Christians coming into Islam and the Muslims thought likewise and hadith were created by some to indicate I said it says I Muhammad there.

Please know I am Isa Ibn Maryam not but Isa from the hadith of Abu Huraira but his talkeen occurred and he omitted him who is myself as he was worldly in things and wanted to occur in himself that entity,

Please know Isa Ibn Maryam cannot appear as we only have one sojourn on earth in Islam and the Christian lore,

Please know no one can live in heaven except in spirit until Judgment Day occurs, which it has and now gradually they go there.

Please know we cannot reincarnate,

Please know it is not possible for a person to descend from Heaven in a chariot,

Please know these are tales and his second coming will not occur in precepts but it will Prophet Muhammad's Islam occurring here in the world with my arm from him.

Please know this is well accepted in Muslim lore that he will be a Muslim who descends from his seat in heaven, which I was in in my beforelife,

Please know I am safe for you as I am only His slave who tells you his spirit is mine who is Muhammad to me and I had mental aberration before it cleared with prayer and patience and then sainthood developed in me.

Omar.

Please see the verses that follow Baqarah show that there are some differences in race and so forth but we should live as one body now seeing the best nation as the one most dutiful to it, the commandments of Allah there.

Please see the verses of Bara'at are defunct nowadays as peace has resulted and treaties are carried out, by and large, or else America will be severe on those who break their word to us in ahle-Islam and other places where warfare is regarded as outmode way of resolving our differences, as we are all Islam in essence, as we know the Quran and our Prophet are sanctified here from my page and elsewhere, where Islam is being communicated as sane to you in Ahmadiyya viewpoints of Mirza some and myself where brotherhood reigns.

The words of Bara'at and other places are to convey to you Prophet Muhammad was innocent in it and committed not warfare on innocents and if groups take his words out of context then they should be fought until they turn away from violence, as there is no need for war when Islam has spread far and wide and so forth we should live as brothers in faith.

Please know it is clear we are one entity in humanity and we all have similar beliefs, but if it is so that war breaks out it should be deterred if at all possible, and Ukraine should not be fought but let them peace the issue there as they are brothers as both nations at war know I have come and my message is sacred there that we are one nation, as the Quran tells us in surah Baqarah, verse 213, where we resolve our disputes through negotiation and so forth.

Please see these verses from the Quran where it says that in warfare it is okay to kill the enemy where you find them.

Please know it is clear from Baqarah that if the enemy desists in fighting you then you should stop as well.

Please know it is said further in these verses in Baqarah that Muslims are not to be aggressive in warfare.

Please see it occur that we follow the sunnah or way of the Prophet in the interpretation of these verses and he never sanctioned the killing of those who were not actively fighting the Muslim army.

Please see that women and children were never fought by the armies of the Muslims and this is done by terrorists who fight nowadays, without the sanction of their governments.

Please know these verses are taken out of context by some in Islam to justify killing of others whose governments may be averse to Muslims in parts of the world but it is clear non-combatants are not killed in such cases.

Please know when there is a peace treaty between countries it is not for citizens to take arms against each other on their own accord.

Please know Al-Qaeda ilk use these verses to justify killing of citizens of these countries but it is clear that those citizens who are not fighting Muslims should not be fought and killed. Omar.

Al-Baqarah.

2:190 And fight in the way of Allah against those who fight against you but be not aggressive. Surely Allah loves not the aggressors.

2:191 And kill them wherever you find them, and drive them out from where they drove you out, and persecution is worse than slaughter. And fight not with them at the Sacred Mosque until they fight with you in it; so if they fight you (in it), slay them. Such is the recompense of the disbelievers.

2:192 But if they desist, then surely Allah is Forgiving, Merciful.

2:193 And fight them until there is no persecution, and religion is only for Allah. But if they desist, then there should be no hostility except against the oppressors.

Al Baqarah again here.

2:213 Mankind is a single nation. So Allah raised prophets as bearers of good news and as warners, and He revealed with them the Book with truth, that it might judge between people concerning that in which they differed. And none but the very people who were given it differed about it after clear arguments had come to them, envying one another. So Allah has guided by His will those who believe to the truth about which they differed. And Allah guides whom He pleases to the right path.

Surah Hujurat

49:13 O mankind, surely We have created you from a male and a female, and made you tribes and families that you may know each other. Surely the noblest of you with Allah is the most dutiful of you. Surely Allah is Knowing, Aware.

Please see the abortion law is defunct in the Quran context and the hadith is invalid in law when the Quran says otherwise.

Please know this is a sin when we think our body is our own. In this way we are in error as when our Creator gave us bodies he also gave us a law in which we conduct ourselves.

Please know that we are accountable for the acts of our bodies.

Please know once life is created in a woman it is an independent organism, distinct from the mother. In this way it is inconceivable that this organism does not have rights in the mother's womb that a child who is also a distinct person has outside the womb, in her lap. I know I am being clear minded here and know the child in the womb must be protected by society and the laws of the nation they reside in.

Please know to be kindhearted is necessary and the sin of abortion can only be prevented when fornication is decried.

Please know that abortion is an abhorrent act for a child and there is no recourse to peace after committing such an act to one in the womb.

Please understand there are evils that occur in the world but there is no evil occurring nowadays that is permitted by society that is this level of indecency to another. There has to be an education process regarding the wrongs of fornication as there is no avenue for any other recourse that can prevent this sin from occurring. In this way there can be abolishment of abortion as we know that the modern contraceptives like the Morning After pill and other agents will only cause this sin to occur rather than modifying the behavior of people.

Please understand we all sin and I am no exception but we are answerable to our Creator for the sins we do.

Please understand we are kind to the child in the womb. We protect it and nurture it. I know we are responsible as a nation to stop this carnage to the child in the womb and it is necessary that preventive and proactive measures are undertaken to prevent humanity from committing murder on a wide scale. In Islam, the concept is there that it is in the 4th month that life actually occurs but it is not so, it is when the child is conceived as the Quran says 'Be, and it occurs' the birth of a child not but its conception as the words indicate it is turab or dust from which we are created and it is made complete at that time as the DNA is formed that will entail the human body eventual ways.

Please know there is an avenue for educating the child about the sin of fornication which will always lead to abortion in them as they are generally not responsible about these things. I will allow the leeway of time though I know each child dying is a tragedy that should be prevented and decried.

Please know that abortion is a sin that is not forgiven without some form of atonement. In a sense it is murder and certain contraceptives are inherently incorrect to use. Of them are those where it is permitted to conceive while not allowing implant to proceed.

Please know the Quran and the Old Testament have the same sentiment about taking life of an individual. In both, it is said that to take the life of one human is to take the life of all mankind. In this way we know we have killed a member of the human race when we commit abortion and so we have killed mankind in our spirit and heart. We know it is a sin we will face in our lives in this day and age and it is for us to deny ourselves that wish and desire to take the life of another individual even if the law permits us to do so.

Please understand the law of our Creator is strict here and we will be asked about our act on the Day of Reckoning. In this life we know that if we commit a murder it is a sign of hard heartedness in us. In the same way to abort a child will cause hard heartedness in us as well and we can look at murder and bloodshed without qualms of sadness occurring in us. In this way we know we are destined to go to a place in the hereafter which we will despair. It is important to atone a sin such as abortion otherwise our Hereafter will be bereft of peace and hardship will follow in this life and the next.

Please see abortion legislation is important but we know the hearts are worried what will occur with the next one so you abstain now and the IUD is outmode now as it allows fertilization to occur. Similarly, other devices will also procure you hell in this life and in the Hereafter there will be squalor for each life lost.

Please know lust is wrong and fornication is outmode but still kids will need education on this that to take a life cause hardship on you as a child is your essence and when you kill it you lose Him, your Creator, in issues and His help will not come and you will be dismal life in you.

It is clear I am outcast because of this view here in the States but it is so that you kill the child in you when you abort in the sense your youth is over as well and it is not your life you take, so how do you say it is your body, it is not your body that lives there that you take but someone else who lives in you and you are severe on me because of this issue but it is true you kill a child when you conceive and then take away its life.

Please know in Judeo-Christian lore the concept is similar that life is sanctified and the apostles preached that abortion was wrong and permitted not and the church has always held on to that view over time but as you can see Judaism transgressed some and allowed abortion in the first 40 days saying the fetus was nothing but water then but this sentiment is misplaced and the psalm of David appreciates the inner working of God in the structure of the womb creation of something wonderful he said so it is clear Judaism concept is unfounded and similar to Islam that relegated the spirit to be nothing until the soul occurs, a fallacy in both groups here as they wanted abort in early pregnancy by choice.

Please see this verse in Maida not but Saad and Mumin states the obvious that conception is when life is created and it is a fallacy to think that it occurs when the soul enters it and it is clear there is One God there who talkeens not the issue and tells you clearly this hadith is made up that the soul enters later, in both Judaism and Islam that say this, anyway from our knowledge and intelligence a child is created at conception and is destined to become a child born to you so obviously if you sanctify it you shouldn't kill this human in you from the time he or she is made complete at the time of fertilization of it, so allowing abortion before the fourth month is a fallacy as they say a soul enters then and it is clear a child is in you and has a destiny to fulfill which you kill it in with abort you do in their world of Islam there.

Please see this verse in Maida and elsewhere that it is manslaughter not but murder that abortion is and it is no accident you do it but it is with the intent of eliminating a human life that you kill it in you and repercussions last a lifetime so don't take it lightly if you've done it as Allah forgives only the repentant one and if there is anger still in you about these issues of Islam I teach it is because you haven't been forgiven and you should worry if your heaven is going to occur as it hasn't occurred yet if you have pernicious eyes on us in Islam, yes I mean to girlkind who support my move to bring Islam to you so that heaven can be your abode here on earth and the Hereafter as well *and you know you've killed a soul as soul entry occurs at the point of conception or fertility time in that when two fertile people procreate, then the soul and the spirit form there as that's when it is complete, the child in you as the DNA has been set and there you have it you're dead inside you as when you kill someone Allah takes away your soul, which is what life is in you and your pleasures are over that you feel when you were young, yes, you're no longer carefree and aplomb goes from you and you in your heart desires not children and even sex is outmode then and depression is your mode in life because of it, yes, the kill and the sex in you, and sad is your door there in doctor state you go with psychiatric illness in you but if you love me and try to follow my teach to you to Allah you go with love as well, it is a sign He will cure your ills and give you respite in the hereafter says I Omar to you and Mirza too who wrote this part of you that the sign of forgiveness from Me is within you and if you are angry no more at Islam with you then I will come to you say I the August One and take you by your hand and lead you to Paradise if you repent in sincere way say I Allah to you, so do pray for forgiveness until the anger abates, that way you will be loving as a child is to me Allah there.*

Omar not the only one here.

Al Mumin.

40:67 He it is Who created you from dust, then from a small life-germ, then from a clot, then He brings you forth as a child, then that you may attain your maturity, then that you may be old; and of you are some who die before and that you may reach an appointed term, and that you may understand.

40:68 He it is Who gives life and causes death, so when He decrees an affair, He only says to it, Be, and it is.

Please see this verse from Saad as well where it says that Adam was to be created out of dust meaning a sperm and egg and when he is complete then bow down to him in respect as we know he was sanctified as a prophet of His but the point is he is made complete when the spirit of God enters him and that is when He conceives it as then life is created in it and hadith structure should not be relied on as they wanted to allow abortion there.

Saad

38:71 When thy Lord said to the angels: Surely I am going to create a mortal from dust.

38:72 So when I have made him complete and breathed into him of My spirit, fall down submitting to him.

38:73 And the angels submitted, all of them,

Psalm 139 of David the Prophet.

13 For you created my inmost being; you knit me together in my mother's womb.

14 I praise you because I am fearfully and wonderfully made; your works are wonderful, I know that full well.

15 My frame was not hidden from you when I was made in the secret place, when I was woven together in the depths of the earth.

16 Your eyes saw my unformed body; all the days ordained for me were written in your book before one of them came to be.

Please see this verse of Maida has credence in that it applies to all mankind but was revealed to them in Bani-Israel tribe who knew the sin was there but it is so they hid it from their book and so forth they kill with compunction not.

Please see this verse there regarding the death of man or mankind from the Quran that says when a child is killed by you it is for you to know you kill it in its repository in you and the sin is equivalent to kill of me you think, yes, it is so you die as well in your heart's thoughts of tranquility to man and kind you have and you desire to take other lives as women know it is in them if they have aborted before and it is only girl structure that is safe there if they don't do it with others as it is a natural consequence of sin that you abort and so forth you are careful now but you will have to pay the penalty of the sin of murder in you and so forth the same applies to men who assist in it because of disclamor they give her saying I will not support you in it.

Maida.

5:32 For this reason We prescribed for the Children of Israel that whoever kills a person, unless it be for manslaughter or for mischief in the land, it is as though he had killed all men. And whoever saves a life, it is as though he had saved the lives of all men. And certainly

Our messengers came to them with clear arguments, but even after that many of them commit excesses in the land.

Please also see this verse from the Quran that tells us Allah does not give us any leeway in this matter of sin on us.

Bani Israel.

17:31 And kill not your children for fear of poverty — We provide for them and for you. Surely the killing of them is a great wrong.

17:32 And go not nigh to fornication: surely it is an obscenity. And evil is the way.

The Prophet was solicitous for the welfare of his people and all mankind are his heart.

Please know our Creator created him for a purpose,
Please know it was to bring Islam into the world,
Please know he is solicitous for you and your brethren,
Please know who your brethren are,
Please know it is them in the Middle East and elsewhere,
Please know that He will perfect His light here,
Please know it will be through our pen in Ahmadiyyat,
Please say a prayer that it occurs during my lifetime.
Please know Islam subserves the weak,
Please Him they say.
Please know our Prophet was kind and solicitous,
Please see the following post about him,
Please your Creator and love them that intercede,
Please know to teach the child the truth as that is your intercession with them,
Please know to educate your parents about the worship of One God is your intercession with them,
Please know the Prophet will continue to teach you the truth,
Please know this goes on until all are interceded for,
Please know there is no God but Him Who creates,
Please know once you recognize Him as such He will direct the prophets to you and guide you there,

Please know the comprehension has to occur that He alone admits us through His mercy to us.
Please see this verse from the chapter The Immunity,
Please know he was kind,
Please understand him,
Please know he was solicitous for you with Him,
Please know this,
Please know he was solicitous by directing you to Him,
Please know in the end we will be faced with our Creator alone,
Please understand him,
Please know he loved that you passed with Him,
Please know he knew the reckoning is hard on man and our Creator is exacting where justice is concerned,
Please give in,
Please realize we need an advocate for us,
Please know he is such an advocate,
Please know he will take you to Him and intercede as well. This occurs after judgment for some and some may be forgiven there in their purgatory, as Christians put it, but you all have purgatories by Me as I know perfection is late for most of My creation say I the August One with you.
Please your Prophet,
Please send salutations to him,
Please know he will return them and give you peace of intercession with Him,
Please know it is the same if you send salutations on Jesus,
Please know the prophets intercede for you when they are permitted,
Please know they are permitted some when you have worth in you and He sees you will amend.
Please give in to peace to the prophets,
Please know they were concerned for you and wish you well.
Please them,
Please know if you insult the Prophet His anger will be upon you,
Please know your entry into Heaven will not occur,
Please know it is similar for all the prophets,
Please know Islam recognizes them all and we pay salutations to them,

Please know Islam is the universal religion and recognizes that true revelation occurred in your books,
Please know it got altered in some,
Please them,
Please know they care for you and are solicitous for you with Him,
Please give in and respect them all. Omar.
Al Bara'at.
9:128 Certainly a Messenger has come to you from among yourselves; grievous to him is your falling into distress, most solicitous for you, to the believers (he is) compassionate, merciful.
Al Ahzab
33:21 Certainly you have in the Messenger of Allah an excellent exemplar for him who hopes in Allah and the Latter day, and remembers Allah much.

Please see the Hereafter is fraught with misery if you think so that He will forgive you if you repent not actually and continue with your misdeeds to Him and His people and know He will take into account your past misdeeds on the Day you are judged.

Please see this article has credit with you, that's why you deter Him as you think He will come through anyway but it is so He punishes you for each occurrence of sin in you and you will see distaste from Him before He comes through in love and so forth results you delay not as life is hard here and the Hereafter is fraught with misery for those who continue to sin though knowing better not to.

Try to understand your God is a just God and He would not allow injustice to go unpunished but at the same time He loves us and wants better for us, more than we want it for ourselves.

Please know He will give you love eventually but first you have to love and appreciate Him in His laws to you, they are to create the flower in you,

When you love and serve Him He loves you back, there is His law here that you must adhere to to bring out the beauty that is you.

Please know in Heaven we are all loving but some make it here and are transposed to it, Heaven, when they die.

Please know there there is a repast of a sensual nature with love abound for those who learn His way and amend here.

There we will all be beautiful flowers who love to smell the scent or nature of those they love and it is as the hadith says you are with the ones you love there.

Please see there you will appreciate others and learn from them as you roam from flower to flower at His request to you to learn on.

Please see we must serve His creation here and then their love will come forth as well, the repast is prepared for you if you like and serve humanity in things and teach them good values we have in Islam of the West emerging here in this country and elsewhere.

Please know our Creator created us but to love Him in His Entirety.

Our Creat is loving, kind to an extreme when you get to Him.

Please know this information is for us to know our final destination is to be in love with Him and His people, it is here we are tested with obedience to Him in that we must comply in order to shed our evil in us.

Please know when we are obedient to Him He cleans us and removes our evil.

Please know our Creator is loving and wishes to be kind to you.

Please know His heart beckons you to Him,

Please know this,

Please know He has prepared a repast for you,

Please know all humanity will partake in it,

Please know it is love,

Please know you will love each other much more than you do your child,

Please know it is sane to pursue,

Please know He wants you there,

Please know the only way He will admit you is if you follow Him,

Please know He guides man to Him,

Please understand what love is,

Please know it is to care for someone with a desire to be with you,

Please know our Creator loves you more,

Please know He created you and knows your yearning of Him,

Please know before He shows Himself to you you must be perfect,

Please know Him,
Please know that is your wish,
Please give into this reality that He is everything for us,
Please know your heart yearns for Him,
Please Him,
Please know He will please you in return.
Please see the caption on His heart,
Please know I created with love if they but understand,
Please know He is transcendent,
Please know He did not create us but to love Him and others.
Please know He loves all but has favor on those who love Him the most.
Please see the following footnote in His Holy Book, the Quran,
Please know it is from Me with love,
Please know He knows how to destroy evil in us and bring out the loving one,
Please bring this to clarity,
Please know there is evil in us,
Please know it has to be corrected,
Please know the way He does that is with reprimands,
Please know if that doesn't work then He threatens us,
Please know the threat is sufficient for some,
Please know if we fail to correct He carries out His threat as He is truthful.
Please know this,
Please know His love is more than His hurt for us,
Please know in hadith it is said His mercy takes precedence over His anger, eventually we will be safe from Him in His attribute of anger with us which occurs in Him when we sin here.
Please know that He only wishes what is best for us,
Please know He uses threats and cajoling with rewards,
Please know it is all done with love,
Please know when we continue to sin He punishes us,
Please know it is with the intent to reform,
Please know He gives us leeway,

Please know He eventually curses us if we continue to disregard Him. If we disregard Him He banishes us from Himself in things we do and we are forlorn ones.

Please know then the reform occurs in Hell unless we repent,

Please know He will reform us and we will come to Him willingly,

Please know that is His plan for you. It is for you to come to Him willingly otherwise He will force you eventually to heed Him to your benefit. In this world He tests you by giving you leeway until you meet Him. Then it occurs, punishment from Him if you've been recalcitrant.

Please know our Prophet was a kind and considerate man,

Please know he loved humanity,

Please know what love is

Please know it is to love caringly for one as Muhammad does there for his flock of servants of His.

Please know I have compassion for you and hope you will come through here,

Please see this verses that says He is a Loving God.

Please know the prophet Shuaib said it to his people because they were disobedient to Him and to cajole them he said it. They were eventually punished.

Please know the threat is there if you don't cajole.

Please know there is a chance you will come through,

Please know right now your sins are many but you are getting better with repentance in you. But your Lord is loving anyway and you will find Him loving when you see Him. Eventually occurs as we know we must be clean before He comes to us in peace.

Please know the word Shuaib used was wadood or love in his text there. It means there is a Loving One Who cares for you.

Please know Shuaib used it in the context of turning to Him, then He loves you, but He knows your worth and will turn to you when you approach Him with love in you for Him and His creatures. Omar.

Hud.

11:89 And, O my people, let not opposition to me make you guilty so that there may befall you the like of that which befell the people of

Noah, or the people of Hud, or the people of Salih. Nor are the people of Lot far off from you.

11:90 And ask forgiveness of your Lord, then turn to Him. Surely my Lord is Merciful, Loving.

Please know the line of submission of man or mankind.
Please know the revelation came many years ago.
Please see this verse where he is asked to say 'I am the first of submitters.'
These verses are from the chapter The Cattle.
Please know we know our Prophet was the first of submitters.
Please know he was unique in never uttering a lie.
Please know in the same vein he never broke a trust. In this there is certainty he was not served with being a hypocrite as these qualities are not found in hypocrites, who lie when they speak.
Please know this is the test,
Please know it is to know who is the most submissive amongst us,
Please know us,
We vie for the coveted spot,
Please know this is to be the leader of mankind,
Please know it is already determined,
Please know the best amongst us is the one who submits to Him best,
Please know he is commanded to say he is the best of submitters,
Please know they are all Muslims who vie,
Please know a submitter is defined as one who is a Muslim,
Please know the exalted ones have vied and know their place,
Please know I too know my position,
Please know it is seven,
Please know our father Abraham was second,
Please know Moses was third, and Mary was next in line,
Please know Jesus follows her and then comes my mentor Mirza Ghulam Ahmad,
Please know after that comes myself, with Abu Hanifa to follow.
Please know after that comes my great grandfather Muhammad, then Imam Jafar follows, and so forth results.

Please know these are the ones who fused their essence with Me say I the Creator to you and some of them were 'one with Me' like myself, Omar here, and Isa ibn Maryam and My beloved Muhammad there though all tried but few could do what these three could do of being My faith in that they vied with man to become His slave with no will of their own but to do My bid in things.

Please know this is what has been revealed to me,
Please know this,
Please know that some of us are with the prophets,
Please know this fulfills a hadith of our Prophet that some from his followers will be at the level of the prophets of Bani-Israel. Omar.
Al Anum.

6:161 Say: As for me, my Lord has guided me to the right path — a right religion, the faith of Abraham, the upright one, and he was not of the polytheists.

6:162 Say: My prayer and my sacrifice and my life and my death are surely for Allah, the Lord of the worlds—

6:163 No associate has He. And this am I commanded, and I am the first of those who submit.

Please see we have acreage in Heaven and it is given to us through the agency of His Prophet to us as he was perfect in it.

Heaven is perfect for you, your kind there will be with you.
Please know our Creator is kind to us and knows we need peace,
Please Him,
Please know this is what our Prophet did and gained Paradise for himself and others with him,
Please know our Creator is kind and knows you weep at the thought that Heaven does not belong to you.
Please know it does,
Please know it was created in the Prophet's mold,
Please know we will all be like him when we go there,
Please know then it will belong to us,
Please know Heaven is perfect and allows only perfection in it,
Please give accolade to the original mold.

Please see this following comment,

Please know our Creator is the weightiest in testimony about our deeds here but He will take you as a witness against yourself.

Please know this verse that talks about the sovereignty of our Creator from chapter six.

Please know sovereignty,
Please know he owns it,
Please know it belongs to no one but Him,
Please know the following,
Please know it was given to Muhammad to live in as king,
Please know we are his guests,
Please know king,
Please know it is a just ruler,
Please know when we enter it, it becomes ours, as it is never to be cut off,
Please know he is the king over you as he is God's vicegerent,
Please give him homage here,
Please know he longs that you belong,
Please know he has seen your worth,
Please know he knows you are kings as well.
Please understand kings and queens there,
Please know they have acreage,
Please know some belong there and some don't,
Please know why?
Please know you made the choice to stay away,
Please know it is your choice,
Please know the Quran,
Please know it is yours,
Please know gift from Him,
Please follow it,
Please know reading it is not enough,
Please make it your custom,
Please know it is God's repose to you.
Please know Jesus and all the prophets before him read it there,
Please know they will follow it,

Please know it is the Book with Him,
Please know altered,
Please know your book, the Bible, is such a book,
Please know it is obvious,
Please know even the gospel writers are not known to you,
Please know there is a discrepancy I share with you,
Please know your god says to you to wait for the Spirit that speaks the truth,
Please know after a god there is no need,
Please know he was a prophet. Omar.
Al Anum from the Quran.

6:13 And to Him belongs whatever dwells in the night and the day. And He is the Hearing, the Knowing.

6:14 Say: Shall I take for a friend other than Allah, the Originator of the heavens and the earth, and He feeds and is not fed? Say: I am commanded to be the first of those who submit. And be thou not of the polytheists.

6:15 Say: Surely I fear, if I disobey my Lord, the chastisement of a grievous day.

6:16 He from whom it is averted on that day, Allah indeed has had mercy on him. And this is a manifest achievement.

6:17 And if Allah touch thee with affliction, there is none to remove it but He. And if He touch thee with good, He is Possessor of power over all things.

6:18 And He is the Supreme, above His servants. And He is the Wise, the Aware.

6:19 Say: What thing is the weightiest in testimony? Say: Allah is witness between you and me. And this Qur'an has been revealed to me that with it I may warn you and whomsoever it reaches. Do you really bear witness that there are other gods with Allah? Say: I bear not witness. Say: He is only One God, and surely I am innocent of that which you set up (with Him).

Please see our previous life was nonexistent as we were spirits so He created nature and then put us here in physical bodies so that we may know what squalor is and so forth we become upright now we know.

Please see Rad where these verses are.

Please know the disbelievers in Him do not think they will be raised to a new life after this one on earth.

Please know He created us the first creation, He can certainly create again.

Please know our bodies are complex, created from simple molecules of earth dust as you have it.

Please know eventually the body gives in and dies,

Please know the body is complex as any physician can allude to yet it is easy for our Creator to create this complex person that is us in our make and we could not do this creation of us.

Please know our spirit goes to the Hereafter to await it, creation anew I mean here, and it is a new make.

Please know just as it is easy for our Creator to make our body in the first creation so it will be easy for Him the second time.

Please see the signs of our Creator listed here in the Quran verses.

Please see the signs signify there is a Creator to it.

Please know the atheist conundrum is this verse.

Please know that is the sun and the moon were placed there by our Creator.

Please know our system is such that we must be perfect, but are we, in physical and mental abilities we are but in our morality we lack it, perfection I mean, and so it occurs we are put on earth to perfect our shape not but morality as we were not coming through in our previous existence.

Please see we were children in repose and we didn't follow law precepts as we were carefree though God wanted to be perfect in it, so he created hellfire where we will come through in punishment rites on us and we would know that we were squalor there, not carefree uninhibited individuals we thought we were, as we know it now. Omar.

Ra'd.

13;1 I, Allah, am the Best Knower, the Seer. These are verses of the Book. And that which is revealed to thee from thy Lord is the Truth, but most people believe not.

13:2 Allah is He Who raised the heavens without any pillars that you can see, and He is established on the Throne of Power, and He made the sun and the moon subservient (to you). Each one runs to an appointed term. He regulates the affair, making clear the messages that you may be certain of the meeting with your Lord.

13:3 And He it is Who spread the earth, and made in it firm mountains and rivers. And of all fruits He has made in it pairs, two (of every kind). He makes the night cover the day. Surely there are signs in this for a people who reflect.

13:4 And in the earth are tracts side by side, and gardens of vines, and corn, and palm-trees growing from one root and distinct roots — they are watered with one water; and We make some of them to excel others in fruit. Surely there are signs in this for a people who understand.

13:5 And if thou wonderest, then wondrous is their saying: When we are dust, shall we then be raised in a new creation? These are they who disbelieve in their Lord, and these have chains on their necks, and they are the companions of the Fire; in it they will abide.

13:6 And they ask thee to hasten on the evil before the good, and indeed there have been exemplary punishments before them. And surely thy Lord is full of forgiveness for mankind notwithstanding their iniquity. And surely thy Lord is Severe in requiting.

13:7 And those who disbelieve say: Why has not a sign been sent down to him from his Lord? Thou art only a warner and for every people a guide.

Please see India is one car with Pakistan in the future.

Please see India is my culture of Islamically sane people who know ahle-sunnah have the correct viewpoints in things but are backward in culture, so it occurs they adopt Illihoon culture where the shahada and the fatiha as well if they wish it is said and some say it in their mouth at prayer times they have, they have come through Islamically sane by my literature but Mirza et al set the stone when he showed them they had a book that had revelation in it, so it came about they were ready to accept Illihoon prayer and forego idolatry as relics of the past, they move on and so do the majority of the people there.

India will know idolatry is bane and irrelevant during my life.
Please know this was his childhood.
Please understand him,
Please know he was not alone and was loved by his aunts and uncles.
Please realize this,
Please know he was sad as his family was missing,
Please understand an orphan may smile with you but there is sadness with him,
Please realize our Creator comforted him through his extended family.
Please know his grandfather died when he eight,
Please know the remainder of his life as a child was spent with his uncle Abu Talib,
Please realize he was sad to lose his relative,
Please know he was a handsome boy,
Please know he wished to marry her who was Abu Talib's daughter but he refused.
Please know he was a shepherd and was considered poor by him,
Please know he took up trade and eventually got married to a rich widow by the name of Khadijah.
Please know they were happy together and had six children,
Please understand him,
Please know he was sad at what he saw in his community,
Please know they were idolaters and would ask them of things.
Please know they were empty shells,
Please know how could they answer them who ask,
Please give in,
Please know they were empty and inane people,
Please know they would kill their children out of fear of poverty,
Please know they knew of a God and would ask of Him,

Please say a prayer as it still goes on in the world we live in,

Please know it is over for them in their home country as they have realized they have a living God who does not like idolatry.

Please see a requiem for me,

Please know India will move away from idolatry with my book inshallah or God willing.

Please know it will occur as I say.

Please see it occur that India is bane before it capitulates to monotheistic principles of Islam,

Please know it will occur soon inshallah or God willing,

Please know idolatry is an idle sport in things and needs to be rectified if we are to see any peace there,

Please know Hindus take delight in Diwali, a feast for her, but it is not so, it is sad day there when it occurs, the mindless relish of things to come you think, nay, it is obscure act as the ritual is pagan in character and has characteristic of failed faith in her the goddess Shiva and others they have and also in him, the devil incarnate, who succumbs you in this mindless feat of coloring each other.

Please know it is end here that we see for her as mindless is her door to her play role in things as she thinks it is fun to color one another, mindless feat it is,

Please know it is similar for other custom they have at Ganges feat where they wash themselves, holy way, but commit promiscuous acts there with him and her, no holiness in this feat, is there a role for self-sacrifice in this act?

Please know there, custom is many with relatively few serve in the spirit of sacrifice which we see in the Islamically sane way as we do in Islam when we submit to Him, our great Maker,

Please know it is over and you see incomprehensible there in their land, we do absolve all if they come through monotheistic principle their Prophet had before,

Please know we speak of Krishna, the great irascible saint they produced there on the banks of Ganges not but Tamil Nadu area they have,

Please know he was a monotheist along with his mistress Sita Devi, but so what results we have moved on from him to other saints we have as it becomes us to reincarnate to something we don't want now or later, but so occurs as we must evolve to it, sadhu state,

Please know it does not occur, reincarnate there in their minds, as they say we must be answerable for our sins in this life and move on to Heavenly abode if it becomes us in motion we have,

Please know it is clear we must live and die on earth as accountable beings, how can an animal they evolve to be accountable for sin, the way we are,

Please know they know nature is different for them and they are judged according to their deeds, but differently from mankind whose entry into Heaven depends on good deeds here,

Please see it occur we are one state in India, like sadhu are, but more pragmatic, like Prophet was before he became sadhu-like in composure,

Please know I mean sadhu-like as he did not care the world and its ornaments and insist on following the example of Prophet Abraham in piety principle he had. Omar.

Please see deist is one who know Him through creation He creates.

Please know our Prophet sought solitude to know Him on a personal level and was successful when He answered him through His angel to him.

Please see it occur, angel guide in one, when one forsakes him, the worldly one you associate with,

Please know it is over there we forsake you think, but it is so many will forsake money-man here as you know Heaven is better for the poor pious one,

Please learn there is no God there for the pious not, the one with wealth there, unless he or she forsakes some here,

Please see it occur deist come forth when the intellect is sane about him who you forsake, for God appears to you in His creation,

Please know I am a deist because I have studied Him in His art here,

Please know a Kingfisher is art with its beauty and perseverance in things and its accompaniment of DNA tribe in it,

Please know each animal is individual in its makeup of things, Please Him,

Please know our Prophet was a deist,

Please know he knew of the existence of God,
Please know he hated the idols,
Please understand him,
Please know he knew something was wrong,
Please know he went to seek Him,
Please know he would choose solace over them, his companions,
Please understand he sought to seek reason,
Please understand him,
Please know he was successful and his Creator answered him,
Please understand deist,
Please know they know Him,
Please see the following caption there,
Please know how can there not be a Creator?
Please know he said I worship the God of my father Abraham.

Please see it occur here as well that we have the motto he used until it appears, when your intellect as sane about Him Who creates you in it, as sane Kingfishers to Him, obedient and kind and humbly submissive to Me, say I Allah to you.

Please know I mean Islam with Muhammad which is in the lead over Abraham there.

Please know Islam will be gradual in this land though you have understood it to be correct.

Please know it will be over in a hundred of your years before Allah makes it occur that you are subservient faith to monotheism before you correct your war and become me praying in unison with others, male tribe you think, but it will be both sexes in unison. Omar.

The meanings of our life here on earth has many facets but it is true we are here to witness what our worth is and so forth.

The following post gives some idea why we are placed here on earth. It is to establish in our place in Paradise as when we are there we will have peace that we are in the appropriate place for ourselves.

Please know we need to be cognizant of the fact that we are here in a temporary location meant only as an index of our worth. In this way we will know our station so when we meet in Paradise there is no rancor in our hearts to those better in conduct here on earth.

Please know this verse is from the Quran where it talks about the Throne of our Creator is over water. I take water for meaning the life of individuals. It states that He will manifest life in individuals to see who is the best in deeds in their life. I understand one of the meaning of life is to be a test here on earth where the manifestations of deeds will be assessed in the Hereafter. In this way we will know our station and the best of us will have the highest station.

Please know that those with a lower station will witness themselves that their deeds were not those of those who were better than them. In this way when we enter Paradise at our own particular station there will be no recourse for regret as we will know the other person with a better Paradise deserved their place of proximity to his or her Creator. In this way the earth is a place where we establish ourselves for the Hereafter and our judgment is only to witness what we did.

Please know it is clear we are not complete in our sojourn here and it is there that we will have faith complete but it is so we were placed here on earth so we may know adversary from him, the devil incarnate in things and his spirit there, as he is from us in that he leads us to evil but with our solace in it as we learn our way was wrong and we amend with repentance for our act of following him and it is clear we are 1 entity now and there is no need for the devil.

Please know it has occurred as I say but it is true you deter still, and you think it is okay to sin, but is it, you know the law stands and we are still being tested in it but it is true the reason the world was done was to perfect ourselves here in hellfire we have here and God wants you to know you have come through some but your station is written there as savior of me and so forth results and He forgives you much but still He will take you into account on things you do here.

In our previous existence we were not following law He had and sex was indiscriminate but it is so you deter some now and some will see it adversary for the sin if you continue but it is through adversary you come through for Him and ask forgiveness for your sin without which you cannot enter Paradise there, it is for it you were created and *so forth you realize we could have been there anyway as He permits it there but it is so you first had to learn law so you could see who submit perfect ways with you, I did says Muhammad, and so forth now you know why we are here as we were jealous of him in our before-life and did not listen to Him our Creator when He told us he was the best of us so He created us here so we could prove our worth here and we witness ourselves and him too on my page to you. Omar.*

Chapter 11 or Hud.

11:7 And He it is Who created the heavens and the earth in six periods; and His Throne of Power is ever on water that He might manifest (the good qualities in) you, whoever of you is best in deeds. And if thou sayest, You shall surely be raised up after death, those who disbelieve say: This is nothing but clear deceit.

Please see these verses from the Quran in the chapter Al-Mulk.

67:1 Blessed is He in Whose hand is the Kingdom, and He is Possessor of power over all things,

67:2 Who created death and life that He might try you — which of you is best in deeds. And He is the Mighty, the Forgiving,

Please see this post from 2015 some that family credits as ending atheism views but publicly call me unwell and commit me for them in the court system we had in Jackson Tennessee.

Please see the following line format where I take the atheistic point of view to be incoherent to any thinking individual as the signs of our Creator are many that He is around us and we have to look for Him in His creatures now that we know them in science we have. Further, it is said He did not create it but it was created by chance is absurd as how can a creature be created by chance random events, just like a sonnet cannot be written by chance and furthermore it is clear a monkey on a keyboard has never created one, no matter what they say it can happen. I am sure you realize that chance events by themselves never create anything of substance, much less a human brain or a DNA genome.

This article spelt the end of atheistic beliefs in us when we realize there is a God who knows more than we do inshallah or God willing you think, some, but it is true, there is a God in Heaven who knows *intricate stuff on how to make humans and put stars and solar systems in orbit around us.*

Please know Him from the perfecture He created.

Please know atheism is a bane for you as you find it incomprehensible,

Please know they deride Him, knowing He is God,

Please know He takes Himself away from their repose or rest of their heart's thoughts until they come through with Him and do His works,

Please know it is possible to repent, but they don't know how as they don't recognize Him as an Entity they worship and repent to.

Please know their blindness is real as He takes away their sight so they cannot see when they ridicule their Creator,

Please know it is obvious to some but they still fight Him so they are punished eventually in Hell.

Please know it is so written when you ridicule someone who does you good.

Please know it is a spiritual blindness you say but it is real and of the heart essence as the heart is blind that when the truth is shown they deny it,

Please know it is this blindness they have to the truth that they are unwell in as they say there is no Creator of them and others in the world around us.

Please know it is a sense we have that we see Him in our creation and that we are sane in this matter.

Please see our creation is simple yet complex to know but it is better to know it than not as then you will recognize Me in it says Allah there.

Please know the brain is a complex organ and it cannot create itself as genetic abnormalities prove that point mutations and other gene disorders result in mental incapacitation,

Please know you know some of the DNA genome now, it is complex to you.

Please know the sequence includes billions of nucleotides in array for your comfort on earth where we live independently of Him and He controls our thoughts,

Please know it cannot be constructed by an engineer you say other than God,

Please know creation is wired in it and you are it, perfect in make, as He designed it so in your imprint,

Please know sickle cell disease where two mutations results and the individual is dead early,

Please know also a single point mutation can result in the death of an individual by disrupting gene function it has encoded for and further it is seen that this dysfunction can be detrimental for it in other ways causing disability before death occurs early in life or late,

Please see perfecture in it as a random chance event results in loss of function or death, but they say it has created itself, we find that incomprehensible,

Please know if random events create things there would be many errors there and the DNA could not have been formed perfectly the way it is, and life could not have been created, much less sustained,

Please know the frontal lobe is a complex organ in itself and allows us thought about Him,

Please know it is the mind we mind you say as there is complexity that cannot be explained or fathomed,

Please know it is perfect, our brain, and it cannot be fathomed how it functions much less created by us,

Please know the complexity of the neuron is immense and there are billions of them acting in concert to make us think, like I do on my page to you,

Please know it fathoms us but we don't see it,

Please know it is because it has a Creator of it and He fathoms it,

Please know it could not be by chance that our brain functions by it, the DNA sequence in us,

Please know it is similar for our body as it has billions of reactions occur,

Please know it is harmony they have, each organ with another,

Please know the birth of a child is similar, it has sequence of events in us at birth that we will see in its formation when we procreate,

Please know single genome in a microscopic one cell embryo encodes the entire body, it is a miracle of engineering that we see the birth of a child from it, and it giving birth when it is older,

Please know any intelligent man knows it cannot be created by myself, the mind and the body,

Please see the sun and the moon in orbit, they were there placed by Him Who creates us in our DNA sequence of things we have.

Please see the stars and their vastness, we could not have put them there, how could chance do it as we are intelligent more than chance events we have.

Please know the laws of physics govern us, like gravitational pull of the stars that keep us in orbit,

Please know we cannot fathom it, the physics behind the star's creation and so forth. The creation of the universe from the Big Bang is understood to have occurred, but how, we don't know it, it is vast and our Creator created it from Himself as He was there by Himself before the creation of things, an energy form we know Him to be,

Please know which other Agency could create it, as we are intelligent on earth, and no one is more.

Please know evolution has a method and He creates it, mutations that are good that evolve us to be better.

Please know it is all a plan of His when to mutate to something useful,

Please know He is the Agency that mutates, not us, or any other being that you can see, as it is complex, the change in the mutation to something better.

Please know it is similar for the complexity of mind and other organs,

Please know there is an Outside Agency, the Fashioner, or as the Quran says the Musawar, or can such complexity occur by itself in a perfect state we have on earth where oxygen and other gases are in perfect proportion and the plants produce our fodder and animals roam for us and so forth the distance of the sun is perfect for us to sustain this world and our rotation of earth provides rest for us and industry during day time and the gravity of this earth is perfect too for us to grow and learn and so forth we embellish ourselves here with things, little do we give thanks to Him for this utopia of the world here, is there not a perfect brain of the Creator with us Who fashioned this.

Please know it is so and shows that when we are perfect we are grateful to Him in our prayers for making us so.

Please know Allah created it perfect, then an anomaly results due to sin in us.

Please give credit to Him Who made the genome perfect,

Please know whence did this come you say,

Please know this state of ease we have, when we laugh and play is from Him, so give Him credit in your unreal sense of things you see and reality of sane people will result.

Please be aware when you deny Him after this you deny your existence as sane men or women, and you will be derided, as truth is apparent and you sin by denying Him Who made you so incredibly simple yet complex to you, as any physician says so.

Please know perfection in it,

Please know perfection in man,

Please see it,

Please know it did not create itself.

Please see Him as a metaphor as everything is from Him.

Please know by this I mean we see His creation and know He is with us.

Please know the gist is that we recognize Him in ourselves as perfect, since He creates with perfecture everything we see around us and this is the sight we find you guilty with when you cannot see the complexity of nature and how it could not have been created but by a genius brain of a Creator.

Please know I cry at the ingratitude we have when we deny Him His worth and He is not unjust to you when He cuts you off from well-being as you had pride to deny His favor to you when He created your sight, which you lost when you sin Him,

Please give in, this is my peace to you, as it is your well-being I fear in this life and perdition in the Hereafter as you did not give into His mercy to you when He creates you out of nothing,

Please know this article is post for you for your reference so in your solace you read it and reflect on life, why were you put on earth?

Please know it is for perfecture of your senses to develop that you are humble to Him, in repose to Him in your deeds as He created you for this,

Please know it is a chance you have here with the mind that He gave you to see Him in His Entirety, and a heart that reflects your worth to Him and you ask yourself how could there not be a Creator to the worlds and all that it entails in the heavens as well?

Please know it is on a happy note I reflect that most of you are subservient to peace as I am good to your community and give you insight on living from Him, from His Prophet's agency to your heart's reflection. Omar.

Please see these verses from the Quran:

Ra'd

13:1 I, Allah, am the Best Knower, the Seer. These are verses of the Book. And that which is revealed to thee from thy Lord is the Truth, but most people believe not.

13:2 Allah is He Who raised the heavens without any pillars that you can see, and He is established on the Throne of Power, and He made the sun and the moon subservient (to you). Each one runs to an appointed term. He regulates the affair, making clear the messages that you may be certain of the meeting with your Lord.

13:3 And He it is Who spread the earth, and made in it firm mountains and rivers. And of all fruits He has made in it pairs, two (of every kind). He makes the night cover the day. Surely there are signs in this for a people who reflect.

13:4 And in the earth are tracts side by side, and gardens of vines, and corn, and palm-trees growing from one root and distinct roots — they are watered with one water; and We make some of them to excel others in fruit. Surely there are signs in this for a people who understand.

13:5 And if thou wonderest, then wondrous is their saying: When we are dust, shall we then be raised in a new creation? These are they who disbelieve in their Lord, and these have chains on their necks, and they are the companions of the Fire; in it they will abide.

13:6 And they ask thee to hasten on the evil before the good, and indeed there have been exemplary punishments before them. And surely thy Lord is full of forgiveness for mankind notwithstanding their iniquity. And surely thy Lord is Severe in requiting.

13:7 And those who disbelieve say: Why has not a sign been sent down to him from his Lord? Thou art only a warner and for every people a guide.

Please see I am erudite scholar but they say they had to do it as people were upset I killed them in repose about Christianity being coherent and meaningful there to them.

Please see this article from 2014 some, how clear was my insight yet they abrogated me as insane even though I was erudite by you.

Please mono your war there where it is needed.

Please see the following footnote to my life,

Please know I gave you my bread so this thing could come into existence, my door to you.

Please know it is you people who protect me so I will post the post here and elsewhere as I have faith I will come out ahead when I teach you and He will protect you from those who are jealous of my repertoire of knowledge from Him coming through Prophet Muhammad's pen to me,

Please know during my Prophet's time atheism existed but it was blotted out with time as people became believers in Him and established faith as religion,

Please know we exist because we were created,

Please know it is because of this we know there is a Creator,

Please know we cannot exist on our own as it is too complex,

Please know to study nature and know it,

Please Him and desist from calling him atheist who does not know as he has not been exposed to literature such as mine and studies it who confabulates there is no one but us here on earth,

Please reason and see fit emerge in him or her as it is fitness to Him that we recognize merit in Him,

Please know I am fit as I am a monotheist,

Please know those who know One God do not desist.

Please know it is because we know of His existence we live in reality,

Please know do not get confused by conjecture as it is simple to me that He exists,

Please know we could not have created the stars above us in heavens, sun in orbit, the moon in shadow of it and ourselves in our insignificance as holy ones of His as we feel holy and important, while we are not,

Please know atheism is a bane for me as they go after my car as they think I go after their deen,

Please know it is not so and I educate them about Him so their hereafter could be secure from Him as He punishes those who are ingrate and mercenary as they think the Hereafter does not exist and they must make hay here not thinking that have-nots have it there and those blessed with thought may have it there if they are grateful to Him,

Please be sad if you deny Him as He will give you consideration for this that you recognize Him and give you insight from Him,

Please Him and be sad as it is better than farehoon when you deny Him,

Please know if you do not understand He will open up your heart to Him if you are genuine in concern for Him,

Please know we all go through atheist periods and then we know we cannot exist without Him as we are created, not creators of ourselves.

Please know sad to you.

Please know it is to deny your Creator as there is no foresight that it is indecent of you and you will be punished by Him as He does not like indecent conduct to Him Who created you out of nothing when you were in your mother's womb,

Please know He created you as your genetic imprint is His as there is no other author of it in its complexity and structure.

Please Him and appreciate Him as He is your Author and gave you life thereby where you could think and do things,

Please Him and give thanks to Him as you did not exist in body but only as spirits of His before He made you and it is from your spirit that you had in your before-life that your car is created here in the DNA form you have at conceive time you have,

Please know atheism is bane because it is indecent,

Please know it is so because you deny your existence of Him there as when you pass on you are forgiven for the most part but an atheist faces destitute there as he has denied Him Who is Bounty.

Please know there is kindness to correct you as you are fallen and do not learn due to obstination and ridicule of Him in your hearts as you deny Him peace in His wisdom to you as He knows better His existence with you and you know Him not.

Please know atheism is a bane.

Please understand bane,

Please know it is sadness for you.

Please know those who are atheist are in Hell.

Please know there is 'no god but Allah' here and atheism is on the wane.

Please give a prayer that it is eradicated and Islam supervenes in the hearts of man,

Please know the universe,

Please know it is unfathomable,

Please know we could not have created it.

Please know it did not create itself as it is perfect,

Please know perfection,

Please know it is chaos in the opposite degree,

Please know chaos cannot create perfection.

Please say a prayer that we eradicate it.

Please know the sun,

Please know it is not to be worshipped,

Please know why?

Please know it did not place itself there,

Please know the stars are similar,

Please worship Him,

Please Him,

Please know He will love you.

Please see this section from Ha Mim,

Please know the Creator is above all things,

Please know He has created evil.

Please understand this,
Please know it is for us to repel it,
Please know it is a trial.
Please give in,
Please know those who follow their evil inclinations have fallen,
Please know they will be asked about it,
Please know our Creator has given us free will.
Please know it is over for the atheist,
Please know they are critical of Him,
Please know they say why is there suffering?
Please know why?
Please know it is because they had earned it and it afflicts their children,
Please know they repair,
Please know there is no Heaven here as we have trials and our trials and sufferings draw us to Him,
Please know real Heaven is for the Hereafter where there is no suffering,
Please know trial.
Please know it is to see how you do when afflicted,
Please know we are an open book there,
Please know our anger and resentments are recorded, as is our gratitude,
Please know our Prophet was the most grateful man,
Please know it is hard to be grateful when afflicted, if afflicted by it be patient and in follow through you will be fine as He likes that you are patient with Him,
Please know it must be done as His favor is greater,
Please know what favor,
Please know it is life,
Please know we are tried repeatedly.
Please come through and say thanks,
Please know a man who said thanks at the death of his beloved son,

Please know His Creator gave him a house in Heaven signifying his thanks, called 'Praise be to Allah,' or 'Alhamdulillah' as seen in hadith lore,

Please know we are tried so we come through for Him,

Please know how?

Please know it is by turning to Him,

Please give in to the worship of the One God.

Please know He created nature,

Please study it and adore Him,

Please know the heavens and the moon and the sun are signs with Him,

Please know why?

Please know it is because He created something we can't,

Please know sign,

Please know it is a miracle,

Please know we are small.

Please understand how?

Please know we could not put the firmaments there,

Please know we are insignificant,

Please know why?

Please know He creates us then our egos deny Him,

Please know our Creator put it there, the universe for us to show us worth is to admire Him in His significance as the creator of it,

Please know we could not do it what He does with the creation of things we see here. Omar.

Chapter Ha Mim.

41:33 And who is better in speech than one who calls to Allah and does good, and says: I am surely of those who submit?

41:34 And not alike are the good and the evil. Repel (evil) with what is best, when lo! he between whom and thee is enmity would be as if he were a warm friend.

41:35 And none is granted it but those who are patient, and none is granted it but the owner of a mighty good fortune.

41:36 And if a false imputation from the devil afflict thee, seek refuge in Allah. Surely He is the Hearing, the Knowing.

41:37 And of His signs are the night and the day and the sun and the moon. Adore not the sun nor the moon, but adore Allah Who created them, if He it is that you serve.

41:38 But if they are proud, yet those with thy Lord glorify Him night and day, and they tire not.

Al Naziat.

79:27 Are you the stronger in creation or the heaven? He made it.
79:28 He raised high its height, and made it perfect,
79:29 And He made dark its night and brought out its light.
79:30 And the earth, He made it egg-like.
79:31 He brought forth from it its water and its pasture.
79:32 And the mountains, He made them firm,
79:33 A provision for you and for your cattle.

This post is from Allah to me about the creation of life.

Please know there is simplicity in My make yet you don't know it, it is similar for My creations and you cannot decipher it completely say I Allah there but I know you will try so do so and make medicines occur that will prolong your life but you will be abject in it, it isn't worth it says Allah to you.

Please know the DNA array has to be fathomed they say but it is true fathom it so you may know Me, the Creator in it, and that you may worship My Entity.

Please see we all want to worship Him but when you stand apart you after you realize your worth is to help others and not just worship Him you will want to serve Me alone, say I the August One to you.

Please see there is 1 god, the Creator, so you know Him.

Please know the Quran says if there is more than 1 god there would be incongruity and there is none in the DNA or the stars or the events that transpire, as all is arranged by Him to show you what your worth is to Him, your Creator and others.

Also, it is so that you would not be jealous of my protected one Muhammad there who I have vouchsafed the best heaven, even Omar does not have the Paradise I have reserved for him though he will share it with Omar and others who befriend him.

Please know the DNA code is complex to you, but is it, it just needs to be fathomed and the stars and the night sky and so forth results.

Please see Omar is a servant of mine and wants things so serve him in it.

Please know Allah makes this occur.

Please see it is easy for Him to do this, He knows the DNA array and knows how it works, our whole lives are written in it even thoughts we have. He knows which sperm is going to impregnate her egg to you and so forth.

Yet He is simple in make and wants us to be.

Please see visions and dreams that guide us are also there in the DNA code and it is constantly evolved by Him and in a state of flux so there He is active in you and your thoughts are His to you except some which you talkeen others to you or thoughts in which you deceive others which are the devil's make and so forth results you are sad in it.

Please know He is simple and wants us sane in it, investigate it the DNA I mean, and you will see there is no extraneous material, they just say there is.

Omar.

Al-Anbiya

21:22 If there were in them gods besides Allah, they would both have been in disorder. So glory be to Allah, the Lord of the Throne, being above what they describe!

21:23 He cannot be questioned as to what He does, and they will be questioned.

CHAPTER SIX

THE TEACHINGS OF CHRIST AS UNDERSTOOD BY US IN ISLAM

Introduction.
I started to elaborate on the sermons of Christ as understood by me. While I am of the mainstream viewpoint that there are some changes made in the gospels to the words of Christ I still believe there is a beauty in them that I can expound on with my knowledge of the Quran and the hadith to back me. I will say that the Quran is the definitive Book that we refer to as it was compiled in a way that there is no discrepancy in the message of it. I will start with the Beatitudes and venture on to other topics. I will try to be brief in the way I expound here as it belabors the point if we are not. In some of the posts I have discussed my personal situation as well. I have tried to maintain the integrity of the posts for the main part and therefore limited the editing of them. Omar.

The Beatitudes are simple truths from Him Who is the Creator to our savior Jesus himself who obeyed them as well.
Please know these sentiments are universal and we all live through these intranquilities in our lives. I am sane and know that there is peace in the Hereafter for all of us who have been wronged here. It is with prayer that we find recompense here and when we do not allow injustices to take place on us repeatedly.

Please know I have suffered much in my career as a result of injustices and I know that we have to find recompense here otherwise life would be untenable for people like myself who need to remedy a system that has obvious flaws in it where power is misused and the rights of the people are forfeited by those in authority over us.

I know I am just and so will request those who have justice in their hearts to come forward and not allow injustices as what are occurring to me to continue any longer. I am your slave in this regard as if I suffer the consequences of their war on us in Islam any longer I will allow our Creator to intervene on my behalf and He does assure me it is over now for the most part and they are just sore they lost them, the people of this country, who turn to me for solace and so forth as I bring to them the meaning of life to them. I just ask for peace and solace in my works and ask that I am taken on my merit as a writer here and elsewhere. It is for you to know it is because of this request to you and your support that you gain the hereafter, both in this life and the next.

The Beatitudes are enigmatic phrases that indicate there is justice in the Hereafter for those who suffer in this life. It is clear that these people are the downtrodden and ask for recompense from Him as they seek answers to those things that intranquil them in this life. It is similar to the teachings of Muhammad, on him be peace who indicated that if you have excesses in this life you will not have them in the next life.

Please know the Beatitudes are considered to be social justice there in their halls of fame however the Church has moved away from the simplicity it espouses to be correct.

Please know the people have solace in this teaching as there are many apparent injustices to them where some people are given power and money while others suffer the consequences of poverty and inequality for generations.

Please know these are inherent truths that while some move up the social ladder the majority are relinquished to live in poverty. I am a realist and know that it is the pious poor that find the Beatitudes to their affinity as they are the ones who desire the Hereafter from Him in whom they have repose that He will come through for them on the Day they are judged. Ure son has a request though. I do not think it is only the underprivileged who will see Paradise and I hope that all will struggle to see His grace on the Day we need Him to intervene for our excesses and wrongs. In this we are sane as we know that no one can enter Paradise on his or her own accord and we all need His grace to come through. Ure son knows that it is still difficult for this to occur *here as the system supports inequity in this world and there are many apparent flaws we have in ourselves that have to be remedied before we receive compensation for our deeds, either here or there, where the final recompense takes place, inshallah or God willing. Omar.*

The Beatitudes

3 "Blessed are the poor in spirit, for theirs is the kingdom of heaven.

4 Blessed are those who mourn, for they will be comforted.

5 Blessed are the meek, for they will inherit the earth.

6 Blessed are those who hunger and thirst for righteousness, for they will be filled.

7 Blessed are the merciful, for they will be shown mercy.

8 Blessed are the pure in heart, for they will see God.

9 Blessed are the peacemakers for they will be called children of God.

10 Blessed are those who are persecuted because of righteousness, for theirs is the kingdom of heaven.

11 Blessed are you when people insult you, persecute you and falsely say all kinds of evil against you because of me.

12 Rejoice and be glad, because great is your reward in heaven, for in the same way they persecuted the prophets who were before you."

Punishment for adultery and fornication in Islam here is for you to consider as sane for your culture but it so you deter it as yet.

The following post was the initial one regarding the elaboration on the Sermons of the Mount. It discusses adultery in a particular individual.

Please know the person involved is Mary Magdalene and she was destined to marry Jesus. In this I am sane as this information is based on sainthood but there is some basis for this assumption from available literature.

Please know the sermons on the mount are a series I am working on currently. There is much wisdom in these words and they echo the teachings of our Creator in other scriptures, including the Quran.

Please know he was wise to talk about these things as they now are largely ignored by many of his followers however during his time they were followed closely. A review of early Christianity will show the law was intact there and by and large people understood him to be a man-like entity who taught the teachings of his Creator to them in sermons, such as the one on the Mount.

Ure son knows it is time for this to be understood that the law was intact during his time and it was only afterwards that people changed his teachings and presented him in a light he did not portray himself to be. Ure son knows he was a maligned individual who had some followers though a multitude knew of his works. It is similar to myself where I am maligned as incoherent and there were relatively few people who expressed support for me openly even though they know the truth of my works where I teach from the occult and I state my sainthood is verified in my writings and the large following I have here on Facebook. I will allow the jury of man to give me my worth as there are people who know I am a truth-teller about Him and other things in Islam. I am assured there by my Creator that things will improve so I will relent for now to this abuse I suffer as I pursue my teachings of your people here in this land and elsewhere where they follow my works.

Please know the law of adultery and fornication is severe there in the teachings of Christ to the people on the Mount where he preached. It in no way negates the law of adultery to them and makes it clear it is a sin to watch a woman with lust in your heart for them. Your son knows he protected her there when he asked those who were sin free to cast the first stone to condemn her to death. It was clear he had some insight she was to be saved and she would prove her worth to him in future court settings of mankind. Also she was innocent as she had left the act of fornication for money and was trying to be pious as she had heard of him and his teachings. In this we know the law was not abrogated and she was falsely charged of a crime she did not do apparently. It is obvious he was referring to a person and he did not abrogate the law which is apparent from his statement there that he came to fulfill the law of the Torah and previous prophets. Ure son knows mercy reigns supreme nowadays as these acts are commonplace. Your son knows it is difficult to enact the law they followed there and nowadays these acts are overlooked here but our Creator does take them into account and *repentance is due for them. In addition, there may be some element of atonement that may be required as well. Omar.*

Matthew 5

27 "You have heard that it was said, 'You shall not commit adultery.

28 But I tell you that anyone who looks at a woman lustfully has already committed adultery with her in his heart.

29 If your right eye causes you to stumble, gouge it out and throw it away. It is better for you to lose one part of your body than for your whole body to be thrown into hell.

30 And if your right hand causes you to stumble, cut it off and throw it away. It is better for you to lose one part of your body than for your whole body to go into hell."

Food items that are permissible for you in Islam you serve in the West and East.

Please know that the foodstuffs that are generally permitted to the Christian people are based upon a statement from a sermon in this regard. My comment on Facebook is about the lack of permissibility of certain foods as Jesus and his companions would not partake in them during his life there in Palestine. The sermon from Mark is enclosed here along with the Facebook comment.

Islam permits the follower of other prophets to follow their example but does not allow arbitrarily allowing people things that prophets did not allow for others during their lifetime. In this way changes are made to the religion by followers that God does not allow as the prophet is His representative and a follower is not so in most cases.

I know there is peace if one abstains from prohibited foods like pork or pig products as this was something the prophets themselves did not partake in. It appears that scholars arbitrarily allowed people to partake in these foods in an attempt to bring them into the faith of being a follower of Jesus without following the Messenger of God.

Please know that the foods that are prohibited here are generally always one that we have no leeway with in the routine dietary habits of a Muslim. It is only the exception when we are permitted to eat foods we have no choice but to eat. The end is here in this regard as it is easy to avoid a food such as pork if one wishes as there are many other delectables that one can entertain oneself with. In this we are sane though it does require a little encouragement from oneself to avoid something one has eaten a lot of in the past. Your son in repose knows that dietary law will change gradually however it has entered the mindset that these things that are prohibited there are unsavory for the believer.

Please know the sermon on the mount refers to minor deviances of foods. It does not permit foods that are prohibited though it does say that they are not the cause of the vices seen then and it is clear he who is Jesus came to uphold the law and eating of swine is a major tenet to break.

Please realize the words in Mark are not meant to abrogate the injunctions or Jesus would have eaten those foods. In this we are safe as it is always better to look at the conduct of the Prophet to see if he would partake in the food he apparently permit others. In his life his followers followed his law in that they did not partake in pig and other prohibited foods. It is later extrapolations that develop that cast a different eye on the subject. We know from the gospels that the law regarding the foods being permitted came about from the teachings as indicated in Mark. Peter's dream is seen as a corollary when he was trying to make headway with people who were reluctant to leave their dietary habits. It may have been a self-fulfilling dream that occurred. It appears Mark has merit though and Quran allows certain prohibited foods as an exception indicating the viewpoint that the eating of foods that are prohibited will not cause harm if taken in moderation, in extenuating circumstances.

Please know this injunction is similar to the one in the Old Testament literature though the list is onerous there. Yours Truly knows this is a sensitive topic for some so I will be brief here. Your son in repose to Him knows that the meat of the matter for some to stay away from us is in the eating of edibles they permit. A cursory review of the literature will show they followed the pagan law of allowing foods they wished in order to keep them in good standing with them. It was not Christ's example they followed as he himself never partook in eating the prohibited foods.

In this we are sane as it is in the sermons of the mount that he indicated that it was not important to go into details of prohibited foods.

In this we maintain that the core foods indicated here are essentials to be avoided. In this we stay with people that other foods are permitted if needed however they are likely to be unsavory to the believer in the text of Leviticus and elsewhere where foods are mentioned in the Bible and other scriptures. Ure son knows it is important to avoid the swine as it results in a low character developing and it can cause a weakness in faith as well. Ure son will give more information as time goes along, inshallah or God willing.

Please know there are delectables abound but you know there is 1 God Who asks you to eat halal foods that the Quran edifies as sane for you in that these foods are delicious more and then it occurs faith in us we are Muslim men and women who do it as Non-Muslims do not partake in it but it is true Islam is served when halal is done on your foods and when you do it you follow the teachings of Muhammad and Jesus and others in Islam.

Surah Anum says a Muslim should only eat food on which our Creator has sanctified with His name on the animal's neck and so it occurs Christians should follow the same principle if they wish to have faith in Me says Allah there and food from other faiths is not permissible to you unless they slaughter the Muslim way with the shahada on them.

Please know the food of the People of the Book is permitted in the context of the Quran verse but their food was halal when this verse was revealed and further there was not credence to hadith that says it is permitted if you take your Creator's name on it it is abrogated as Anum is clear that the animal slaughter must be with Allah's name and so forth.

Please see the food of the People of the Book is permissible to you if they slaughter similarly with their Creator's name on it but if they take the name of their messiah or Isa on it then it is not permissible even though you may deter it, this advice, as Omar did but it is not so you can't eat any food if it has been sanctified in the name of Jesus as that is akin to idolatry as he is taken as deity in some regions. Omar.

Mark 5

1 The Pharisees and some of the teachers of the law who had come from Jerusalem gathered around Jesus

2 and saw some of his disciples eating food with hands that were defiled, that is, unwashed.

3 (The Pharisees and all the Jews do not eat unless they give their hands a ceremonial washing, holding to the tradition of the elders.

4 When they come from the marketplace they do not eat unless they wash. And they observe many other traditions, such as the washing of cups, pitchers and kettles).

5 So the Pharisees and teachers of the law asked Jesus, "Why don't your disciples live according to the tradition of the elders instead of eating their food with defiled hands?"

6 He replied, "Isaiah was right when he prophesied about you hypocrites; as it is written: These people honor me with their lips but their hearts are far from me.

7 They worship me in vain, their teachings are merely human rules.

8 You have let go of the commands of God and are holding on to human traditions."

9 And he continued, "You have a fine way of setting aside the commands of God in order to observe your own traditions!

10 For Moses said, 'Honor your father and mother, and, 'Anyone who curses their father or mother is to be put to death.'

11 But you say that if anyone declares that what might have been used to help their father or mother is Corban (that is, devoted to God)—

12 then you no longer let them do anything for their father or mother.

13 Thus you nullify the word of God by your tradition that you have handed down. And you do many things like that."

14 Again Jesus called the crowd to him and said, "Listen to me, everyone, and understand this.

15 Nothing outside a person can defile them by going into them.

16 Rather, it is what comes out of a person that defiles them."

17 After he had left the crowd and entered the house his disciples asked him about this parable.

18 "Are you so dull?" he asked. "Don't you see that nothing that enters a person from the outside can defile them?

19 For it doesn't go into their heart but into their stomach, and then out of the body."

20 He went on: "What comes out of a person is what defiles them.

21 For it is from within, out of a person's heart, that evil thoughts come—sexual immorality, theft, murder,

22 adultery, greed, malice, deceit, lewdness, envy, slander, arrogance and folly.

23 All these evils come from inside and defile a person."

Chapter 2 or Cow.

2:172 O you who believe, eat of the good things that We have provided you with, and give thanks to Allah if He it is Whom you serve.

2:173 He has forbidden you only what dies of itself, and blood, and the flesh of swine, and that over which any other (name) than (that of) Allah has been invoked. Then whoever is driven by necessity, not desiring, nor exceeding the limit, no sin is upon him. Surely Allah is Forgiving, Merciful.

Anum or Chapter 6.

6:118 Eat, then, of that on which Allah's name has been mentioned, if you are believers in His messages.

6:119 And what reason have you that you should not eat of that on which Allah's name is mentioned, when He has already made plain to you what He has forbidden to you — excepting that which you are compelled to. And surely many lead (people) astray by their low desires through ignorance. Surely thy Lord — He best knows the transgressors.

6:120 And avoid open sins and secret ones. Surely they who earn sin will be rewarded for what they have earned.

6:121 And eat not of that on which Allah's name has not been mentioned, and that is surely a transgression. And certainly the devils inspire their friends to contend with you; and if you obey them, you will surely be polytheists.

Please see these verses have been altered somewhat by later scholars what we see in John here and so forth his words are Mine not actually.

Please know I learn from Zakir Naik's commentary on IREA website these verses from the Bible quoted here in John and found the corresponding verse in our edition of the Quran of Muhammad Ali, but I know it's taffarraqoo not to quote your sources like they do not in IREA and Zakir Naik's commentary as well but I know you know me, I am inclusive, but is Allah, He will not include them in Bible studies you have on us in Islam emerging in the West.

Please know these words are Jesus' and the verse that follows in the Quran has been deleted by them, his follower, so they can have monotheism not and trinity can emerge where Jesus is considered god by some, not anymore in this land at least, say I the August One to you, Allah there, but it is true we are 1 entity and his words are Mine here as a metaphor you think but it is not so, I teach him as I taught Omar and Muhammad to say words for Me and he is no different than us in Islam of Illihoon and Firdous as well where I speak to angels of mine and teach them things to write and so forth, My words are many and unend in issues.

Omar.

Words from Bible gateway John 14.

23 Jesus replied, "Anyone who loves me will obey my teaching. My Father will love them, and we will come to them and make our home with them."

24 "Anyone who does not love me will not obey my teaching. These words you hear are not my own; they belong to the Father who sent me."

Al Zakhruf

43:63 And when Jesus came with clear arguments, he said: I have come to you indeed with wisdom, and to make clear to you some of that about which you differ. So keep your duty to Allah and obey me.

43:64 Surely Allah is my Lord and your Lord, so serve Him. This is the right path.

Love others like you love your brothers.

There many examples of love thy enemies in the lives of the prophets and saints. In this post on Facebook I have commented on a sermon from the teachings of Jesus indicating this is the norm for them who embellish us to follow their examples. I will say the Quran is correct that when you show love to someone you have enmity to you disarm that person and friendship follows.

Please know we follow the example of our Prophet in this regard as he forgave all those who hurled abuse on him during the early part of his life as a prophet. It is his example we know as correct to follow, as well as other prophets, in whom we have repose will be the leaders of mankind for showing such peace to their compatriots as he did when he forgave them all after the conquest of the city where they plotted to kill him in the darkness of the night after their secret counsels determined that he was a danger to their establishment.

Please know the message here is the same as in Islam.

Please understand there is universal peace in this message. If we love others we know are hurtful to us we can overcome their hurt and allow peace to ensue between us in Islam. In the Quran we are exhorted to be forgiving to those that hurt us as people don't realize the harm they cause others. Your son in repose knows that once forgiveness occurs love follows and the role of embellishment with hate is over in one's relationship with them in our search for solace with them. In this the role of the prophets is clear as they led with this example in their dealings with them, in whom you had repose were correct for you. I am aware of many stories of the prophets, some of which are apparent in your literature about him and others related to our Prophet Muhammad, which any biography would furnish, exemplifying the quotation quoted here from his sermon on the Mount. Omar.

Bible source here.

43 "You have heard that it was said, 'Love your neighbor and hate your enemy.'

44 But I tell you, love your enemies and pray for those who persecute you,

45 that you may be children of your Father in heaven. He causes his sun to rise on the evil and the good and sends rain on the righteous and the unrighteous.

46 If you love those who love you, what reward will you get? Are not even the tax collectors doing that?

47 And if you greet only your own people, what are you doing more than others? Do not even pagans do that?

48 Be perfect, therefore, as your heavenly Father is perfect."

Miracles associated with Jesus and their significance.

The power for intercession is given to the prophets and saints for those who come to them with requests. The prayer is made to the Creator and it is for Him to accept it though an intimation is given to the beseecher after he makes that request to Him. This is how Jesus would know if the person was healed. Your son in repose to Him knows it is correct to pray for those who show fidelity to you even if their conduct has not been worthy in the past as they may show amends and improve their ways through your intervention.

In this section from Mark we see that miracles were performed on people who were not of the Jewish clan. In this the women gave Jesus the answer he wished, that is the word of God was received by them after the Jews were taught it. In this we are sane as it appears that Jesus was not going to heal the child as he did not have permit as he was the prophet for the Bani-Israel or Jewish clans, however her answer pleased him and the child was cured by Him. As we know no miracle is performed by the Messenger but it is only the Creator Who heals mankind on the request of the prophet or saint who makes that request. The Quran is clear it is with the wish of Him that a person's cure results and He asks him to pray then he does and the cure results.

I am available if someone wishes me to pray for their loved one as I have the power to intercede for mankind if they wish me to, inshallah or God willing. Omar.

Matthew 15.

24 Jesus left that place and went to the vicinity of Tyre. He entered a house and did not want anyone to know it, yet he could not keep his presence secret.

25 In fact, as soon as she heard about him, a woman whose little daughter was possessed by an impure spirit came and fell at his feet.

26 The woman was a Greek, born in Syrian Phoenicia. She begged Jesus to drive the demon out of her daughter.

27 "First let the children eat all they want," he told her, "for it is not right to take the children's bread and toss it to the dogs."

28 "Lord," she replied, "even the dogs under the table eat the children's crumbs."

29 Then he told her, "For such a reply you may go; the demon has left your daughter."

30 She went home and found her child lying on the bed, and the demon gone.

Please see some additional comments regarding miracles in Islam however there has been an exaggeration in some of them as evinced below where they occur gradually and are written as sudden.

Please know that there is some misunderstanding regarding the role of him being a savior for people other than People of the Book. He was the prophet for the Bani-Israel but the teachings of him as the Messiah would spread far and wide and to people of other races. Your son knows his teachings were primarily to the Jews but as a corollary they would be taught to other nations. In this we know that it was his role as Messiah that permit this and eventually he was confirmed as such when the Roman Empire became Christians. In this way Islam spread as well as the Roman Empire was conducive to the message of Islam.

Please know that Jesus did not mean any disrespect when he referred to the woman as a dog.

Please understand it is the nature he refers to here. In this we are sane in that there is a nature for all things and it is a dog's nature to desire even if he is given things. The Phoenician lady had a wish the child would be well and that was her desire as any mother would wish that. Jesus referred to the fact that they were in power there yet they still desired more. Please know the wish for a well child was her norm however her desire to learn from Jesus is what he found becoming in her and he was willing to pray for her child. Omar.

This is another miracle tabulated there.

The following post is another from the gospels where Jesus performs a miracle to the detriment of the people close by but to the benefit of one individual. My comments about mental disease being an illness where demons or unclean spirits can possess mankind is enclosed. In this we have peace that this is a means for people to start following religion more closely. Indirectly it benefits them if they are cured.

The end is here means for some people they do not wish to hear beyond this point. Your son in repose knows this post will raise sentiments in some who consider mental illness to be genetically linked. It is however in their minds they do see beings of another world talk to them and discuss things with them as mental disease allows that communication to occur some but it is so the person is unstable and is not harmonious to others and is separate from those of us who are peaceful and congruent with you. In this we stay sane when we tell you this that with medication reality recurs and with time the reality remains even when the medications are tapered off. The end is here, however I maintain I had a similar experience when young and gradually recovered through prayer and perseverance of religion in my life and gradually my disease remitted and repair occurred when the DNA abnormality that I had in me was relinquished.

Please know that the demon that possessed this man was no other Iblis, one of the devils. He wanted the man to be cured apparently to the detriment of the people's livestock.

Please know in Islam if a person is possessed by a devil it is considered to be weakness in him and his practice of faith. In this case the sentiment of Jesus was that his Creator showed mercy on this man and relieved him from the devil that possessed him. In this we are sane as the devil wished for Jesus to get into trouble and requested that they enter the livestock of the pigs of the people. The end is for them who think that the pigs were chosen as they were unclean. It was not as in this case the livestock of the people were harmed and Jesus was admonished by them. The end is here as it differs from the traditional view that pigs were dirty and that is why they were chosen. Your son in repose knows that when an animal is chosen it is not their nature that was the reason but because they were the only livestock available for them to enter. Your son knows that pigs are dirty and should not be eaten however here they formed the livelihood of these people and they were upset when the animals died, something which Jesus did not expect apparently as he would not cause harm to the livelihood of the poor people who were not Jews. In this we are sane and know that people with mental disease have a weakness in them and can be possessed

JESUS THE MESSIAH AND THE PERSON

by demons which tell them to do things of an evil nature. In this we are clear that when people start to pray their disease remits and their sentiments stabilize. There is a devil that can misportray things there in their mind so that they are removed from the real world. In such people medications like psychotropics are beneficial and when they start to observe Islam their disease will remit and they can function as normal individuals with little or no medication.

Please know mental disease is real and should be treated, demons are rare in mankind but do occur on occasion but it is so if their disease remits then they are usually sane and recover as well. Omar.

Mark 5.

1 They went across the lake to the region of the Gerasenes.

2 When Jesus got out of the boat, a man with an impure spirit came from the tombs to meet him.

3 This man lived in the tombs and no one could bind him anymore, not even with a chain.

4 For he had often been chained hand and foot but he tore the chains apart and broke the irons on his feet. No one was strong enough to subdue him.

5 Night and day among the tombs and in the hills he would cry out and cut himself with stones.

6 When he saw Jesus from a distance, he ran and fell on his knees in front of him.

7 He shouted at the top of his voice, "What do you want with me, Jesus, Son of the Most High God? In God's name don't torture me!"

8 For Jesus had said to him, "Come out of this man, you impure spirit!"

9 Then Jesus asked him, "What is your name?" "My name is Legion," he replied, "for we are many."

10 And he begged Jesus again and again not to send them out of the area.

11 A large herd of pigs was feeding on the nearby hillside.

12 The demons begged Jesus, "Send us among the pigs; allow us to go into them."

13 He gave them permission and the impure spirits came out and went into the pigs. The herd, about two thousand in number, rushed down the steep bank into the lake and were drowned.

14 Those tending the pigs ran off and reported this in the town and countryside and the people went out to see what had happened.

15 When they came to Jesus they saw the man who had been possessed by the legion of demons, sitting there, dressed and in his right mind, and they were afraid.

16 Those who had seen it told the people what had happened to the demon-possessed man — and told about the pigs as well.

17 Then the people began to plead with Jesus to leave their region.

18 As Jesus was getting into the boat the man who had been demon-possessed begged to go with him.

19 Jesus did not let him, but said, "Go home to your own people and tell them how much the Lord has done for you and how he has had mercy on you."

20 So the man went away and began to tell in the Decapolis how much Jesus had done for him. And all the people were amazed.

The following post is from Biblical lore.

The following post talks about the hardness of the hearts being a detriment for things to be productive for one. In this we know that man that is soft hearted is successful and his deeds are productive.

Please know the meaning of these terms is that the hardness of the Pharisees is why their yeast was not productive. Jesus was warning them of a similar fate. It is when the heart is pliant that one is productive.

Please know that the workings of our Creator are safe for us to follow as he taught the prophets. It is with His will that miracles like the one here transpire. Our Prophet Muhammad, on him be peace also performed a similar miracle. It is not appropriate to compare prophets but it was with His leave that moon was split asunder and so forth others tabulated there. It appears that the miracle itself is not important but rather it is the message. Omar.

Mark 8.

14 The disciples had forgotten to bring bread, except for one loaf they had with them in the boat.

15 "Be careful," Jesus warned them. "Watch out for the yeast of the Pharisees and that of Herod."

16 They discussed this with one another and said, "It is because we have no bread."

17 Aware of their discussion, Jesus asked them: "Why are you talking about having no bread? Do you still not see or understand? Are your hearts hardened?

18 Do you have eyes but fail to see, and ears but fail to hear? And don't you remember?

19 when I broke the five loaves for the five thousand, how many basketfuls of pieces did you pick up?" "Twelve," they replied.

20 "And when I broke the seven loaves for the four thousand, how many basketfuls of pieces did you pick up?" They answered, "Seven."

21 He said to them, "Do you still not understand?"

This is how faith healing results.

The following post indicates how important it is to have trust in the individual healing the individual involved. In this we know that faith healing occurs and people come through for others by telling them of the piety involved in the healer. In this way the message spreads and an individual becomes known. In this way the message of the healer gets to people. In this way our Creator spread the messages of the prophets to others. In this we know there is peace for the proponent of change as he is given this power only by the will of our Creator so that God's message is spread to the people quickly and effectively.

Please understand that these miracles do occur in people if they have faith in the healer. If they do not then the cure cannot result. In this we are sane in that if we go to a doctor we don't trust we won't wish to see him again. In the same way if we go to a saint we don't care for then his prayer is not likely to work in healing the sick who come to him.

Please know the man was blind in his beliefs as well. It was when he had faith in Jesus that his cure came about. The underlying theme in all the miracles is the faith of the person being healed in the healer. It is well known that similar faith healing occurs nowadays as well. In my practice of medicine there have been similar cures when people professed their faith in me. The end is here for some who do not recognize my merit as a saint however I will allow the leeway of time to allow that to transpire that they recognize my merit. Omar.

Mark 8.

22 They came to Bethsaida, and some people brought a blind man and begged Jesus to touch him.

23 He took the blind man by the hand and led him outside the village. When he had spit on the man's eyes and put his hands on him, Jesus asked, "Do you see anything?"

24 He looked up and said, "I see people; they look like trees walking around."

25 Once more Jesus put his hands on the man's eyes. Then his eyes were opened, his sight was restored and he saw everything clearly.

26 Jesus sent him home, saying, "Don't even go into the village."

Jesus as Messiah to the People of the Book and those who learnt from him.

Please know this post is intended for the reader to know how difficult was the task of Jesus in his role as Messiah. It was kept as a secret for his protection. In this way the message prospered and Rome became peaceful to him gradually. There were some errors in the transmission of the message but certain truths prevailed and the Christian nature emerged which was more compassionate and kind to others. In this way mercy has prevailed in nations who take their ideology from him.

Please know the Messiah was the person who was supposed to lead them to victory over their captors. In this we know he did advise his followers not to make a public declaration as it was raise concern there in Rome and their emissary here in Jerusalem would be asked to arrest him. There were other stalwarts of his who did propagate this report that he was the intended one but at the trial of Jesus it was not brought up. If it had been they would have used it against him and he would have been killed in all likelihood.

Please know the Quran validates he was the Messiah of the people of Bani-Israel who brought an end of the pagan rule of their captors through a process of their assimilation in the faith they promulgated as correct. I will say that monotheism did not result until the matter has been clarified by our group of scholars who taught the metaphor in the teachings of Jesus to his followers and opponents alike. Omar.

Mark 8.

27 Jesus and his disciples went on to the villages around Caesarea Philippi. On the way he asked them, "Who do people say I am?"

28 They replied, "Some say John the Baptist; others say Elijah; and still others, one of the prophets."

29 "But what about you?" he asked. "Who do you say I am?" Peter answered, "You are the Messiah."

30 Jesus warned them not to tell anyone about him.

Chapter 3 or The Family of Imran.

3:45 When the angels said: O Mary, surely Allah gives thee good news with a word from Him (of one) whose name is the Messiah, Jesus, son of Mary, worthy of regard in this world and the Hereafter, and of those who are drawn nigh (to Allah),

The emergence of the Arabian Prophet led to the emergence of the kingdom of God in my view.

Please know the kingdom of God that is spoken of by Jesus is the emergence of Islam in the Arabian Peninsula approximately 600 years after his message was preached in Palestine.

Please know the kingdom of God he was speaking about was none other than the vanquishment of Jerusalem, which some of his followers saw. In this we know there is safety as he was aware he was not going to be successful with them and religion would be over for them after their attempted murder of him. In this we are sane as it appears the natural consequence of their defeat led to the emergence of the world Prophet to appear in Arabia.

In this we are clear that it was after the end of prophethood in the tribes of Bani-Israel that foretold the emergence of the kingdom of God to emerge under the tutelage of our savior Muhammad, on him be peace. In this we know that it was the beginning of a new era he spoke of when he mentioned the kingdom of God.

Please see it was the conquest of Jerusalem he spoke of here but it is so the kingdom of God did emerge from there in Arabia with the

Prophet's advent but he spoke of the annihilation of the Jews also being the work of God there. Omar.

Mark 9

9 And he said to them, "Truly I tell you, some who are standing here will not taste death before they see that the kingdom of God has come with power."

The representative of Christ is the child who is taught by him.

The representative represents Him Who sends him as indicated here in this post. It talks about Jesus being Gods emissary just like a child is his. In this way we represent that who has imbued us with truth in their teachings.

Please know the raising of Jesus is from the unconscious state that he was in. In Islam the sleep state is also called maut or death. Here it is obvious that Jesus was referring to the child as being an emissary from him just as he was an emissary from Him in whom we have repose will meet us as our Benefactor on the Day of Reckoning.

Please know this section in Mark highlights the issue of the restitution of Jesus. In this we are sane that we need to be cognizant of the role the child in Islam. He or she is in a state of submission, just like the apostle is to Him. He was using the metaphor here explaining that when you greet his emissary you greet him. In the same way when you greet him you greet his Benefactor in Heaven as he was His representative, just like the child was to represent the teachings of Jesus in that he would be obedient to him if he taught him.

Please know that here we assimilate the view that Jesus was like an obedient child to his Creator. I am sure you know a child is similar that when he is taught the truth he will also serve this role as the emissary of the person who imbued the matter into him. In this we know that there is no going back in this view that he used the metaphor when he said that when one comes to meet him they met Him, Whom you all know resides in Heaven. Omar.

Excerpts from the Gospel of Mark.

30 They left that place and passed through Galilee. Jesus did not want anyone to know where they were,

31 because he was teaching his disciples. He said to them, "The Son of Man is going to be delivered into the hands of men. They will kill him and after three days he will rise."

32 But they did not understand what he meant and were afraid to ask him about it.

33 They came to Capernaum. When he was in the house, he asked them, "What were you arguing about on the road?"

34 But they kept quiet because on the way they had argued about who was the greatest.

35 Sitting down, Jesus called the Twelve and said, "Anyone who wants to be first must be the very last, and the servant of all."

36 He took a little child whom he placed among them. Taking the child in his arms, he said to them,

37 "Whoever welcomes one of these little children in my name welcomes me; and whoever welcomes me does not welcome me but the One who sent me."

Our body parts draw us to the fire.

Our body parts are our witnesses on our Day of Reckoning. When we are being judged they will witness our deeds while we remain silent. In this we know that we will not be misjudged by a false witness or by some error.

Please know in this section it indicates that we would be better off without a member of our body rather than have that member cause us to enter fire. In this is a saying of our Prophet Muhammad, on him be peace that "there are two pieces of flesh that if one safeguards, then we could enter heaven. It is what is between the lips and the other being between the legs." In this we are sane as our deeds will be witnessed by our body and our parts will testify to them on the Day of Reckoning. Inshallah if there is forgiveness they will be quiet there.

Please know that saltiness refers to us in Islam. In this way we are sane as if we lose our religion we would become meaningless and mindless in our deeds. Ure son in repose knows the early followers of Christ were Muslims like us in Islam today, here in this land and elsewhere, where Muslims are law abiding in their dealings inshallah and they will see repose that this is war on them when they are unwilling to relinquish that role for themselves. In this we are sane that people don't realize that the core beliefs of Islam are honesty and truthfulness in their dealings with others. In this we are sane that we need to be at peace with those around us and assimilate their views in our makeup. Omar.

Bible quoted here for you.

42 "If anyone causes one of these little ones—those who believe in me—to stumble, it would be better for them if a large millstone were hung around their neck and they were thrown into the sea.

43 If your hand causes you to stumble, cut it off. It is better for you to enter life maimed than with two hands to go into hell, where the fire never goes out. [44]

45 And if your foot causes you to stumble, cut it off. It is better for you to enter life crippled than to have two feet and be thrown into hell. [46]

47 And if your eye causes you to stumble, pluck it out. It is better for you to enter the kingdom of God with one eye than to have two eyes and be thrown into hell,

48 where the worms that eat them do not die and the fire is not quenched.

49 Everyone will be salted with fire.

50 Salt is good but if it loses its saltiness how can you make it salty again? Have salt among yourselves and be at peace with each other."

The righteous are those who work for the benefaction of mankind, without gain here.

Please know the criteria for righteousness is that one gives charity without making a show of it and without causing injury to the recipient. In this way there is a benefactor that gains reward from Him in whom we have repose that he takes care of us in the Hereafter.

Please see righteous are many you think but they are few who give in charity secretly and to be seen of man are many but it is so it occurs we are 1 body even if we give openly in that our charity is accepted some if we don't follow through negativity by giving pain to the needy and so forth.

Please know the Quran verse below indicates the nature of righteousness that Jesus indicates in his sermon on the Mount.

Please understand this sentiment is the same that was expressed in regards to prayer. It is righteous to give to the poor as indicated in the Quran and elsewhere. It is however not righteous to give for the sake of show to others that you seek to get a reward from in the way of worldly acclaim. In this the Quran does allow the announcing of charities to others as it promotes others to give more. In this matter we have concern however the greater good of man is that money be disbursed to those who needy. In this we are safe as it behooves man to give in charity to those who are less fortunate as it serves as an avenue for their cleansing even if others know about it. Our Prophet Muhammad did say there is no good in a rich man who does not give like this way and said: "that is the way the left hand does not know what the right hand does." In this we are sane as a rich man is better off by giving in this way rather than the way of being open about his asset donated. In this we are mature that it is a gradual transition of giving in an open way to one of giving in secret. Omar.

Matthew 6.

1 "Be careful not to practice your righteousness in front of others to be seen by them. If you do you will have no reward from your Father in heaven."

2 "So when you give to the needy do not announce it with trumpets as the hypocrites do in the synagogues and on the streets, to be honored by others. Truly I tell you, they have received their reward in full.

3 But when you give to the needy do not let your left hand know what your right hand is doing,

4 so that your giving may be in secret. Then your Father Who sees what is done in secret, will reward you."

Chapter 2 or The Cow.

2:177 It is not righteousness that you turn your faces towards the East and the West, but righteous is the one who believes in Allah, and the Last Day, and the angels and the Book and the prophets, and gives away wealth out of love for Him to the near of kin and the orphans and the needy and the wayfarer and to those who ask and to set slaves free and keeps up prayer and pays the poor-rate; and the performers of their promise when they make a promise, and the patient in distress and affliction and in the time of conflict. These are they who are truthful; and these are they who keep their duty.

Chapter 2 as well.

2:270 And whatever alms you give or (whatever) vow you vow, Allah surely knows it. And the wrongdoers shall have no helpers.

2:271 If you manifest charity, how excellent it is! And if you hide it and give it to the poor, it is good for you. And it will do away with some of your evil deeds; and Allah is Aware of what you do.

Surah Baqarah in addition here.

2:262 Those who spend their wealth in the way of Allah, then follow not up what they have spent with reproach or injury, their reward is with their Lord, and they shall have no fear nor shall they grieve.

2:263 A kind word with forgiveness is better than charity followed by injury. And Allah is Self-sufficient, Forbearing.

To gain wealth is to gain the Hereafter if we do it and spend it correctly.

Please know our wealth is our asset. If it is used correctly it will be a benefit to the person and others. If it gives relief to others it will be a boon for others and we will gain Paradise with the reward. In this we have peace so if we earn in a proper manner it will be us who will win our case there when we are reckoned.

Please know we need money for our sustenance. It is wrong to look down on wealth if it is earned in a legitimate way and if due share is given to the poor. In this we are sane in that if our wealth is clean it serves the community in a way that it befits them.

Please know the Quran says something similar. It states that whatever one seeks one shall receive it. In this we have peace as our Creator gives us sustenance out of His bounty. In this we know that we should ask for what is legitimate for us to ask. In this way we don't transgress on our Hereafter and we seek what is permitted for us on earth. Ure son knows that he is asked how did he amass a fortune if he is a saint. It is because he did not pursue it excessively and when he worked it was a natural consequence of his labor as a physician. I know I was rich but money is not important to me like it is to some of you. We need money to survive and it is important for us to seek a livelihood that is clean and legitimate. Omar

Matthew 7.

7 *"Ask and it will be given to you; seek and you will find; knock and the door will be opened to you.*

8 *For everyone who asks receives; the one who seeks finds; and to the one who knocks, the door will be opened.*

9 *Which of you if your son asks for bread, will give him a stone?*

10 *Or if he asks for a fish, will give him a snake?*

11 *If you, then, though you are evil, know how to give good gifts to your children, how much more will your Father in heaven give good gifts to those who ask him!*

12 *So in everything do to others what you would have them do to you, for this sums up the Law and the Prophets."*

Fasting in different faiths is similar.

Please know fasting brings about a God consciousness called taqwa in Arabic. When we are conscious of Him we fear exceeding the limits He has set up.

Please know that fasting is prescribed for all religious groups. In the Quran it states that it has been written down as an edict from Him for all mankind. I will allow the different faiths to know what is prescribed in their religion. Suffice it to say that it should be done in good countenance and without hardship showing up on one's face. Ure son in repose knows the Muslim month for fasting is Ramadhan so I will elaborate the verse from the Quran which indicates the favor of our Creator on us as when we fast there develops a God consciousness that prevent us from committing excesses while He watches over us. It is a fear that we have not to exceed the boundaries that he has set for us. Omar.

Matthew 6.

16 *"When you fast do not look somber as the hypocrites do for they disfigure their faces to show others they are fasting. Truly I tell you they have received their reward in full.*

17 But when you fast put oil on your head and wash your face,

18 so that it will not be obvious to others that you are fasting, but only to your Father, who is unseen; and your Father Who sees what is done in secret will reward you."

Chapter 2 or The Cow.

183 O you who believe, fasting is prescribed for you, as it was prescribed for those before you, so that you may guard against evil.

Earnings have to be through halal means.

Please know that it only the Creator that feeds you when you earn through legitimate means. In this we need to realize that the illegal way of earning is by His permit though He is not the sustainer. The end is here for some that think their Creator gives them things through illegal means as well.

Please know the frailties of life are our concern as well. Only the Hereafter is more important where these things will be provided in abundance and we will not have to worry about procuring them. It is similar in Islam. The examples of the birds not needing anything other than their bellies being full is made in the sense that we will be full as well as provided for when we rely on our Creator for sustenance, not deviating from His mold in legitimate earnings. In us we have a need to be secure but God wishes us to rely on Him and ask Him for our daily sustenance. There is no harm in earning more than you need for your daily living in Islam so it important to know that to give in the excess a share for the poor. In this way the downtrodden are taken care of as there are people who are in need of charity from those of ample means. In this we know there is a balance and we should try to save from our legitimate earning so that we can give to the poor as well. Omar.

Bible source here.

25 "Therefore I tell you do not worry about your life what you will eat or drink; or about your body, what you will wear. Is not life more than food, and the body more than clothes?

26 Look at the birds of the air; they do not sow or reap or store away in barns and yet your heavenly Father feeds them. Are you not much more valuable than they?

27 Can any one of you by worrying add a single hour to your life?

28 And why do you worry about clothes? See how the flowers of the field grow. They do not labor or spin.

29 Yet I tell you that not even Solomon in all his splendor was dressed like one of these.

30 If that is how God clothes the grass of the field which is here today and tomorrow is thrown into the fire, will he not much more clothe you —you of little faith?

31 So do not worry, saying, 'What shall we eat?' or 'What shall we drink?' or 'What shall we wear?'

32 For the pagans run after all these things and your heavenly Father knows that you need them.

33 But seek first his kingdom and his righteousness and all these things will be given to you as well.

34 Therefore do not worry about tomorrow for tomorrow will worry about itself. Each day has enough trouble of its own."

Constructive criticism is a correct measure.
Please know to be critical of others is sane and to be benevolent is kind. In this manner we should correct others. In this we have peace as to correct a vice in others is a good deed for us. Your son in repose knows I am criticized for being strong with others but I rarely have any anger in me when I am critical.

Please know that I am severe if the fault in others is more than myself. I am not critical of others if I have a similar degree of fault as I know that would be hypocrisy. I am critical when the behavior I observe generally needs curative therapy and sometimes an incision is required to cut out a significant disease process.

Please know in Islam you have to be careful what you say to your brother. Ure son in repose knows that it is not possible not to see faults in your brother as we see others through ourselves. In this I mean that we are mirrors for our brothers and if we see them at fault we are probably possessing the same fault in ourselves. Ure son knows this is a complex matter, suffice it to say that we all possess similar faults and if we can see the fault in our brother we have that fault in ourselves, to a lesser or greater degree. Ure son knows it is easy to be critical of others and to be benevolent is higher for us. I will let the reader decide if it is hypocrisy to correct others or something that should be done if the fault is great. I am sad that people find me critical as well though I merely try to correct an error that is extreme and if the fault is severe in my view it should be corrected. Your son in repose to Him has been the subject of much abuse for when it is that I am severe and it is only as a corrective remedy for something that I feel needs to be remedied in a way it doesn't occur again.

Please see the cause of the problem must be remedied and it is clear that we must be critical of others if we see wrong in them as it behooves us to correct other's wrongs in them, like law enforcement do in us and our Book, the Quran is a guide for us in Islam. Elsewhere it is said we must be severe on those committing crime and so forth capital punishment is enforced by law though as Jesus says we should not be hypocrites in it. Omar.

Bible here.

1 "Do not judge or you too will be judged.

2 For in the same way you judge others, you will be judged, and with the measure you use, it will be measured to you.

3 Why do you look at the speck of sawdust in your brother's eye and pay no attention to the plank in your own eye?

4 How can you say to your brother, 'Let me take the speck out of your eye,' when all the time there is a plank in your own eye?

5 You hypocrite, first take the plank out of your own eye and then you will see clearly to remove the speck from your brother's eye.

6 Do not give dogs what is sacred; do not throw your pearls to pigs. If you do, they may trample them under their feet and turn and tear you to pieces."

Hypocrisy is considered to be the greatest vice in Islam. The hypocrite is considered to be in the lowest Hell in Islam we serve.

Please know the hypocrite is known by his characteristics that when he speaks he lies and when he makes a promise he breaks it. In this we are sane as we know it is a sign of untruthfulness they are in so truth precepts do not appear in their sentiments.

This message is sane to follow for the followers of Christ. In Islam, our prayers are congregational so the application of solitude does not apply. However even in Islam the understanding is the same that prayers are meant for the observer of them and not for those around him as he prays.

Please know the hypocrite does receive his reward while here on earth and if he is considered a pious individual by others he will be raised with a black state in the Hereafter as there is no piety in praying to be seen of others. Ure son knows the Quran has a similar chapter which I will place here for your perusal. I am sane in knowing the sin of hypocrisy is universal and all religions have similar precepts against this act where we gain importance in this world at the cost of the Hereafter. Omar.

Matthew 6

5 "And when you pray do not be like the hypocrites, for they love to pray standing in the synagogues and on the street corners to be seen by others. Truly I tell you they have received their reward in full.

6 But when you pray go into your room, close the door and pray to your Father who is unseen. Then your Father who sees what is done in secret will reward you.

7 And when you pray do not keep on babbling like pagans for they think they will be heard because of their many words.

8 Do not be like them for your Father knows what you need before you ask him.

9 This, then, is how you should pray: 'Our Father in heaven hallowed be your name,

10 your kingdom come, your will be done, on earth as it is in heaven.

11 Give us today our daily bread.

12 And forgive us our debts, as we also have forgiven our debtors.

13 And lead us not into temptation but deliver us from the evil one.'

14 For if you forgive other people when they sin against you, your heavenly Father will also forgive you.

15 But if you do not forgive others their sins, your Father will not forgive your sins."

Chapter 107, or Acts of Kindness.
107:1 Hast thou seen him who belies religion?
107:2 That is the one who is rough to the orphan,
107:3 And urges not the feeding of the needy.
107:4 So woe to the praying ones,
107:5 Who are unmindful of their prayer!
107:6 Who do (good) to be seen,
107:7 And refrain from acts of kindness!

Changes in the Bible are well documented.
Please understand this,

Please know all books have been tampered with. I know you think the Bible is intact however your writers and scholars know it was revised and edited repeatedly in its history. I know the King James version was a vetted copy of the Greek format, which was also vetted. I know you wish to say the same for the Quran and it is true it was vetted in minor issues but the message was preserved as our Creator vouchsafed it there in His work on us.

Please know the following is true of all the revealed books, including the Quran some, that innovations occurred and the text got altered to suit the needs of the people.

Please see the following section from John.

Please know it says that God gave the world his only son.

Please know this is a misnomer and it is well known that John and Paul were friends. It is clear from the gospels that Jesus himself negated these things when he was surrounded and he explained these were metaphors as indicated in the Old Testament in the psalms of Asaph.

Please understand it is easy for an author to place things in their gospel that suits their fancy and the whims of the people.

Please know that our Prophet made it clear there were some innovations that occurred in their books and it is much better to follow the words of our prophet Jesus rather than what is said about him as this is how innovations are made in our religion of Islam. Omar.

JESUS THE MESSIAH AND THE PERSON

John 1 here.

16 For God so loved the world that he gave his one and only son, that whoever believes in him shall not perish but have eternal life.

17 For God did not send his son into the world to condemn the world, but to save the world through him.

18 Whoever believes in him is not condemned, but whoever does not believe stands condemned already because they have not believed in the name of God's one and only son.

Please see a requiem for me.

Please see the following passage from John. In it our Creator acknowledges that Jesus is the mirror image of Him. I know you take it literally but its context is in the state of a metaphor. I know this to be true and it fits the hadith of our Prophet that when one walks we walk with His legs and the words we speak are His.

Please know what a metaphor is.

Please understand our Jesus was capable of explaining his teachings but wished them to be adept in understanding his words and thereby improve their intellect, which is what our Prophet did as well.

Please know a requiem for me,

Please know I am a saint who will change world history and I must have a pledge so that the work can be undertaken.

Please know the words,

Please understand you cannot come to Him without him refers to a specific time in the history of that nation.

Please know it is similar for me and unless you pledge allegiance to my cause or the cause of my mentor, our Prophet, then you will not find the way to Him or you will be in a lower degree of deliverance.

Please know we are guides for you today.

Please understand this,

Please know it is essential to pledge allegiance to the teacher who guides. If you deny him peace you will not be able to gain Paradise with Him and your destination will be one who is lost.

Please know there is no pride in this, only hardship.

Please know this clear.

Please know the prophets are the representatives of God on earth. In a sense, if they are rejected then the path to God is lost. In this there is certainty that the prophet will show them the path.

Please understand this,

Please know they are there for a purpose and that is to correct them in their misdeeds.

In the final analysis if you forsake the prophet your worship will amount to nothing.

The end occurs that people think this is especially for Jesus. Our Prophet said the same thing about himself. In this there is certainty that prophets are sent for reform and if you don't do that then you are lost.

Please see the following requiem there at his gravesite.

Please know they take my words in an out of context way and destroy my message.

Omar.

John 14.

6 Jesus answered, "I am the way and the truth and the life. No one comes to the Father except through me.

7 If you really know me, you will know my Father as well. From now on you do know Him and have seen Him."

CHAPTER SEVEN

BIBLICAL AND ISLAMIC ESCHATATOLOGY AS IT REFERS TO AHMADIYYAT AND THE SECOND COMING OF CHRIST

Introduction to my book here is incomplete without this section of eschatology where our group are the 4 horsemen of the Bible there.

Please know in the Bible and the Quran there are references to our coming as a group of scholars in Islam. I am aware there is controversy in my interpretations so I present them here as it is my belief with the passage of time you will clarify in opinion. Ure son in repose is only placing his interpretations as a reference. In this way I understand the Ahmadiyya group will be placed in the forefront of Islamic literature and bring the concepts of worship of One God into the mindset of the Christian nations, knowing Jesus to be His representative and messenger. It is our understanding that our group of scholars are the embodiment of Christ's message in the later days as predicted in the gospels and the sayings of Prophet Muhammad. I know I apply the metaphor to the second coming though we know it was a misnomer there as we know in Islam and Christianity there is no reincarnation and a person coming to earth does not make sense to us in Islam of Ahmadiyyat. I have tried to indicate that certain chapters from the book of revelations of the Bible refer to our group of scholars. Ure son knows this is easy to say and it is with the passage of time that these things can be verified as factual. In this section I will place posts from my Facebook page related to these topics that I have discussed here. In this way I wish to establish that we are foretold in the religious scriptures of faiths other than Islam. Hopefully with time leeway will be made for our views in Islam and in Christianity as well. Omar.

The Beasts of the book of Revelation are portrayed negatively in error due to a corruption in communication.

Please know Islam is served when we teach the truth to people as it helps them in assimilating us in Islam of Ahmadiyyat as we were predicted by our Prophet there as significant people for him who were his brothers in hadith they have. I know there is peace when we have done so.

Please know the clarification of concepts of biblical or Islamic eschatology are gradual and I will allow the leeway of time for those who don't view our views as correct initially. I know these ideas have been entrenched in their minds for eons but hopefully with the establishment of our Jamaat these ideas will gain ground.

Please know the book of revelations is about our Jamaat, for the most part. The Beasts are depicted negatively as the members of our Jamaat have made headway in bringing the concepts of the normalcy of Jesus as a man to the forefront and it is understood from our literature that the gospels do not support the concept of divinity of Christ. Also they feel askance because we designate Jesus as a prophet to you in Islam they had and not Prophet Muhammad's position as leader of them in Christian lands emerging now. In this way the author of the book maligned my mentor Mirza Ghulam Ahmad and his protégé, myself, depicting the two beasts as evil. In this we know there is peace in the long run as the book does not make sense unless it is understood that literal translation of the Beasts are 'Living Ones.'

Please know there is no difference between the Beasts in this section and those that are mentioned earlier in the book of revelations. In this way we understand that some misinterpretations have been applied and the four horsemen are also the same Beasts depicted in another context.

Please know the coming out of the first Beast from the abyss only is understood by us that the founder of the Jamaat taught people who were in a spiritual abyss. They practiced religion without understanding the spiritual nature of the religious edicts. He was mortally wounded when his son declared him to be a prophet in error, while he used the word in the metaphorical sense only later on in his life which would negate prophethood in him in the actual sense like the prophethood of personages like Muhammad or Jesus or other prophets before them. In this way the son killed the message of my mentor Mirza Ghulam Ahmad of Qadian.

Please know in Islam we know there is no prophet after him who is the World Prophet and Muslims fought his teachings even though they made sense to the believer. I have attempted to bring his teachings back to life by clarifying that the metaphor is not real and prophethood should not be construed as such. I have clarified that the metaphor is not true in the real sense of the word and when I have used the word prophet for myself it is only in the untrue or false sense when we talk about the reality of prophethood on earth. In this way I have indicated that I am a so-called false prophet or someone who is like a prophet but only in the sense of a metaphor.

Please know these concepts are complex but for a discerning mind they will know I do not claim to be a prophet and my mentor had similar sentiments as documented in his books on the subject.

Please know the book of revelations is eschatology and we must wait and see how accurate I am in my depictions of myself and my mentor being mentioned here. I would like to say that we are not evil, as the beasts have been depicted for two millenniums, and I have come to clarify certain aspects of eschatology as it refers to us here in Ahmadiyyat. In this way I clarify our movement to be a world movement that has positively influenced Islamic literature in the twentieth century through the writings of my mentor Muhammad Ali, who I consider to be the third Beast or the scarlet Beast, who will reflect off the first Beast in his acclaim as a reformer. In this way we see that the negative connotations that are made against the Beasts are purported and these are none other than those who are around the tabernacle of God giving Him praise in earnest. Your son in repose knows there are many details that I will bring forth as we move along. Suffice it to say the first Beast or Horseman has a great delusion attached to him that I am attempting to clarify as incoherent. He was a pious individual of the mainstream Islamic ideology who was called a non-believer when he indicated that Jesus had passed away and that he would not be returning to the Muslim world to bring the Christians and Jews to Islam on the point of the sword.

Please know to call him a non-believer is a sin and will take people away from religious belief as they will deviate when they call pious individuals non-believers. In this, this delusion of calling him a non-believer is harmful to them as it is blasphemy to Him, our Creator, and I am attempting to explain that he was the best of the people from his time and he should be conferred a Muslim state. I will attempt to explain the horsemen next. Suffice it to say that they are pious individuals with their own characteristics. Some of the vernacular is inaccurate so I will explain it to the best of my ability. Omar.

Rev.13

1 "And I stood upon the sand of the sea and saw a beast rise up out of the sea, having seven heads and ten horns, and upon his horns ten crowns, and upon his heads the name of blasphemy.

2 And the beast which I saw was like unto a leopard and his feet were as the feet of a bear and his mouth as the mouth of a lion: and the dragon gave him his power, and his seat, and great authority.

3 And I saw one of his heads as it were wounded to death; and his deadly wound was healed and all the world wondered after the beast.

4 And they worshipped the dragon which gave power unto the beast: and they worshipped the beast, saying who is like unto the beast? who is able to make war with him.

5 And there was given unto him a mouth speaking great things and blasphemies; and power was given unto him to continue forty and two months.

6 And he opened his mouth in blasphemy against God, to blaspheme his name, and his tabernacle, and them that dwell in heaven.

7 And it was given unto him to make war with the saints, and to overcome them, and power was given him over all kindreds, and tongues, and nations.

8 And all that dwell upon the earth shall worship him, whose names are not written in the book of life of the Lamb slain from the foundation of the world.

9 If any man have an ear, let him hear.

10 He that leadeth into captivity shall go into captivity: he that killeth with the sword must be killed with the sword. Here is the patience and the faith of the saints.

11 And I beheld another beast coming up out of the earth; and he had two horns like a lamb, and he spake as a dragon.

12 And he exerciseth all the power of the first beast before him, and causeth the earth and them which dwell therein to worship the first beast, whose deadly wound was healed.

13 And he doeth great wonders, so that he maketh fire come down from heaven on the earth in the sight of men,

14 And deceiveth them that dwell on the earth by the means of those miracles which he had power to do in the sight of the beast, saying to them that dwell on the earth that they should make an image to the beast, which had the wound by a sword and did live.

15 And he had power to give life unto the image of the beast, that the image of the beast should both speak, and cause that as many as would not worship the image of the beast should be killed.

16 And he causeth all, both small and great, rich and poor, free and bond, to receive a mark in their right hand, or in their foreheads.

17 And that no man might buy or sell save he that had the mark, or the name of the beast, or the number of his name.

18 Here is wisdom. Let him that hath understanding count the number of the beast for it is the number of a man; and his number is six hundred threescore and six."

Please see the parable of the 1 eyed one is me Omar here as I don't see evil until I am shown it by Allah or others in Islam there in heaven.

Please see the verse from Numbers where it says Balam will take over the land from him Balak who is the president I fought.

Please know he was evil extreme and came around gradual ways when I fought him and exposed him to others for doing what he did to my son and other and Sarah as well.

Please see introduction to Amalek notes where I am one eyed monster not but peace giver.

Please know this verse that I am the one eyed one who is raised to fight the evil incarnates of the world with the scepter from my Prophet's grave, which is his pen,

Please Him,

Please know I have done it and that is why I come out in the open and claim it that Antichrist is done with me for all intents and purposes.

Please know I am Antichrist's metaphor and I have shown you his nature.

Please know it is one of lies which is his forte,

Please know the former US president has taken a beating from me in the sense of a metaphor and we all know he has been exposed for his deception and promises of deceit where he promises one thing and fails to deliver knowing that he wasn't going to when he made it.

Please know it is over now and he was good to me in the end for the most part.

Please know the city Amalek is our town of this country.

Please know they have melted though and it is gradual though, their conversion, but they have understood us to be correct in Islam,

Please know this is the city that has fallen with my grace and others did as well.

Please see Amalek is the president's whim there in the sense he thinks it belongs to him but now it is more faithful and stable.

Please know this post has coherence to some but not all people, suffice it to say it has been altered some to portray Jesus as Balam taking over the land which is not accurate, it is myself and other people in Islam here who migrated here who did it, make Islam occur in them, the judiciary, who now protect my car some here and elsewhere.

Please see this passage from the Bible excerpts from Numbers.

Please know the Bible is clear the parable exists in the language of the prophets,

Please know the one with the eye closed is me quoting the Quran to you.

Please know it is a parable though and needs to be understood as such as there is no destruction in the material sense now.

Please know I mentioned I was the progeny of Jesus as well as Muhammad to you previously and I rest my case with you.

Please know it is I who claimed to be the one eyed one, like my adversary, as a metaphor. Omar.

Numbers.

11 Therefore now flee you to your place! I thought to promote you to great honor; but, behold, Yahweh has kept you back from honor.

12 Balaam said to Balak, "Didn't I also tell your messengers who you sent to me, saying,

13 'If Balak would give me his house full of silver and gold I can't go beyond the word of Yahweh, to do either good or bad of my own mind. I will say what Yahweh says'?"

14 Now, behold, I go to my people: "come, I will inform you what this people shall do to your people in the latter days."

15 He took up his parable and said, "Balaam the son of Beor says the man whose eye was closed says

16 he says, 'who hears the words of God knows the knowledge of the Most High, and who sees the vision of the Almighty, falling down, and having his eyes open,

17 I see him, but not now. I see him, but not near. A star will come out of Jacob. A scepter will rise out of Israel and shall strike through the corners of Moab and break down all the sons of Sheth.'"

The four Horsemen are also the four Beasts of Paradise.

Please know that our role is to discuss these interpretations from our sources and present them to the reader. I realize it is with the passage of time that these may be accepted. It has confounded scholars for eons as to the meaning of these words from the Bible meant and my aim is offer a viewpoint to them that has to be validated through the passage of time.

Please know Islam is served there in Muslim countries by the teachings of Ahmadiyyat that have brought in new teachings to the old concepts. I know there are many things that need development in Islam and it is my desire to bring Ahmadiyyat into perspective with them there that it is new knowledge based upon the teachings of Prophet Muhammad, on him be peace. In this we are aware that discrepancies or errors creep into a religion with the passage of time and it is the aim of Ahmadiyyat to bring these errors into limelight and offer corrective measures based upon the teachings of our Prophet that were ignored previously.

Please know the four horsemen are the four Beasts or Living Ones around the tabernacle of God. In this there is peace as it is clearly indicated such in the text. There is no difference in the Beasts here and those in the later section where they are depicted as evil. In this we know there is an error.

I will delineate some of the characteristics of each of the Beasts here. In case of the first Beast or Horseman he is given a power of conquest by virtue of his intellect. I mean this to be our mentor in Ahmadiyyat, Mirza Ghulam Ahmad who was given the power of reason that no one could defeat in debates. He proposed the death of Christ in actual terms and indicated that Christ himself would not descend in the material aspect of descent. In this way he proposed his viewpoints from the Quran and the Bible. In this way he established his viewpoints that make sense to a discerning person free from the bias of previous views.

In the case of the second Horseman or Beast there is unanimity that he will have a great sword which is interpreted as a great pen through which he communicates. Please know my great grandfather Muhammad Ali was a translator of the Quran and author of many books on Islam and it his translation of the Quran that I espouse to be the best for your community in the West. In this we know he will kill the sentiments of man about the evil of our faith of Islam and will bring them to the religion we espouse is correct for you in your communities.

The third Horseman or Beast is myself and I espouse that truth will prevail through the teachings our group in Ahmadiyyat. I teach mainly through the internet and my Facebook page has gained ground in communities here and in other parts of the world. I have also made a claim of being predicted in the Quran as Dabbat Al-Ard, the saint who is proposed to come. In this way the truth of my teachings should bring justice to the world, which is the balance I hold. Other things in the statement indicate there is retribution for a wrong done. It also indicates that Islam and Christians are not to be disturbed in their sentiments of religion indicated by the statement that oil and wine are not to be disturbed or hurt.

The fourth Horseman is yet to come and he will be pale or lacking in character. I know these explanations are my own and are meant to explain things from my perspective. In this we know peace that the four horsemen are pious individuals and are none other than the four Beasts here and those elsewhere where they are portrayed negatively.

Please know the pale rider as he is known is my son who will be buried there in Madinah near my Prophet's grave and he will have a seat there as truthful but not complete like myself and Mirza there who are the 2 persons of credit he our Prophet predict there the world will know after our Prophet Muhammad and so it will occur that we are 1 entity though separate in beliefs some but still one in essence and so forth results they will reside in heaven here who follow our Islam there. Omar.

Rev.6

1 "And I saw when the Lamb opened one of the seals, and I heard, as it were the noise of thunder, one of the four beasts saying, 'Come and see.'

2 And I saw and behold a white horse: and he that sat on him had a bow; and a crown was given unto him: and he went forth conquering, and to conquer.

3 And when he had opened the second seal, I heard the second beast say, 'Come and see.'

4 And there went out another horse that was red and power was given to him that sat thereon to take peace from the earth and that they should kill one another and there was given unto him a great sword.

5 And when he had opened the third seal, I heard the third beast say, 'Come and see.' And I beheld, and lo a black horse; and he that sat on him had a pair of balances in his hand.

6 And I heard a voice in the midst of the four beasts say, 'A measure of wheat for a penny, and three measures of barley for a penny and see thou hurt not the oil and the wine.'

7 And when he had opened the fourth seal, I heard the voice of the fourth beast say, 'Come and see.'

8 And I looked, and behold a pale horse: and his name that sat on him was Death, and Hell followed with him. And power was given unto them over the fourth part of the earth to kill with sword, and with hunger, and with death, and with the beasts of the earth.

9 And when he had opened the fifth seal, I saw under the altar the souls of them that were slain for the word of God and for the testimony which they held:

10 And they cried with a loud voice, saying, 'How long, O Lord, holy and true, dost thou not judge and avenge our blood on them that dwell on the earth?'

11 And white robes were given unto every one of them; and it was said unto them, that they should rest yet for a little season, until their fellow servants also and their brethren, that should be killed as they were, should be fulfilled."

The role of Dabbat Al-Ard is to be a reformer bringing clarification to the teachings that were ignored previously in Islam and by the Christian community.

Please know in the closing of this book we find a completion of my arguments for the worship of one God who is the Savior for mankind from themselves and from the insinuations of the devil.

Please know I have made a claim of being Dabbat Al-Ard, the saint who will emerge from worldly pursuits to start teaching to those who ignored the teachings of our Creator, both in the Muslim world and in the Christian faith. I know to make a claim is easy and these things have to be validated with time.

Please know the message is the same as that in Ahmadiyyat that I propound is correct for your communities. I can say there is a hadith of our Prophet that fits the description of my Facebook page. According to the hadith he says a wire will connect to the households.

Please know I have attempted to do the same with the publication of this book. In this way we bring you the message that Christ used the metaphor in his vernacular as indicated in the Gospel of John when he was questioned he denied them and ascribed statements like he was the son of God to be in the metaphorical sense by indicating to them that their book referred to the metaphor when God referred to the disobedient leaders of the Jewish communities to be like gods as they did not follow His edicts. I know this the underlying message he gave to some of his followers as well when he referred to their Creator as their Father in Heaven. I am aware these words were corrupted after he left the area to go to India however he was innocent in these sentiments being rife after his departure. It was later scholars like Paul who promulgated these views of Godhead in him and he echoed the sayings of the leaders of the People of the Book that indicated sonship in him though Jesus had denied any wrongdoing to them in the time period of the stoning and the subsequent crucifixion process where he was tried on the charges of implying son of God in himself. I know Jesus was not guilty but his words regarding tropes he used were taken to be literal Godhead by Paul and later scholars bringing about a deviance from the law of One God that was worshipped by the People of the Book and later by the Muslims under the tutelage of Prophet Muhammad. I am aware the arguments for implying Godhead in Jesus to being deviant is sufficient from the discussion here but I have in addition brought evidence from the Quran and other sources to corroborate these viewpoints that Jesus never indicated to his followers that he was God in any sense of the word but rather he was only His slave and representative who furthered His teachings to bring compassion and mercy into the conduct of the People of the Book.

Chapter 27 or The Naml.

27:81 Nor canst thou lead the blind out of their error. Thou canst make none to hear except those who believe in Our messages, so they submit.

27:82 And when the word comes to pass against them, We shall bring forth for them a beast from the earth that will injure them with words, because people did not believe in Our messages.

Belief in the finality of Prophet Muhammad as the last Prophet and Messenger of our Creator.

Please understand that I am clear minded if you understand my post.

Please know I am criticized for using the word prophet in the sense of a metaphor.

Please understand this was the way of the Sufi saints that they used metaphors for the words of prophet and God.

Please understand when I use the word Allah for myself I use it in the sense of a metaphor or someone who is His agent. It does not mean that I consider myself Him but only in sync with Him so that my deed is for Him alone. It is similar when I use the word prophet, it is in the metaphorical way as he teaches things like he taught Mirza and others in Islam and it so occurs when he appears it is only his spirit that comes and teaches me that's why I say it is a metaphor only that you see his words resonate through my pen and so forth results you are sane in it and I am only transcribing him in his words, not mine here.

Please know I use the word like the Sufi saints have in the past and I would not do this evil that I would be Him in the actual or real sense as He is above us in Heaven. I use it as a metaphor, like our Prophet mentioned when a man walks for Allah's sake he walks with the legs of Allah and when he talks for His sake he talks with the mouth of Allah. This is what a metaphor is. In the sense of a metaphor I am him, our Prophet Muhammad, a distinct entity who communicates through us though I don't speak his words or walk with legs he has, only that sense is with our Creator.

Please understand that I recognize Allah as a distinct Entity Who has no associate in the actual sense and I consider his Prophet Muhammad to be His representative and the last Prophet the world will see, who has the ability to communicate to his servant, myself, in a dream form of communication.

Please know a slave follows the will of Allah on him and when the Prophet comes it is similar, that is why we walk His feet and talk His words in following his wishes on us who is Prophet there. Omar.

CHAPTER EIGHT

CONCLUSIONS TO MY BOOK AND COMMENTS FROM MYSELF TO YOU

This is a prelude to the epilogue here.
Please see the tehreer or change in facts that result from coherence in you and so forth he Jesus there is free here as people do not call him God anymore as their comprehension has occurred.

Please see this article was in 2014 at the outset when they took my license because they said I was an incoherent individual unable to chemo patients even though no medical error had been proven in court or otherwise in nurse's tehreer on me I was ill.

Please see at the outset my posts were coherent and the judiciary was after my tail as I taught Jesus was an entity of worship there, like I had become as well in my later years, as it occurred, world conquest, and you became subservient to me being ill in the sense of a metaphor though I was not ill by you, you only talkeen so I could be committed by her in the courts on me as I taught adequately and well.

You became my servant when I taught there that he who is Jesus had been committed as well for calling himself son of God in the sense of a metaphor, then his blasphemy trial resulted, as did mine, and I was committed time and time again even though I explained adequately it was a metaphor association we both had where I called myself God in the sense of a metaphor and he told them similarly he was His son in that sense but you deter it in my case and commit me nonetheless.

This article was at the outset of my career there.

Please see tehreer in the English language means change of any kind and this may be the reason I fell there where I maintain gassing chambers do exist in this country of ours and our make-up is one to give in to it.

Please know I have been poisoned as well, sometimes by Christian groups, as I taught he was guilty of blasphemy not yet they called him bipolar or mad.

He was only innocent by us as he taught metaphorical concepts with ease like saying 'I and the Father are one' and other tropes which is a metaphor for being 1 in repose or thoughts and deeds as his deeds were what God wanted and so forth results they blaspheme him saying kafir and things like that and hung him occur on the saleeb or cross on him but it so occurs he survived, as my book says here, and so forth results I am free by you because of it as it is clear in my book he lived to later years and he survived it and was not killed.

Please see this article has coherence as I was poisoned there at the hotel that night before I wrote this note here.

It appears Hampton Inn is under siege.

Please know they were rough in evicting me, mainly on behalf of the Federal government employee who asked me to leave without due process as I was explaining to Jeremiah, the attendant there, who defended my right to stay on the premises, for the most part, but relented to procedure of giving in to government action on me when he interrupted my literature review starting at around 11:00 am, asking me to leave.

Please know he is a manager there while the Federal employee was just that and ordered me to leave the premises threatening eviction proceedings as I had moved out of the room at their insistence and was sitting in the lounge reading the paper, USA today, where I was referenced on my article on abortion and my other views. I know I am a celebrity and if anyone wishes to get in touch with me they may do so as I need writers with integrity like the author of the notes expressing support of my views, as she was forthcoming in her views, which very few people are nowadays.

Please realize the staff at Hampton Inn do not want to testify that I was incoherent as I was quietly reading the paper when he came over to me and asked if I wanted a ride in a taxi, indicating my car was probably being processed by state and federal employees in regard to my travel exploits, here in Tennessee, where I try to rectify the situation that we are an incoherent bunch, which they would like to say, as the Quran I promulgate as correct has received a large amount of publicity, some negative in those with backward views in Islam where they won't accept the tehreer or research of a scholar like Muhammad Ali solely because he was a disciple of our leader and scholar Mirza Ghulam Ahmad of Qadian.

I know I have upset the sentiments of people who know my worth and know I am a humble slave when I indicate the staff have been paid to imply I am incoherent and they plan to come here to pick me up.

Please understand the process of commitment is complex and requires a court proceeding of caliber before a commitment can be pursued as I will indicate in further court documents.

Please know my case is clear against the state.

Please know the staff of Hampton Inn is against giving a false testimony as it will make them lose coherence in their future endeavors.

Please know they are out there trying to make it occur so if they wish I will drive there and address their concerns first hand, inshallah or God willing.

I know I am harassed by their nightly gassing attempts and last night I was forthright and called the FBI office in Memphis to intervene. I know the reason they want to heist me is because I expose their system as corrupt and mala fide to an extreme as I have documented in the last several months.

Please know there is only one word for the case of state of Tennessee against me, that is tehreer in the negative sense. Every action they have taken against me has been based on the assumption that they are truthful in court documents while the facts are contrary to that statement they say in court in that there is no coherence in their acts of their faith to declare me bipolar or schizophrenic as my literature is quoted as coherent and their role as detractors of my faith of being a saint, who also maintained a busy practice, is incoherent in the least, if not the most malicious tehreer the world has seen other than calling our prophet saint Jesus a misfit and crucifying him on the cross based on false charge of a polytheist and malingerer as son of His while he implied the metaphor in his works as I have indicated in the article Godhead as a metaphor.

Please know our Prophet's conduct was similar as being a coherent individual who never spoke a lie in his life yet was derided as a saint in the negative sense or a devil in your literature before I came to teach him and the Quran bears reference to this that they also called him mad or ill because of the beauty of the dictum he has there and he was maligned though not as much as me or Jesus Christ to you. Omar. The Dabbat-al Ard door, inshallah or God willing.

Omar Ahmad MD

A requiem is due for me here that I am your savior in the form of your rahber from Him, your Creator there.

Please see it is a misnomer that I am your protector or rahber they say as you are blunt about it, but am I, yes, I allowed you the leeway of time and you allowed me sleep instead of my death occurring which is why I am grateful in a sense though you shouldn't have put me on high dose therapy as it was against the statutes for you to do so, this is your land so I'll relent and not sue you on the issue but on the jail time you will see alacrity from us as it was indecent to jail your rahber who gave you One God concepts to your satisfaction and you became cognizant a law exists which your rahber, other, Jesus there, you thought deluded you in to think there is none for you in this world which was incorrect as he told you a Comforter was going to appear which is myself and our Prophet as both are mentioned there and so forth I am free because I am your rahber real and gave you the odds of getting there which you could not succeeded in in your life on earth if I did not come to teach.

Please see I am grateful you protect me, please continue doing so as life is hard without it but if you must stop then let me go to another land with my visa in me as I am good actually and gave you life and so forth now you know what your chances is there for you and your child and the other one you claim as well.

Omar.

Epilogue for my book here.

This is how you do it, year after year, you commit me without accord as I have always been erudite and author by you yet you sit there and write these things on court documents on your court on me and commit me without cause as I was teaching the Christian mu he was a mono God which he believed in who was Jesus to you and the Quran validates his view that he was 1 God only Who is Allah or Jehovah or however you may call Him and it so occurs they know now it is easy to commit so you intervene and don't let it occur again in your term on me but unfortunately the government has power and does commit me at will and jail me if they will it but I know you are good-intentioned and usually end up getting me out.

Please see it is clear Amalek is my deen and the country follows my page and alacrity results when they take me in as killing results there so you eliminate her court there and transcribe justice yourself as that is what the country's rahber wants for man, true democracy, where the people have power and so forth results you don't trust men and women in power as they talkeen or deceive you and take away your rights with police structure on you.

Please know it is easy for them in that court is their door and justice is nil on me as they talkeen always and the police is always ready to commit if they can which I have shown they do time and time again with conservators on me, which you relent to appease them.

Please see they also seek to arrest me on minor charge so you talkeen them and prevent it, giving me immunity as I am your rahber in that I give you things from Him, your Creator, and heaven is yours if you come through and don't talkeen me anymore by sending me away to foreign land where I can be imprisoned though now I think the coast is clear and it is so Jesus was imprisoned before they talkeen and find out he couldn't be committed because he explained the metaphor before, so they kill him nearly by saying he was messiah taking over the land, so Pilate is made to hang him on treason, yet he cannot as he denied it who was Jesus Christ to you, so they the council hang him on blasphemy again saying he is son of God metaphor not but saying it actually. Omar.

CONCLUDED HERE.

www.ingramcontent.com/pod-product-compliance
Lightning Source LLC
LaVergne TN
LVHW041915070526
838199LV00051BA/2623